Preface

The ancients nomadized with their flocks and herds for the sake of finding pasture and hunting grounds. Wittingly or not, they spread the seeds of primitive civilization all over the world. However, this process seemed endless in the age of small-scale production, when people were completely isolated from each other, though the crowing of their birds and barking of their dogs were within earshot. Some of them remained in their native land for their whole life; others devoted their whole life to exploiting new frontiers. The socialized large-scale production has given a great impetus to human flows. The globalization of the economy has expanded human activities to every corner of the world.

Nowadays, human beings crisscross this blue planet, reaching far beyond the boundaries of their ancestors. They have greatly expanded their sphere of activities, particularly due to the advent of modern transportation tools. Xun Zi (Hsun Tzu), a great Chinese philosopher of two thousand years ago, said: "Horse riders, though not fleet-footed, can travel thousand miles; Boat sailors, though not good swimmers, can get over turbulent rivers." We should now add "Aircraft flyers, though not winged, can travel through the sky." Aircraft makes it possible for travelers to reach the other side of the planet within a single day. The advancement of transportation means has greatly increased the traveling ability of mankind.

Traveling facilities have greatly promoted exchanges as well as collisions

among different cultures and social systems. People around the world learn from each other, condone each other, and intermingle with each other. Thus, they have moved forward and diversified the culture of mankind. They have rendered our planet into a more colorful and wonderful place. Human beings of modern day have gradually grasped the concept of "citizens of the global village" while they strive for existence and development.

As Confucius is quoted in the *Analects of Confucius*, "Within the four seas all men are brothers." This simple and plain ideal of the ancient time has been accepted by more. According to DNA sequences and structures, scientists infer that mankind may probably evolved from the same ancestor, that is, "Lucy", who lived 3,200 thousand years ago in the East African Great Rift Valley. Her descendants probably left Africa about 60 thousand years ago and spread to the rest of the world and then evolved into races of different colors with different languages. This archeological finding has provided genetic basis for the idea of "Within the four seas all men are brothers."

For more than one hundred years before the turn of the last century, China was self-isolated and cut off from the outside world. But its gateway was forced open by imperialist powers with modern guns and cannons. After the new China was founded in 1949, some foreign powers imposed a blockade and embargo against the new nation. It was not until the end of 1970s that China opened its door and ushered in a new era of open-door reforms. A large number of Chinese have visited foreign countries and numerous foreigners have come to China. This inflow and outflow of

tourists have added splendid colors to a world culture.

Many Chinese feel like they are on another planet when they visit foreign countries of completely different cultures. Probably the same is true to foreigners who visit China. When walking down the street foreign visitors would be followed and stared at by curious Chinese kids, which would make them uneasy and uncomfortable. This scene of looking at foreign visitors as E.T. really runs against the Chinese tradition of hospitality. It would also make the Chinese feel uneasy and ashamed too. Fortunately as more and more foreigners come to China, people become inured to foreign faces. The Chinese people perform the duties of host to foreign friends as the old adage tells them to do: "To be joyful to have friends come afar." The Chinese people try their very best to make foreign guests "feel at home", whether they come to China on business or on pleasure trips.

Some Chinese have settled down abroad; some foreigners remain in China. Both of them have taken a foreign land as their home and successfully mingled with the local society. The ancients roved about seeking rich pasture for their domicile; and it's nothing strange for contemporaries to choose places favorable for their existence and advancement in life. Europe and America have attracted some Chinese with their advanced science and living styles; China has attracted some foreigners with its high-speed economic development and a long-standing civilization. "During the 1980s, Chinese went to America seeking their dreams," as an American said. "Now it's time for Americans to come to China with opportunities everywhere." The enterprising spirit is an important link in human genes and it's the instinctive human nature to

go after opportunities.

We have interviewed a number of foreigners living and working in China. During these interviews, we found all of them have, more or less, "a Chinese complex". They like Chinese culture, and are happy with their life and work here. Many of them have taken China as their home. Of course the Chinese people have never regarded them as outsiders. Leading a comfortable life and intermingling joyfully with the local folks, they share a similar sense of happiness, though their experience may be different. The Chinese call them "Lao Wai", or old foreigner. The phrase does not have a negative connotation and is a type of greeting to friends coming back from afar. "Lao Wais", with sentimental feelings to China, have deeply touched Chinese people. The achievements of these "Lao Wais" would be an inspiration to friends abroad.

It is interesting to have personal interviews with these "Lao Wais". Through these interviews people can see the changing China and the changing life of "Lao Wais" much better. So it is meaningful to share with others their experience living and working in China. The interviewees are all common people and their accounts are all common stories. But many times these stories have rocked our spiritual world.

During the course of working on the book, we have got assistance from many friends. We cannot possibly express our full, sincere thanks to them. By sharing these touching stories with our readers, we hope this book will bring us joys of colorful life and food for thought.

Lu Yang
October, 2007

Contents

Personal File

Name: Eric Abrahamsen

Chinese Name: Tao Jian

Nationality: American

Occupation: Self-employed

Time in China: 5 years

East Meets West
A Young American's Cultural "Switch"

Eric Abrahamsen is a handsome young American who has chosen a very Chinese Internet alias "Suo Zhuzi"— a common name meaning "Locking Post". To everyone's surprise, he was elected to be a moderator for a well-known Chinese literary forum called "Reading Life". He is currently occupied with compiling and translating 15 contemporary Chinese short stories for a collection to be published by Penguin, a famous British publishing house.

 a little over six feet five, Eric literally towers over most Chinese when walking down the streets of Beijing or attending parties, like a camel standing out among a flock of sheep. Given his height, many Chinese people consider it a pity that Eric didn't play for the NBA. Having lived in China for just five years, his mastery of the language is extraordinarily admirable. He possesses a huge vocabulary, pure pronunciation, and an intimate knowledge of the latest lingo and expressions. Many people believe that his work as a free-lancer provides him with a great opportunity to exploit his linguistic skills. With his mastery of English and Mandarin, it would be another pity and waste of talent if he were not involved in cultural exchange.

When complimented on his mastery of the Chinese language and his humor, Eric reacts modestly, sometimes even blushing a bit. Eric's charisma and gregarious nature have made him popular throughout Beijing, especially within cultural circles. As a result, Eric always has a helping hand whenever he finds himself in need.

Eric recently found online fame with a six-month stint as a moderator on the "Reading Life" online forum. He has generated mild fanfare among Chinese online members excited to see an exotic "mottled bamboo" on the forum. The trend these days among the Chinese is to replace online words with their homophones. As you might have guessed, the Chinese pronunciation for mottled bamboo is the same as the Chinese pronunciation for moderator. Note that the level of "mottled bamboo" is not just given to anybody. Only a person who has attained the highest acknowledged writing level is allowed to serve as a moderator, and given the power to edit and delete other people's posts. Who could have imagined that a person whose mother tongue was not Chinese could occupy this position of "pointing to the mountains and rivers and setting people afire with his words"? Just imagine how high a Chinese level he has achieved! This of course has aroused a great interest among the news media. Why, even when we arrived at Eric's home to conduct an interview we found a group of cameramen from a TV station busy shooting a program with Eric.

A Foreign Student at the Central University for Nationalities

Still basking in the glow of newly wedded bliss, the cheerful-tempered Eric granted whatever was requested. The cameramen recorded his daily work as a free-lancer and even asked him to bake bread, grind coffee beans, and do other household chores in front of the camera to show their audience the graceful demeanor of an aproned husband. When not satisfied with the shot, the TV crew would require him to repeat the shot over and over again. It reached the point that even the cameramen felt it was asking a little too much of Eric. However, Eric kept assuring them that it was okay, saying "not a problem" in Chinese. No one present could conceal their smiles as Eric said this in a typical Beijing accent, with a heavily-emphasized final "r" sound that even many Chinese southerners cannot pronounce well. His tone and manner were very much that of a young guy from Beijing's backstreets — full of honesty, generosity and tolerance.

Despite being tormented by the TV crew, Eric showed no trace of fatigue as he sat down for his interview with us. The interview began with the topic of how he ended up coming to China.

Eric's ancestors immigrated to the United States from Northern Europe about a hundred years ago. Besides his height, the only real remnant of his Norwegian heritage is his name. Starting on the subject of his passion for China,

Eric said, "I actually first visited China when I was 10 years old on a trip with my family. We entered China via Hong Kong, passed through Guangzhou and arrived in Beijing. The magnificence of Tian'anmen Square and the Forbidden City left me in … well, awe. Yes, I was in great awe. Of course I also climbed the Great Wall. However, I didn't feel any sense of pride of being 'a true man who sets foot on the Great Wall'. I was probably just too young to understand."

At the University of Washington, Eric majored in international relations. When selecting a country for the main focus of his study, he wrote down China without a second thought. Was it because of the impression of his Beijing trip as a ten year-old child? Perhaps the allure of an ancient oriental culture? Eric shook his head at these suggestions and responded, "I can't really say. I didn't really have a reason behind my choice." It turned out that Eric's unintentional choice would have a profound influence on his life journey, leading him to his current career success and even helping him tie the knot with a Chinese girl.

One of the requirements of the international relations program at the University of Washington is that students must take two years of language courses related to the country of their focus. Rather than study Chinese in the America, Eric found that he could meet this requirement by enrolling as an exchange student at China's Central University for Nationalities, which had a study-abroad program with his university. Before his departure, he concentrated his efforts on Chinese for three straight months. He also asked his teacher to pick out a Chinese name which was "Tao Jianyou". Excitedly, he arrived in Beijing. He felt confident about his Chinese when taking courses at the UW to the point where he even admired his own talent for language. However, Eric experienced a rude awakening once he got to Beijing, and discovered that he could neither make himself understood nor understand others. "Too depressing," said Eric with an exaggerated expression as he recalled the experience.

That wasn't the only thing that had him depressed. "I only realized that I forgot to bring a coffee grinder when I arrived in Beijing. I am used to freshly brewed coffee and can't go back to the instant stuff. OK, forget it then. But it wasn't until I started getting daily pounding headaches that I realized I was addicted to caffeine. However, asking my family to send a coffee grinder all the way from the States wasn't the most practical of solutions. I was later told though that one could get a coffee grinder in Beijing. I rushed out immediately to get one. When I got to the store I found that not only did the store have a coffee grinder but all the name brands were there too. In reality, anything you could want, you can find in Beijing." With the ability to make his own coffee again, the headaches disappeared.

However the language problem proved to be a bit more challenging to solve than the coffee one. It's a good thing that Eric is not only smart but a hard worker as well. With the favorable language learning environment, Eric made huge strides in his Chinese. His progress really skyrocketed when he met his schoolmate Ma Dongxiao from the English Department of CUN.

It is probably a short cut in foreign language learning: to have a sentimental sweet transnational marriage with a native of the foreign language that one is

studying. In the process of emotional exchange, the dating lovers would surely improve their linguistic skills by teaching each other their mother tongues. Unlike many other foreign students who speak fluent Chinese but are afraid of reading and writing, our fellow-student Tao boasts all-round excellence in listening, speaking, reading and writing. This should be attributed to mutual study and progress with his fellow-student Ma.

At CUN, around 80-90 percent of the student body is composed of Chinese minority nationalities. Ma is a member of the Muslim Hui nationality whose customs differ from the Han — the ethnic Chinese majority. However, when it comes to language, there is no difference at all between the Han and the Hui. Consequently, Ma provided Eric with a perfect linguistic environment. With the aid of his fellow student at CUN, Eric made daily progress in their dual world.

Foreign Son-in-Law of a Chinese Family

Speaking honestly, Eric's oral Chinese was still lacking by the time he graduated from CUN. This was partly due to the fact that the "dual world" that he shared with Ma simply hadn't existed long enough. His speaking ability was still not quite up to par when he paid his first visit to Ma's family in Changchun, Jilin Province. Ma's parents, artists by trade, were people of traditional Chinese culture. The arrival of their daughter's international date took them a bit by surprise. The father, in particular, was having trouble with the idea. In private, the father scolded the daughter for her decision. "There are so many nice young Chinese guys out there. How on earth did you end up with a foreigner? He can't even speak Chinese well."

The next time that Eric would meet Ma's family was after he had lived in Beijing for quite some time. His speaking ability was no longer an issue. He had also become familiar with the Chinese way of life and thinking. Because of his knowledge of the Chinese culture, people looked at him differently. The would-be father–in-law began to warm up to him as well.

During this trip to Changchun, they had to stay longer than planned as they

were confined to Ma's home because of the SARS situation. This unexpected layover surprisingly resulted in great leaps of progress in both Chinese and love. It also resulted in the parents finally approving of the relationship. As a result, the mention of the SARS incident conjures up nothing bad or horrible for Eric. Instead, a slight feeling of sweetness and pride comes to him as he described the moment saying, "This is truly what you call 'turn bane into boon'," he said in a meaningful way.

After having spent four of his five years in China dating Ma Dongxiao, the couple ended their long distance love race in the sacred bonds of holy matrimony. They set up their love nest in a rented two-room apartment. Eric works at home as a free-lancer while Ma works at a radio station. They still communicate in both English and Chinese. The newlyweds don't have high materialistic expectations but value the quality of their cultural life. All their friends wish that the two can live forever in their honeymoon.

As his wife is Muslim, Eric gave up eating pork when he began dating her. "Giving up pork is out of respect for the customs of my wife's people. I do it for

the sake of love — not out of religious reasons. With so many other foods on earth, it's not a big deal. Besides, it helps avoid high cholesterol."

Both of them enjoy dabbling in the kitchen with their "ok" cooking skills. So it's no surprise that cuisine cultures from the East and the West are frequently intermingled in their little world. Their day jobs keep them busy and so they often have dinner with each other outside as well as at home. When eating out, they make an appointment to meet at a particular restaurant and leave directly from their respective offices. They enjoy eating out this way as it gives them a sense of occasion, meeting each other like secret lovers.

With different cultural backgrounds and different modes of thinking, is there any need to adjust their way of life when meeting relatives from their respective families, even if the couple loves each other dearly? "Of course there is," said Eric when asked. "They have different ways of expressing feelings. The Americans are a little more straightforward and the Chinese have a somewhat soft and warm way. I can't really say which way is better." He appreciates the Chinese consideration shown for others and also favors the independence of Americans. He and his wife take good, but not routine, care of each other. Now Eric can automatically "switch over" between the two cultures, treating American in the American way and Chinese in the Chinese way. "This 'switchover' is not hypocritical," Eric emphasized. "I use these two styles sincerely, and they come from the bottom of my heart."

That accounts for the ease with which Eric switches between two different cultures.

An Exotic Mottled Bamboo

After graduating from CUN, Eric worked as an editor for two years at *That's Beijing* an English daily-life magazine. The work load was quite heavy. In addition to his responsibilities as an editor, Eric had to conduct one or two interviews for each issue.

Interviewing is a difficult job. First, to make an appointment by phone is a

critical hurdle and Eric finds it daunting. It is a problem because these interviews are set up by phone — a most difficult task for foreign students of the Chinese language. The difficulty lies in the fact that in a face-to-face conversation, a person's body language and facial expressions help convey even the subtlest of meanings. Even if you can't understand a word or two, you can get the basic gist of the conversation. Over the phone, you lose those advantages as you can't see the other person. If your hearing comprehension wasn't good enough, you were going to be in trouble. However, as he interviewed dozens of people ranging from officials to scholars to artists, the timid beginner was even able to "fool" the people he was setting up interviews with. As long as the conversation on the phone was kept short, the other party had no idea he wasn't Chinese. Image the surprise of the person being interviewed upon discovering that they had been speaking to a foreigner.

His career as a free-lancer began after two years in the editing job. Out of his love and understanding for the Chinese culture, he was determined to do something for East-West cultural exchange with his mastery of the language.

He found great pleasure and interest in the Chinese internet. Two year ago, with help from the Chinese writer Xu Xing, Eric registered at the well-known Chinese literary forum "Reading Life".

"I don't know if I was the first foreigner frequenting the Chinese forum," said Eric. "But I am sure nobody knew I was a foreigner for a long time." In addition to his Chinese name "Tao Jian (his Chinese buddies shortened "Tao Jian-you" because they thought it didn't quite sound right), Eric has another name — the aforementioned "Suo Zhuzi" — that was thought up by his wife. Hoping their boys to grow up strong and sturdy, Chinese farmers would give their kids names such as "Suo Zhu" or "Zhuzi" meaning Lock or Pillar. Along with such a rural name as Suo Zhuzi, and his smooth Chinese writing, Eric "fooled" a large contingent of netizens. Through his own postings and the reading of other's posts on the forum as well as rich vocabulary encountered while surfing the internet, Eric furthered his Chinese cultural attainments with each passing day.

His buddies did their very best to help put Eric in the position of moderator

for the "Reading Life" forum. They not only thought that "Comrade Suo Zhuzi" had the ability to be a moderator but that it was nice and interesting as well for an American to play that role on a Chinese forum. Jokingly following Mao Zedong's style in his article "In memory of Norman Bethune" writer Xu Xing made a posting to the forum: "Comrade Suo Zhuzi, maybe a member of the Republic, or the Democrat or some other parties of the United States, was in his twenties when he was sent by a no-body-knows person to China. He made light traveling thousands of miles to help us in our BBS cause."

As a moderator, Suo Zhuzi exercised his powers, including deleting postings. An American deletes posts written by Chinese in a Chinese forum! He never thought he would be doing such a thing before and it made him feel a little strange. However, it was very helpful in deepening and widening his contacts with Chinese cyber friends and proved beneficial in bettering his Chinese. With support from friends and timely advice from his better half, Eric performed his job without a hitch. Although he occupied the "throne" of moderator for a term of only six months, Eric's story as an "exotic mottled bamboo" has been on everybody's lips in the online world.

Envoy of Cultural Exchange Between East and West

At present Eric is expanding his reading horizons into many other pure literary forums such as tianyaclub.com, my.clubhi.com and qingyun.net.cn. With a great interest in Chinese literature, he would spend a lot of time on reading novels which many native young Chinese couldn't do at the present day. His favorites include works by Wang Xiaobo, Su Tong, Yu Hua, Zhu Wen and Han Dong. Recently he has been focusing on the collected works by Lu Yang. He has immense interest in translating these works into English. On his desk a copy of "A Chinese-English Dictionary" he has been using for the past two years is completely dog-eared, vividly demonstrating his hard work.

Eric believes that many of today's Chinese novels are excellent. However, because publishing channels are filled with difficulties, they cannot be efficiently

brought to the international market. Additionally, Americans' knowledge of Chinese literary is woefully lacking and fragmented. Therefore, it is imperative to set up open international exchange channels for the purpose of spreading Chinese works. He has already started the process by contacting some American literary magazines and recommending certain Chinese writers and their works in hopes to arouse their interest.

As previously mentioned, Eric is working on a collection of Chinese short stories for Penguin. "The stories that I have picked versus the stories that you Chinese natives would have picked are somewhat different; I would not necessarily pick up what you Chinese would think good," he said. "To the Chinese my selections may be a little unexpected. Anyway these are stories selected for readers from the English world. It would only be natural for 'Penguin' to consider the feelings and opinions of an American." After this project, Eric of course has further aspirations. "I want to be in the book business. Specifically I want to be in the business of promoting excellent contemporary Chinese novels to American readers. I also hope to translate these works into English for the American people."

He has conducted the major part of his career in Beijing. "I can't leave now. There are simply so many cultural resources here. Wouldn't it be a pity and a waste if I don't make full use of them?" Of course, Eric makes a short trip back to the States every year. After all that's where his roots are. To Eric, even though China is still developing and lags behind the US, it is full of vitality, just like the luxurious and exuberant paddy fields he saw in Guangdong during his trip when he was ten years old. Beijing in particular is "a city with plenty of vigor and everybody has their dreams, goals, and future plans in mind, even though it is a bit untidy, dirty, dusty and windy in spring." He said, "To the contrary, America has a beautiful environment and a well developed society, but people there lead an overly comfortable life, lacking goals and hence motivation. Pursuing is always more vigorous than possessing."

Like many Americans in Beijing, Eric plans to "watch the fun" of the 2008 Olympic Games in Beijing. He may then return to the States with his wife. There he may go to graduate school or even start a family. The couple doesn't have to worry about family planning restrictions (the one child policy) in China since Ma is a Muslim minority and Eric is an American citizen. And what then? "Back to China of course." During the course of the interview, we've noticed that word "back" always comes up when Eric mentions either the US or China. He's truly taken both sides as his homes. Destined to travel between the two cultures for the rest of his life, he will have to switch between his ways of thinking and life accordingly.

"On your return to China, will you consider settling in other cities like Shanghai or Guangzhou?" we asked him. "No way! Beijing is still the place to be," answered Eric. "Shanghai and Guangzhou are flourishing economically, but Beijing is still the cultural center." That's right. "If you want to be a cultural worker," said a movie conductor, "You have to be born in Beijing even if you have to be reincarnated as a dog!" Bursting into laughter, Eric agreed completely.

Translated by Yang Yaohua

Personal File

Name: Michael Williams

Chinese Name: Dalong

Nationality: American

Occupation: Finance

Time in China: 6 years

To Dream of Being a Dragon

Michael Williams, a young man from Phoenix, in the United States, claims to have all the most typical characteristics of a mixed-blood person — intelligence, good looks, and even more a warm heart. An accidental trip opened the door to China, hence starting a brilliant life. He is the subject of this article Dalong.

One day in November 2006, I came to interview Michael Williams, the vice president of Lingo Media's Beijing Office, in his office on the 11th floor of Dongfang Yinzuo at Dongzhimen.

I knew Michael Williams' name was Dalong before I came, because it was printed on his business card. He is the third foreigner I know who has the Chinese name Dalong. The other two were so named because they were born in the year of the Dragon. I wondered whether the foreigner I'm going to interview today was also born in the year of the Dragon. So as soon as I met him, I couldn't help asking him right away, "Are you called Dalong because you were born in the year of the Dragon? "

"No, I was born in the year of the Rabbit," Michael smiled.

"Why did you call yourself Dalong then?" I continued.

"I like 'dragon' because I like Li Xiaolong, a famous Kungfu movie star known as Bruce Lee. So I named myself after him."

"Do you have a surname in Chinese?"

"Yes, Ma."

"Ma? Why?" Obviously, it has no relation to his English name Williams.

"Look at me," Dalong pointed to his face, "I've got a long face like a horse, so I chose Ma as my surname."

"You're very funny," I smiled. This way of greeting immediately removed the sense of formality and enlivened the atmosphere.

An Accidental Trip to China

Michael was born in Germany and migrated to the United States with his parents at the age of nine months. His father is half German, half British, and his mother is half Polish, but both were born in the US and both are American. Michael smiled and said, "Actually I'm a typical mixed-blood, with multinational blood in my veins."

Michael's home is in Phoenix, Arizona, in the United States, where most of the people are white, and some Mexican, but few Chinese. He grew up surrounded only by white people. When he was a little boy, he knew nothing about China. In his own words, "My understanding of China was zero."

"What made you want to come to China?" I felt very surprised. I know a lot of people who decided to come to China because they had heard of China, knew something about it, or were curious. But being absolutely ignorant of China, what had made Michael travel all the way from his hometown to the remote east — to China?

"I came to China completely by accident. In 1997, during the spring break of my last year in college, I went to Hong Kong with some of my classmates. That was my first trip to Asia. Hong Kong to me was just like New York in the States — a prosperous city full of busy working people. Before our trip come to an end, we went to Guangzhou for one day. That day left a very deep impression on me. I saw many beggars in the railway stations, and the city was dirty and messy at that time. It gave me a very bad feeling. Compared with Hong Kong, it was a completely different world. I felt sad for those poor people and really

wanted to help them and do something for them. After graduation in 1997, with the help of the Amity Foundation, I went to teach English at a normal school in Shandong, in northern China. With me was another American boy, Robbie, who was one year younger than I."

He told me once that he used to be a missionary, which reminded me of the main male character of the novel *The Thorn Birds*. To me, a priest is an occupation, someone who works for the Church. But where in China was the need to hire a foreign priest? Had he come to China just to be a missionary?

"I'm a Christian, and a missionary, but this wasn't due to the influence of my family. Being a missionary is not my profession. I only worked in my spare time for the Church in college and spread Christianity. So after I decided to come to China, the Amity Foundation helped me find a teaching job in a school, and supplied me with an air ticket. The school provided accommodation and paid me 1,000 *yuan* per month.

One thousand *yuan* can maintain a normal living standard for a Chinese person. But for a foreigner, this sum doesn't quite seem enough. "Was that little money enough for your living expenses in China?" I was a little bit concerned.

"It was enough because I didn't need to pay for lodging, and moreover, the school was located in a remote place where there were few opportunities to spend money. So one thousand *yuan* was more than enough for my monthly expenses. Of course it depends on how you choose to live. I'm an industrious person, never dip into my purse. Besides food, which cost me about 300 *yuan* per month, I saved the remaining 700 *yuan*."

I had never imagined he would be so good at housekeeping.

"To tell the truth, I love to travel. I thought that, since I'd already made it to China, I should go to more places and visit various scenic spots. In addition, there are advantages to being a teacher — winter and summer vacations. You can make full use of this time to travel."

"Where have you been?"

"I've been to a lot of places…."

"How did you travel, by plane?" I asked.

"I was making so little money each month, how could I afford to travel by plane? I took a train each time."

"Hard sleeper?"

"No, mostly hard seat. Sometimes it was difficult to get tickets, so I bought standing tickets. I remember once I went to Xi'an by train and there were no seats left. I stood in the corridor of the carriage. At that time the carriage was swamped with people and the air was filthy. A farmer-looking man standing beside me struck up a conversation with me by asking me where I was going. Upon hearing that my journey would be quite long, his expression became very sympathetic. Then he laid a big pack on the floor saying, 'Come sit down, brother, sit on my big pack. We can sit back to back and even take a nap.' At first, I refused. But seeing his sincere look, I agreed. We sat back to back all the way. At that moment, I heard a Chinese say something to him, complaining that I should have taken a plane, but instead was making trouble and squeezing into a train with them. The farmer-looking man retorted angrily, something like he must have his reasons for taking the train. Not every foreigner was a money bag or a rich person. We should take care of him. Hearing that, I was deeply moved."

"Is there anything that you are unaccustomed to in China? Have you ever run into anything that has made you unhappy?"

"One thing made me very angry. That was in 1998 when I was still working in Shandong Changwei Normal School. In the summer of that year South China was heavily flooded. Everyone in my school donated something to express their concern and condolence for the people in the flooded regions. I was no exception. I took 200 *yuan* from my monthly savings and donated it. But for some reason they wrote my name on an honor roll and posted it on a wall. Moreover, they put my name at the very beginning. Seeing this I was very angry, so I went to see them. But they told me that the amount of money I donated was the largest, so I should be praised and others should be encouraged to learn from me. I explained to them that I donated money to show my love, not to win praise. I didn't want others to know about me, as it was a simple thing that anyone should have done. Doing good deeds doesn't need to be repaid. "

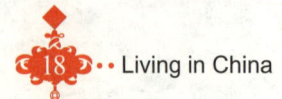

His words touched my heart deeply. I have met some foreigners and most of them don't like to receive praise when they do something good. To them, it's natural to do good things. It's the basic way of being an upright person, and doesn't need to be mentioned at all. In China, on the other hand, people see things differently. We like to give praise as an encouragement, and a way to teach others, so that good behavior is spread from a point to an area. Looking at Michael in front of me, I suddenly felt he had a bit of Lei Feng's spirit of doing nameless good deeds.

The Secret of Success in Learning Chinese

Michael speaks Chinese fluently, in a soft voice. If you couldn't see him, you might mistake him for a broadcaster somewhere in China.

"Your Chinese is excellent. Where did you learn it?"

"Before coming to China, I learned a little bit of Spanish and French in college, but spoke them both poorly. After I came here, I started learning Chinese by myself. At the very beginning, Robbie, who came with me, spoke Chinese better than I did. So wherever he went and whatever he did, I followed him like a shadow. Later, I made up my mind to study Chinese hard. Soon, my Chinese surpassed his, which made him very upset."

"He must be jealous of you. Do you have any good methods or knacks for learning Chinese?"

"My student introduced some books to me, and taught me."

"I know your wife is Chinese. She wouldn't happen to be that student, would she?"

"No way, it wasn't her, but she is the reason why I studied so hard."

Michael laughed, and his face lit up with happiness. "Wow Dalong, you even had a teacher-student love story! Please confess how you tricked her into falling in love with you." I questioned him quickly. He didn't mind at all, but told me everything in detail.

"Her name is Wang Xiaohui. I had noticed her soon after my arrival, but

she didn't have much of a reaction to me. She is a pure girl, clever and pretty. She never expected that she would make friends with me and love me. I didn't express myself to her and kept only a teacher and student relationship. We didn't break this kind of relationship until a few days before I went back home to the States. I told her that I liked her and she said that she liked me too. I was afraid I would never see her again once I left here. If I didn't say it at that moment, I would never have another chance, and might regret it all my life."

"Did she agree?" I asked.

"She was surprised, but she agreed."

Michael was obviously immersed in happy memories, and the clock seemed to have turned back to the year 2001.

Michael went back to the States carrying with him the love he had found in China. He was not lonely then because his heart was fully occupied by her, Xiaohui. He was full of anticipation and confidence. After he went back, he took a MBA course in Arizona State University. Two years later, he graduated

and found an ideal job in a pretty big company. Everything seems to be going smoothly, so why did Michael return to China?

"The second time I came to China was for her. I missed her and longed to live with her."

"Then why didn't you ask her to study in the States?"

"She was studying, too. She studied very hard and not long after I left she successfully passed the entrance exam for graduate school at Peking University. So I decided to make a sacrifice and come to China for her sake."

"Your coming to China meant you gave up the good job and high salary you already had. Were you willing to give it up? Didn't you feel any regret?"

"If one doesn't have love, why should one work?" Michael replied firmly. Just these few words revealed how deeply he loves her. I really admire his courage and perseverance toward love. "After arriving in China, I went to work at the Wall Street English School and she studied at Beijing University. We lived very close and took care of each other in life."

The Most Romantic Thing

"You must have had a very romantic and happy life while you were living in Beijing, didn't you?"

"Absolutely. Well, I'll tell you a very interesting story.

"I love riding my bike. I used to race when I was at the university in the US and I think that having a girl sit on the back of the bike is the most romantic thing that you can do in China. I also really enjoy watching movies where couples ride together because it is really nothing that you would ever see in the US. Maybe a scene about riding around in the rain while the girl holds an umbrella for the two of them, or even a family with the father carrying a mother on the back and a baby in the middle — to me this is really a great thing that is unique about China. The problem is that it is illegal on the streets of most cities.

"One time, my then girlfriend and I were riding around Beijing. We came up to a stop light and she got off the bike to walk to the other side to where she

could get back on the bike. Unfortunately, a police officer saw us and came over to lecture her. I told the officer that she was from Mexico and wasn't able to speak any Chinese. She was wearing a hat from the Southwestern part of the US and she could pass for a Mexican girl, and the officer looked at me kind of dumbfounded. He then told me that my Chinese was really good and he was still confused as to why the girl with black hair was Mexican and not Chinese. I told him that Mexican people also have black hair and brown eyes. He found it fascinating to speak with two foreigners who were riding a bike late at night in Beijing. Anyway, he gave me a patient lecture on traffic safety….

"After that, he told me to be careful with the girl on the back and not to let anyone else see us riding around otherwise we would have to pay a fine.

"I thanked the police officer and rode away to pick up my wife on the other side of the intersection. After we were far enough away she punched me in the arm for lying."

"When did you get married? Did the marriage procedure go smoothly?" After the story, I learned they were already married. I felt happy for Michael. After giving up his job and waiting for many years, he finally lives with his beloved happily forever. But somehow I was still curious. Weren't there any complicated and moving stories behind the marriage? Unexpectedly, my question indeed resulted in a story.

"We got married in 2005. Speaking of marriage, things were not that smooth. Her parents didn't agree at the very beginning, especially her mother."

"Why?"

"A mother usually loves her daughter the most, and thinks her daughter should find the best and most handsome boy. You know, as I told you already, I've got a long face and don't look that handsome…."

"What did you do then? "

"It wasn't a big deal. I just went slowly and waited for my chance. Well, I was fortunate to have an opportunity to be on TV."

"On TV? As an actor?" I opened my eyes wide and looked at him.

"No. Do you know there is a program called 'Absolute Challenge' on

CCTV? It's a televised employment program done by employment units. Applicants exhibit their talents on TV, answer various questions raised by the examiners, then the company chooses the winner from among the candidates."

"I've seen it. What position were you applying for? Did that help your marriage?"

"Well, I was a teacher at the Wall Street English School. They planned to hire a service manager, so I applied for the job. After a series of TV contests, I won. Her parents and family members watched the program. Her family members all praised me, saying I was so capable and highly dedicated, and would surely have a bright future. Her relatives and friends also persuaded her mother to accept me. My talents and sincerity finally moved her mother. Now her parents treat me very well, regard me as their own son, and hide nothing from me. Now they live with us."

Protecting Environment Starts from Me

"Where do you live? Have you bought a house in Beijing?"

"Not yet. At present we live in a rented house in Chaoyang District."

"How do you get to work, by taxi or by car?"

"I take the subway every day. It's very convenient, isn't it?" Michael's reply shocked me. A foreigner going to work every day on the subway, like us. On second thought, it is quite natural. It is very convenient to get from Sihui to Dongzhimen — just take the No. 1 line to Jianguomen, transfer to the No. 2 loop line, and go to his office. Saying this, Michael took out a subway pass from his pocket. I once again opened my eyes wider, saying, "You've got a monthly pass. How did you get it?" I know it's very hard to get a subway pass, even for Chinese people.

"A friend gave it to me," Michael looked very proud of himself. "But," he changed the subject and continued, "once I got on a crowded subway, and I overheard one man say, 'this foreigner doesn't drive, but prefers to squeeze in and out with us.' I immediately said to him, I do it for environmental protection. If there is one more driver, there will be that much more gas emission polluting

the environment. I could drive or take a taxi to work. If you don't care, neither do I. Anyway, this is China, your own country…."

I was moved by his seriousness. If a foreigner can work for environmental protection, why can't we, in our own country?

Speaking of the environment, Michael was off again on a favorite subject.

"The landscape around Arizona is some of the most distinct in the world. There are really high mountains in the north that have snow on their peaks in May and pine trees that are green all year around. The middle of Arizona has a lot of red rocks from the iron in the dirt. When it rains, the mountains turn a very bright red. Southern Arizona is mostly desert where tall Saguaro cacti grow.

"My wife had never seen that sort of difference in forestation before. She loved the Saguaros around my home, but she thought the trees and the mountains up north were even more beautiful. As we were driving through the forest one day, she asked me who planted all of the trees. I told her that they were all natural and that nobody had planted them. She didn't believe me though, she thought I was just kidding, so she asked me again. I told her that it was true that nobody planted all of those trees, that over the years they just came out of the tiny seedlings. She still thinks that I was joking and that the people who settled the west in the 1800s were the ones who came out and planted the trees."

I understood perfectly what his wife was thinking. We have a tree planting festival on March 12th each year. In our minds, trees must be planted by people. There is a Chinese saying, "When earlier generations plant trees, posterity will enjoy the cool shade."

While were chatting, I suddenly felt concern for the next generation of his family. I asked him what he planned in that regard. Michael smiled again. I sensed there was some good news coming. Sure enough, he told me that his wife was two months pregnant. From his eyes, I can see he was also very much looking forward to his future child. He dared not guess whether it would be a boy or a girl. He said he'd rather it was a boy. If it was a girl, she would be awesomely attractive, a beauty for sure. Everyone says that mixed blood is the most beautiful, don't they?

A Busy Career

The second time I met Michael was at a Canada-China Business Council Conference. Dressed in a business suit, Michael looked especially impressive. Now he's the Chairman of the Canada-China Business Council. "When did you switch jobs to do this?" I asked surprisingly.

"This is my volunteer part-time job, without any salary," Michael smiled. "My official status is still the vice-president of Lingo Media Beijing Office. This volunteer job can provide me with opportunities to meet many Canadian and Chinese businessmen. It is also a kind of promotion and marketing for the business and brand of the company."

In fact, Michael's company is a provider of English language learning materials. As early as 2001, they signed a contract with the People's Education Press to compile a series of English learning textbooks for primary and middle schools, including *PEP Primary English*, *Starting Line*, *Beginning English for Young Learners*; they also co-published *Subject-based English* and *English in Business Communication* with the Foreign Languages Studies and Research Press. In 2006, Michael's company Lingo Media signed a co-publishing agreement with Jiangsu Publishing Group (Phoenix Publishing Group) to publish a complete set of English textbooks for vocational schools called *Vocational English for Colleges*, including listening, speaking, reading and writing courses, after-school reading and teacher's materials. Michael spent all his time on promoting this series of materials. He helped the Yilin Publishing Press with marketing promotion and teacher training from vocational schools who use this series of materials for teaching. Therefore he often shuttles around big cities, makes full use of his good Chinese to communicate with teachers, and listens carefully to their opinions and suggestions. During all this his wife supports him fully and is never a drag on him. Whenever he mentions this, a proud and happy smile emerges on his face, and he thanks God that he has married such a good and virtuous wife.

On May 24, 2007, Michael went to Xi'an as usual for a routine training lecture to local teachers at vocational schools. But this time he was really reluctant to leave his home and his wife, as her expected date of delivery was right around the corner. He was afraid that if the child was born, his wife wouldn't be able deal with it alone. But when the expected time arrived, the baby gave no sign of coming out. His wife, Xiaohui, consoled Michael, "You go ahead. It's OK. There should be no problem. The baby won't come out that soon. I can manage myself." So Michael left for Xi'an. The day he set out, he received a call from Xiaohui that evening saying that her water had broken, a sign of delivery. Michael, in Xi'an, got really worried. What should he do? He was going to give a training lecture in the early morning, just a few hours away. How could he leave at this crucial moment? He was faced with a difficult situation. On the one hand was the safety of his wife and the baby, on the other was the expectations of the teachers. He didn't know which side to choose. At last he decided to remain for the work. He immediately called his secretary in the Beijing office and asked her to go to his home and take his wife to the hospital, and at the same

time comforted his wife and gave her strength.

On the morning of May 25, after Michael finished his presentation of the course materials and the training lecture, he apologized to all the teachers and explained his situation to them. Then, he returned to Beijing as soon as possible and dashed to the hospital. That evening, their daughter was born. Watching their new-born daughter, Michael smiled wholeheartedly, for his family had got another beauty. He gave his daughter the beautiful name Leah Michelle Williams, but he hasn't decided on a Chinese name yet. However, he has made a plan for his daughter in the future. He hopes she will be a diplomat and do a lot of practical work to promote friendly relations between Chinese and American people. He said, "My daughter, my wife and I will move back and forth between China and the United States for sure in the future."

Written and translated by Li Shujuan

Personal File

Name: David Drakeford

Chinese Name: Da Wei

Nationality: British

Occupation: Self-employed

Time in China: 5 years

A Briton Arrives in Beijing

David is from Bristol in the southwest of England. As it is difficult to find really good jobs in England, David arrived in China in 2002, with bright hopes and expectations, and began his colorful life here.

I made my first contact with David on the telephone. I could tell by his distinctive Queen's English that it was an Englishman on other end of the line.

In a quiet, cozy corner of the Dongzhimen Pizza Hut I had a face-to-face chat with Dawei, the young man I had talked with on the phone. A Briton with a cherubic face, he looked like a teenager but said he was approaching his thirties. This has completely changed my long-held opinion that all foreigners look older than their actual age.

His full name is David Drakeford, and he didn't need to rack his brains when picking his Chinese name: Dawei, the most common, off-the-shelf Chinese equivalent of "David".

David is from Bristol in southwestern England, a city to the west of London. After growing up in a village in an outlaying area of Bristol he went to college at Bridgewater, where he majored in sound engineering.

"Isn't life in the UK pretty good? Why did you come to China?" I came directly to our topic after an interchange of civilities. "Nowadays there are so many Chinese youngsters who go to college in the UK with high hopes that they can carve out careers abroad."

"I just wanted to come here to browse a little bit after I left college."

"Is it hard to find jobs in your country? I heard it is not so easy." I was really curious about the different employment situations in the UK and China. China

has a big problem in providing suitable jobs for all of its college graduates.

"It's not so easy for job seekers in England either," David assured me.

David came to China in 2002. Dalian was his first port of call, a coastal city with beautiful surroundings, similar to his home town. There David landed a job as an English teacher. After four months, he started looking for something bigger, just like any young people who thinks the grass is always greener on the other side.

First Visit to Beijing

At the beginning of 2003, full of bright hopes and expectations, David arrived in Beijing by train and started his life here.

"East or west, home is the best," as a Chinese saying goes. At home you are always comfortable and away from home you are always on the verge of trouble. It is even so for a Chinese person in China, let alone a foreigner stranded in a foreign land, far away from his kin. "Where did you stay first when you came?" I couldn't refrain from asking.

"I stayed in a hostel near the Jinghua Hotel," David said, "for thirty *yuan* a day."

"Only thirty *yuan*? That's cheap. How were the amenities?"

"Well. How shall I put it? I had to share a room with other people. There was no computer."

"Did you get a job offer before you came?"

"No. I just wanted to come and so I came."

"You really are terrific." I spoke highly of his courage. It would be absolutely unthinkable for a conservative person like me to do such a thing. Who would have thought that a foreigner, a complete stranger, could dare to venture out in this bustling metropolis? "Since you knew nobody in Beijing, how did you manage to find a job here?"

"On the Internet," he said casually.

Indeed, at a time when the Internet is everywhere and information flows unobstructed, it has become indispensable to life and makes things much easier. A great deal of things which used to be very complex and hard to tackle are now a piece of cake. Without doubt, David is one of those who have benefited from the Internet.

David started his job hunt in an Internet cafè. A few days later he found an English teaching post with the private Shane English School and a monthly salary of 7,000 *yuan*. This was his first job in Beijing, and the starting point of his entry into the social circles of Beijing.

In the Shane English School, David met teachers from Australia, Canada, the USA and the UK as well as Chinese teachers. He worked four hours a day, and spent the rest of his working hours learning Chinese.

"It is easiest for foreigners to get English-teaching jobs, isn't it?" I asked him.

"Yes. Most Chinese schools need foreign English teachers since the whole country is crazy about learning English. That's why it's easy for native English speakers to get a job," David concluded. "But not all of them qualify for the job. Some speak good English but don't know how to teach. Some have questionable behavior. Some are alcoholics. Some even come here just to escape being pestered by a wife at home."

David has learned this from his own work experience and from contacts with colleagues. Actually, we Chinese also know that not all foreigners who work in China are the best. Their qualifications vary — some good, some poor. To my knowledge, some foreign teachers have been sacked by their students for poor teaching.

David's contract with the school expired in 2004 and he was somewhat homesick. After a three-month pleasure trip around China and in Hong Kong, he went back to the UK, with no plan to come back again.

"What's brought you back then?" Staring into his eyes, I tried to read his mind.

"Well, I had trouble finding a really good job in England. I saw an advert once for a position in the company which made the cartoon *Chicken Run*. They were hiring a PA for two managers. I really liked the sound of the job and managed to get an interview."

"What happened?" I had no sooner finished asking than I realized that the answer to my question was obvious. He was sitting here talking with me, wasn't he? Anyway, I still looked at him, waiting for the rest of the story.

"The interview was pretty weird. There were two people playing different roles with entirely contradictory viewpoints. I was supposed to find a middle ground, I guess, but I sort of lost my bearings. Besides, I didn't like one guy who was quite boorish. Maybe that was required by the role. Anyway, my answers

were unsatisfactory to them, and the result goes without saying." He still revealed a trace of regret when mentioning the interview, though it happened years ago.

"And after that?" I asked.

"After that I couldn't get a job that I wanted. I thought about going to South America where jobs are readily available, but the pay is so low that you can't have a decent life. We have to work to live, right? So I decided to go back to China."

Second Visit to Beijing

On his second visit to Beijing, David was once again faced with the problem of finding a job, but this time he was no longer a stranger in a strange land. Thanks to his previous teaching experience in the private school, he had several buddies who could offer him some help.

On the recommendation of a former Chinese colleague from a private school, David got a job recording English texts for middle school listening tests. It was not enthralling but happened to be congruous with David's major in sound engineering at college. It was not demanding, requiring only his mother tongue and voice, but no doubt this job offered him new prospects. Later on he started recording with friends. They provided English recording services to the Noah Company for its handheld dictionaries and to other companies for their English learning CDs and multimedia products. During this period, David learnt the real meaning of the Chinese word "*guanxi*" or "social networks" and grasped the importance of *guanxi* in daily life.

"Tell me how you found out the meaning and importance of the word *guanxi*." I was a bit surprised to hear, for the first time, a foreigner with only middling Chinese pronounce *guanxi* perfectly. Keenly interested, I asked him about his understanding of the Chinese word.

"I heard this word when I first came to China and thought it was curious. In our country, we rarely resort to *guanxi*. I came to realize its importance when I got the first recording job. There were sections of dialogues in the English listening tests which took place between a man and a woman, so I had to have a

female partner. I found a young English woman who often did this kind of work for other companies and even for China Central Television. She was grateful to me for the money-making opportunity, and in turn recommended me for more recording work. This showed me the importance of *guanxi*. Why didn't I figure this out earlier? I was really stupid." I couldn't hold back laughing, looking at his young face wearing a kind of "discovering the new world" expression.

"Actually, you started weaving your real social networks or *guanxi* in the private school. Without that Chinese teacher, you wouldn't have been able to get the first recording work and by doing the recording, you helped the Chinese teacher too. In fact, *guanxi* is beneficial to both sides. Look at the Chinese character " 人 " for person, isn't it like two people supporting each other by leaning against each other? Of course it would be totally different if you misused *guanxi* by pulling strings."

He nodded in agreement. Requisite business dinners and drinking-binges are common practice in China, as are the social networks or *guanxi* that see large numbers of desirable vacancies filled by friends and family. "In Beijing, perhaps more than any other city, foreigners seem to follow this model." He wrote an article "Mixing Business with Pleasure" for a magazine, in which he fully describes his understanding of *guanxi*.

"Where is your favorite place to go?" I asked.

"Bars."

"For drinks only?"

"No. Not for drinks but for meeting new friends."

"For *guanxi*, right?" I seemed to catch on to what he was saying.

"I like to go to the Bookworm in Sanlitun. Every time you go in everybody simultaneously turns round to look at you."

"Why?" At this point, a common scene in American cowboy movies flashes into my mind: A strong, burly guy enters a bar, and all those inside turn round and look the stranger up and down with suspicious eyes.

"They want to see if the newcomer is someone they know. If he is they will call him over to join them."

"So that is a pretty good place for social life. You can make new friends, meet old friends, expand your social circles and rake in more business."

"You're right," David continued. "People go to different bars for different purposes. If I want to see a band, I'll go to Yu Gong Yi Shan."

"Do you like music?" I asked him.

"Yes, I do. I like to make music with MIDI — Musical Instrument Digital Interface."

When I asked him to show me a piece of his music, he admitted with an embarrassed smile that he always started off with a bang but ended up with a whimper, and hadn't finished any yet.

Being Embarrassed

In addition to music, David loves writing and photography too. While engaged in his recording, he regularly contributes articles to magazines and newspapers as a free-lancer. When we switched the topic to photography, David told me a story that really embarrassed him a great deal.

One day his camera went missing. Unfortunately it went walkabout on the same day he had a cleaning lady at his house, which gave him grave cause for suspicion. He made the mistake of enquiring about her credentials to one of the lift operators and the rumor was spreading before he was even out of earshot. Xiao Xie (Little Xie), the cleaning lady, along with a satisfied customer of hers, knocked at his door to have a long chat with him. "They told me what I had already found out: she had been working many years at the building with no previous troubles or blemishes on her record," David said. Many repetitions of this central argument threw up some interesting points however. "Although she isn't well educated," the neighbor told David, "her heart is the same as yours or mine." At this Xiao Xie appeared a little piqued, but she was starting to win David over. The only way for him to salvage the situation was to invite her back next week at full pay. "Her reputation is now as clean as my floor, and I got a safe for my valuables."

A Ferocious Cab Driver

David has gradually gotten used to Beijing life. Take riding taxis for example. When he first took taxis, he would always look at the face of his driver. One day, he came across a cab driver who opened his eyes to what a real "a wheel-dominator" was like.

He hailed a taxi on the far side of a moving bus. The driver made a bee-line for the curb, displacing the full-to-bursting vehicle and further grounding an innocent cyclist. This was the driver who was soon to take him across a large and chaotic city at top speed.

The number on the driver's registration card was low: "000486". Too low, thought David. Years of negotiating the streets had taken their toll. His driving was moderately scary but it was worse while they were stopped: lack of stimulation caused him to rattle his metal cage a few times to get David's attention. Here is the dialogue between the taxi customer and the driver.

"So … what time did you start work?" David hazarded.

"6 o'clock start, 12 o'clock finish."

"Six hours a day?"

"Eighteen."

The driver noticed that the taxi in front had a flat tire and honked his horn, but the warning was lost in an orchestra of cab calls. He persisted, even running a red light to try to help his taxi-brethren, according to David.

"Where are you from? England? Ah, a gentleman!" The driver reasoned before directing a burst of the vilest possible language at a private car.

"He missed the exit to my road and dutifully thumped the meter off, soon the G-force of a sharp left turn led us back the right way. I was left on the curb, hoping that the looming taxi price hike might translate somehow into some rest and relaxation time for these stressed delivers of fragile human cargo, but with so many other claims on the proposed extra 0.4 *yuan* per kilometer it seemed unlikely that 000486 would be getting much rest soon."

Happy Life in Beijing

"How is your life in Beijing? Is it passable?" I asked him, thinking life couldn't be easy for a foreign guy wandering alone in a foreign land.

"Not so bad."

"Have a girlfriend?"

"Yes."

"Do you plan to stay on in Beijing?"

"I'm not planning to live here permanently, but I guess it would surprise me if I left." Taking a sip of his coffee, he went on. "Are you happy in Beijing? Somebody asked me this recently. Of course there are certain key factors that contribute to our daily happiness, a decent cup of coffee perhaps or a salesman understanding our Chinese without pulling out a calculator (see this normal price of 40? If I press 'minus' and then '2' you can visually appreciate the bargain!). There are the unexpectedly good days: Is a calm, proficient taxi driver plus jam-free roads what the Chinese mean by 'Double Happiness'?"

"The glass may be half full or half empty but at this stage in life there are plenty of refills yet to come." Stirring his coffee with a spoon, David continued. "All in all I think that my presence here — as I do have a choice of almost any city in the world — confirms my satisfaction and yes, my happiness."

David got excited when talking about his plans for the future.

"I have many plans but my first China dream was always to have a band of my own. Chinese girls have nice voices." He said it was pipe dream for him to set up a band at present because it took too much money, and he did not have the financial muscle.

Maybe this is David's dream. Only he who has dreams will build momentum in life and enjoy happiness.

By Li Shujuan
Translated by Yang Yaohua

Personal File

Name: Jonathan Kos-Read

Chinese Name: Cao Cao

Nationality: American

Occupation: Actor, TV Host

Time in China: 10 years

Speak of the Devil…

A handsome American young man by the name of Cao Cao, has been hosting "The Seventh Day" program at Beijing TV station, and he has turned the show into a big screen hit. He has also played many roles in movies and TV dramas, and is well received by Chinese audience because of his sunny appearance, pure Chinese with a typical Beijing accent, his sly but honest facial expressions and offhand jests. And most importantly, he has impressed his audience because he has a unique known-to-all Chinese name which he picked out from Chinese history. Yes, he has greatly benefited from his connection with the historical Cao Cao.

*J*onathan Kos-Read intentionally picked out the well-known historical Chinese name "Cao Cao" (pronounced ts'ao ts'ao) for himself. It seems just a little bit odd to the Chinese. Looking at this young American, who wore the trace of a sly smile during our interview, I felt there was something improper about his choice of name, but couldn't say what. Anyhow I had to admit that he was very clever to use this exalted name picked from China's history to impress people.

Cao Cao (A.D. 155-220) was a renowned statesman, strategist and poet of the Three Kingdoms Period (220-280) of Chinese history. With his great strategic talent and far-famed literary genius, Cao Cao enjoyed a mixed reputation as being "a capable minister in an age of tranquility, a treacherous pretender in an age of chaos". Characterized vividly but somewhat distortedly in the classic novel *Romance of the Three Kingdoms* written during the Ming Dynasty (1368-1644), the name Cao Cao has ever since been synonymous with a crafty arch careerist, a capricious man capable of being base as well as being great, a man whose personality mixes vehemence and wantonness with cunning and suspicion. The English idiom "Speak of the devil and he will appear", when translated to the equivalent Chinese idiom — "Talk of Cao Cao and he will appear — has a more or less negative connotation.

The great Chinese writer Lu Xun spoke out against the unfair portrayal of Cao Cao, emphasizing that "Cao Cao was a man of great ability, at the very least

a hero. Despite not being his follower, I have nevertheless always admired him".

Sharing Mr. Lu Xun's attitude, Jonathan picked the Chinese name Cao Cao for himself. Following this choice, he has had a smooth life and a successful career in China. In a word, the junior Cao Cao has benefited a great deal from his association with the senior Cao Cao.

A Foreign Face in "The Seventh Day"

In 2006, a handsome foreign face showed up as an anchor on "The Seventh Day", a very popular TV program put out by Beijing's BTV station. This young American man, active in Beijing's streets, would conduct random interviews, learn some amazing skills from others, or play games with the people passing by. One time he'll do morning physical exercises with the elderly, the next time he stops dating lovers and asks them to publicly display their affection for each other, and yet another time he teaches foreign visitors how to speak Chinese. His audience bursts into hearty laughter at his constantly surprising tricks and finds amusement in their seemingly plain urban life. "The Seventh Day" became more interesting and both his program participants and the audience were tickled pink by his fascinating tactics. Not long after, this young American had left a deep impression on his viewers with his typical Beijing accent, both sly and honest facial expressions and endless games — not to mention the well-known name Cao Cao.

At the end of each show, he says to the camera: "See you next week on 'Talk of Cao Cao and he will appear'." His audience eagerly looks forward to seeing the show at the same time next Sunday.

He puffed up a bit with pride when mentioning the origins of the program "Talk of Cao Cao and he will appear." "They asked me to come for a sample show at first," he said. "Then an idea popped up in my mind and I said 'See you next week on 'Talk of Cao Cao and he will appear'. So BTV, thinking it would be a bad idea to put someone else in instead of me, kept me in the program for the following week." Actually Cao Cao's little trick was highly praised by his

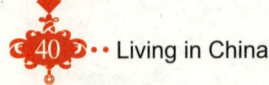

colleagues. "Talk of Cao Cao and he will appear" is one of the most familiar idioms to Chinese people, and it is quite interesting to hear it uttered by a foreign Cao Cao. What's more, how could they give up such a charming outdoor host like Cao Cao!

Beijing residents came to know Cao Cao well from the program, as did audience in other parts of the country, since BTV programs are also broadcast outside of Beijing via satellite. He admitted that it was "The Seventh Day" that increased his popularity. In fact, Cao Cao had previously acted in dozens of TV dramas — providing glimpses of his face to Chinese viewers. However, the cast of a drama is usually pretty large, with more than a hundred names in the credits, which pass quickly on the screen. An audience wouldn't be able to pick up all the names in a blink of eye, except the stars. That means there are numerous TV actors/actresses whom the audience recognizes by face but not by name. Therefore, it is rather difficult to rise to prominence in the entertainment industry. Cao Cao, however, gained some fame both inside and outside show-biz circles because of his advantage over others with his famous name. But it is "The Seventh Day" that has made him a household name and increased his popularity.

In 2007, BTV has invited Cao Cao to be the guest anchor for its series — "Glimpses of Beijing". He has brought a keen sense of humor and depth to the program. This makes the program fantastic and touching, drawing both domestic viewers and those abroad, and allowing them to deepen their understanding of Beijing. TV viewers can also find his playful smiles on some gala occasions, such as BTV's annual competition of "Arts from Our Land" which is performed by foreigners. Inviting a foreigner to host a Chinese TV program is an example of "making things foreign serve the needs of China", and introducing China to the world using Cao Cao is an example of "making things Chinese serve the needs of the world". This is indeed a paragon of East-West cultural exchange.

Cao Cao has been as busy as a bee. Every week, he has to do a program for "The Seventh Day", host "Glimpses of Beijing" plus some evening galas, and help with programs for variety shows. In addition, he writes a column in a foreign language magazine. All these things are only his "side occupations".

His regular occupation is in the show biz as a movie and TV star with endless contracts offered to him. "It's good to be busy," I joked with him. "That means the people here need you." Since he had a busy schedule, we had to squeeze the interview into a half day following the shooting of a TV program and before his flight to join his group in Shenyang.

Learning Chinese To Be "Cool"

When I called him to make the arrangement for the interview, Cao Cao considerately proposed meeting me half way in order to spare me the trouble of going across the city. However, since I knew he had bought a house in Beijing and gotten married, I was quite curious and wanted to see with my own eyes the happy domestic life of this successful public figure. Therefore, I insisted on paying a visit to his home.

When I knocked at the door, I heard a little doggie yelping from behind it. Cao Cao had no sooner opened the door than the doggie jumped to the cuff of my pants and yapped crazily. "Sima Qian, don't be naughty," he admonished. Wow! Giving a little Chihuahua a name like that! I was amazed again at his unique way of thinking.

Noticing my amazement, he began to explain while seating me in a chair. "I thought highly of Sima Qian when I was reading his *Records of the Historian*. Typical historical records were written either in the form of chronicles or following sequences of historical events. It is rare to see one using historical figures as a vehicle. By portraying the individual figures, Sima Qian depicted historical arenas and events from different angles, helping readers have a deeper understanding of history. Sima Qian is great and extraordinary. That's why…." That was why he named his pet dog after Sima Qian, the great historian of 200 B.C.

It is beyond reproach for westerners to name their pets after their heroes. Cao Cao's admiration and respect for Sima Qian come from the bottom of his heart. All this tells us that his knowledge of Chinese culture is comprehensive and profound. But I am sure that someone would thoughtfully pass me a clinical

thermometer or simply suggest I should see a doctor if I were to tell people that I held Sima Qian in my arms while interviewing Cao Cao.

I asked him about his original reason for learning Chinese in an attempt to dig up the roots of his "passion for China". "I learned Chinese only to make me look 'cool' so I could draw girls' attentions," he said seriously, without a sign of joking. "I took art courses in high school. I once entered a national art competition but only won the third prize because I didn't display my skills very well." He still seemed disappointed at not taking the first. However, the third prize winner found favor in the eyes of an arts professor at New York University because of his artistic potential. "My teacher told me to go straight to the New York University School of Arts and major in performance and movie direction. In order to graduate, you need to earn certain credits, one of them being a one-year course in a foreign language." Cao Cao found nothing interesting in Italian, Spanish or German. "I really wanted to learn Chinese, which is quite different than these Western languages. It would be cool to speak it," he said. "Maybe girls would like me if I spoke that language."

His previous knowledge of China may have been limited to the General Tsao's chicken he had had at a Chinese restaurant. "Pretty delicious," as he smacked his lips. I guess "General Tsao's Chicken" is probably the same dish as the famous "Cao Cao's Chicken" from Bozhou, Cao Cao's hometown in Anhui Province. Perhaps fearing that "Cao Cao's Chicken" wouldn't make much sense to American customers, restaurant owners in the US changed it to its current name. My mere guesswork could not be proven without further research and Jonathan drew no hasty conclusions either.

Learning Chinese inevitably got him involved in Chinese culture. He pondered the commentaries and notes of different critics when he read *The Arts of War* by Sun Zi (Sun Tzu), a strategist of the fifth century B.C. He thought Cao Cao's commentary was the most striking of all. He adored Cao Cao when he read the novel *Romance of the Three Kingdoms*. "I think he is the coolest figure in the novel. He is intelligent, rebellious and a bit devilish. In my eyes, a man like him is really cool and must appeal to girls. I wanted to be as cool as him and so I named myself after him."

The process of picking out a Chinese name for himself was not without twists. At first he gave himself the name "Fen Zi Shu Shi" or "Vertical Molecular Formula" because he favored natural science. "A name of four characters! Are you Japanese?" his teacher said shaking his head. Then he decided to pick Cao Cao. The teacher didn't agree either. Jonathan said, "Then call me 'Qin Shihuang' (the first Emperor of the Qin Dynasaty, 221-206 B.C.)." "That's enough," the teacher replied. "Call yourself Cao Cao then." With this annoying but funny student, his teacher was really at a loss at what else to say. After "bargaining" back and forth, he finally got away with his "plot". American student Jonathan Kos-Read now had the Chinese name "Cao Cao".

To the teacher's surprise, fellow student Cao Cao would be a booming star in China! "If not for the name of Cao Cao, I don't think I would have had such success." That's true. The name is so resounding that it instantly catches people's attention whenever he introduces himself. It would be hard to imagine that he wouldn't become famous.

Cast in Fifty Movies and TV Dramas in Eight Years

After his graduation from college, He came to China just to "browse" around the country. He was instantly fascinated and decided to stay. "China has a long history with lots of historical relics. China is developing at a rapid speed as well. I come across new and changing things every day. It is quite encouraging and interesting."

It has been ten years since Jonathan first set foot on Chinese soil. "The first two years I did only odd jobs such as an English and biology teacher, an employee at CNN and so on. I did so many jobs. I was even a store owner." In China people call a job that does not match with one's training as "employment in a job out of one's line". Fortunately he benefited a lot from his two years of "jobs out of his line". He took advantage of these two years to steel himself, learn from life, observe society and build up experience. He was therefore well prepared for

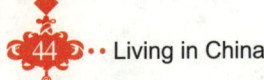

putting his image on the screen. "In the last few years I acted in more than fifty movies and TV dramas, like *No. One Restaurant, Bloody Romance, The Last Imperial Concubine, Break out the Encirclement, Never Give up, Ode to Yan'an* and so on. I am grateful to Director Teng Wenyi for giving me an opportunity during those days, which brought me — an amateur — into the show biz circle."

In the previous years, when Chinese directors needed a foreigner for a role in a movie or a TV drama, they would usually cast a Uighur (a member of an ethnic group in northwestern China) or a person of mixed Chinese and Western blood for the part. Later on they began hiring one or two foreigners to take the special part. But in most cases, however, these foreigners not only lacked professional training but also had a language problem. "In fact there are so many guys on Broadway who are more professional and more handsome than I am," Cao Cao said. "But among the foreign actors in China, these who are better looking don't speak Chinese as fluently as I do. And those who speak better Chinese aren't better looking. As a student specializing in performance, I have a combined superiority over others. That's the reason why Chinese directors prefer me. With a sunny and healthy image, along with his artistic talents, the six-foot Jonathan has the all-round ability to play villains as well as positive characters.

He has a clear appreciation of his footing in the field of arts and that's why he went to China instead of Broadway for career opportunities. This is more or less like David Beckham joining the Major League soccer team — the L.A. Galaxy. "Those who play soccer better than Beckham aren't as handsome as he is and those who are better looking don't play better. It was absolutely the right choice for him to go to America, just like it was for me to come to perform in China."

Asked about the actors and actresses he had worked with, he blurted out Siqin Gaowa, Li Youbin, Jiang Qinqin, Tian Hairong along with many more — a long list of shining stars. Many of these have become his good friends.

He acted as a spy taskmaster in a recent TV play. In his stage photos, he looked grave and stern with a cold stare, quite unlike the affectionate and elegant fiancée he played in *Princess De Ling*. He disclosed nothing about the plot of the play. But it would be good to leave you in suspense. Surely, he will present another new artistic image to his Chinese audience.

A Bond Between the Two Brings Them Together

An old Chinese saying goes like this, "If there is a bond between them, the two will meet though they're a thousand miles apart." In the case of Jonathan's affinity for his wife Li Zhiyin, "a thousand miles" is not the right measurement; it's more like "ten thousand miles".

In 1998, when he was 25 years old, friends started talking about the topic of his marriage. Asked what kind of girl he would prefer, he said, "First the girl shouldn't be too naïve; secondly not too obedient but candid; and thirdly she should have a little meat on her bones." That is Cao Cao! He is a quite different from the common man with his unconventional criteria for a spouse. He would like a girl to have her own ideas, individual character and refined tastes. He was not interested in today's fashionable "bony" girls who try to be lovely

and compliant like endearing little birds. His prayers were answered, and the "Aphrodite" he had dreamed of rose from the foam of the sea.

One weekend a girl with a beaming round face appeared in front of him. After a brief introduction to each other, Cao Cao asked her three questions. He believed the answers to these three meticulously conceived questions would reveal her personality in an instant. By the way, Jonathan's father is one of the leading psychologists in America. The courts often rely on his dad's psychological test results to decide cases. Nurtured in the family's tradition of learning, Jonathan has a rudimentary knowledge of psychology. I don't know how his father would react to his introduction of psychology into love affairs though.

"Why is this foreigner so sassy?" was the girl's first reaction. But after his explanation, Li Zhiyin, a sophomore majoring in finance, began thinking seriously about the answers. For the sake of their privacy, Cao Cao didn't want to disclose the questions and answers. But one thing is for certain, Li's answers moved Jonathan's heart while his candidness and unique style moved her, too. Following the introduction came a date. Li's mediocre English forced Cao Cao to use more Chinese. He quickly improved his Chinese with his linguistic talent and love as motivation.

Once he was invited as a guest to Beijing TV's "The Eighth Zone". During the show, the two hosts gave him a shotgun quiz on his Beijing dialect with very obscure words and expressions. Cao Cao passed easily and got his "qualification diploma". He made an affected "acceptance speech", which carried the TV studio audience away with roars of laughter. Asked for the best ways to learn a foreign language, Cao Cao recommended, among others, dating a pretty girl as one of the best. "You will have so much to talk about with the girl you love. So you have to try your best to convey to her your intimate feelings. You will use gestures if you cannot do it verbally." He exaggerates these gestures with his long limbs. "You have to use all means to make yourself understood, so you are forced to enlarge your vocabulary." The hosts, convulsed with laughter, unanimously agreed it was the best "secret recipe" to learn a foreign language.

Cao Cao became well known in show biz for his role as a documentary

director in a 1999 movie. From then on his performing career in China took off, with contracts coming one after another. His relationship with Li and their mutual attachment strengthened with each passing day. Cao Cao had found success in both love and career. While filming a movie in Yunnan Province, in 2002, Cao Cao almost lost his life in a small mountain village bordering Myanmar. He contracted appendicitis, but treatment was delayed for three days because of the humble local medical conditions. That led to a perforated appendix that worsened into peritonitis. He was hurried on a night flight to the provincial capital Kunming for a surgical operation. Zhiyin, who was then in Shanghai on business, immediately put aside her work on hand and flew to Kunming to look after Cao Cao.

When Cao Cao came to his senses after the surgery, he found in Zhiyin his guardian angel. Not knowing how to take care of the sick, the dainty girl tried her best. Three days later, her company prompted Zhiyin to go back. Worried to tears by the news and loath to part from each other, the two decided to remain together and melted into a smile again. "Forget Shanghai. Everything will be fine." Having gone through this bad break, Cao Cao firmly believed that he had found his better half and proposed to Zhiyin. Instead of exchanging engagement rings, their keepsakes were a jade pendant and a jade bracelet. Cao Cao always admired the historical Cao Cao's deviation from orthodoxy. Zhiyin and Cao Cao, who both hated common customs, even the symbolic ring of marriage, got married with only a marriage certificate issued from the relevant government

department.

Financially Li Zhiyin runs the show at home and has the final say in spending. Cao Cao is glad to be financially "handcuffed". She specialized in finance and so it is wise "to make the best use of her talent" and let her control household matters, he thinks. Every time he returns home from a movie shoot, Cao Cao hands all the money he earned to his wife. She allots him 100 *yuan* a day (equivalent to $12 US dollars) as pocket money. For any special expenses he has to submit a "budget" to her for examination and approval. Of course, the wife also tries to learn and pursue his hobby of collecting works of art. She goes with him to "nose around for treasures" and allocates money for it.

Like all newly-wedded couples, Cao Cao and Zhiyin are "adapting to each other". They have some disagreements caused by their different cultures as well as their differences in personality. To Zhiyin, Cao Cao is not a man of calm temper. Whenever they have a spat, it is always Cao Cao who is first to reconcile and apologize. But he also points out her faults and asks her for an apology. This kind of masculine clear-cut reasoning indeed makes the innately emotional woman feel both fond and annoyed.

Although the two are at cross-purposes every now and then, they are assured of their loyalty to each other. Cao Cao was absent from home for periods of time due to work. He sometimes has beautiful actresses as his performing partners. In order to put his wife at ease, Jonathan made a gentleman's agreement with her that whenever he has to do a romantic scene, he would call her first to tell how the scene would be played out and how pretty the actress was. Only then would he proceed with her approval. But Zhiyin never "abused her veto power". She took time to pay him short visits and sometimes even stayed with the crew in order to take care of the matters in his daily life. This transnational couple's deep affection for each other aroused admiration and envy from his crew colleagues.

Zhiyin is now expecting. She has quit her job and now enjoys rest and relaxation at home — no more accompanying her husband to shooting sites. Cao Cao has been happily collecting ideas for a girl's first name that matches the

Chinese surname Li. I asked him how he knew it would be a girl, since Chinese hospitals are prohibited from revealing gender results from ultrasound scans. Delighted, he said, "I am a foreigner and they leave one side of the net open for me." I assured him that his coming baby would be very pretty as it is said that babies with mixed blood usually inherit only the beautiful aspects of each of their parents. Upon hearing this, Cao Cao beamed with smiles.

Every Day Is a Good Day

Jonathan makes a handsome income out of writing, TV hosting and performing in movies. They purchased an apartment in a fancy community in the Panjiayuan area. When they bought it as a development future, it was an empty lot; as Jonathan put it, just "a mass of air". The price they paid per square meter was 8,000 *yuan*, which has now risen to 13,000 *yuan*. The neighborhood is friendly and most of the residents are from Japan and Germany, just like a diplomatic quarter. But Jonathan has so far not found any of his fellow countrymen in his neighborhood.

The apartment, high up on the 25th floor, is decorated in such a refined and elegant way that the owner's cultural tastes are clearly displayed. Through the windows the scenic Longtan Lake is just within sight. The balcony is big enough to accommodate more than a dozen people for a party. Cao Cao often invites friends to have barbecues and chats on it. They ramble over the world's affairs, just like the historical Cao Cao and his arch rival Liu Bei, "over a cup of wine, discussing who the hero was in their world of turmoil".

He has decorated his study in a manner that follows oriental culture blended with hints of the West. A single step inside the door, one can see a human-sized Buddha statue, causing one to wonder how he managed to "invite" this heavy piece of stone up to the high rise. "I was only able to move it up here with the help of a half-dozen men," he said with pride. "One person alone can't even move it an inch." This Buddha statue and the stone Lord Guan standing in the sitting room's corner have added a rich cultural aroma to the home. Bookcases reaching to the ceiling are filled with foreign and Chinese books. "I love history. On the first shelf are books of European history, on the second Chinese history.... I am also interested in the art of war," pointing at the shelves standing against the other wall, Cao Cao said. "Those are all books about war." He has a limitless reading horizon. His special fondness for war history is not limited to reading only. "I often play historical war recreations on the computer, and even on a sand table, with friends of the same interest. Take Alexander the Great's conquests in 334 B.C. Imagine what the world would have been like if the young king of Macedonia hadn't died from malaria so soon; if he had not turned his sights to the Ganges after he had conquered the Persian Empire; and if he had, instead of marching down to the Indian Subcontinent, advanced east into Warring States Period China?"

My comment on his "military maneuvers" was: there is no "if" in history. But it is great fun to "fight on paper or on the computer". Just imagine what the consequences would have been if the brilliant Greek and Chinese cultures collided and the kind of war scenario that would have resulted if the troops of Alexander the Great fought against the armies of the seven powerful warring states of China. Of course it is a sort of game that challenges the mind.

"We are not 'fighters on paper' and not 'fighters on the computer' either," he earnestly stated with a serious looking. "They are serious war simulations on a military sand table. All war models are strictly made based on the historical references." To him, it seems unbearable to lump together his "academic war study" with laymen's computer games. I suddenly realized that, with such earnestness and persistence, he might have made himself another Officer Jonathan — and of course there would have been one less movie star in China — if he had been admitted to West Point Academy instead of New York University. But there is no "if" in life either. Anyway it is still good enough to have this as it is.

Jonathan has frequent gatherings with some young American "wanderers in Beijing" in the Bookworm, a café in Sanlitun Street. This is a self-organized group of writers who, out of their own free will, introduce China to the outside world. At these get-togethers, they try to make their articles as perfect as possible before publication. Everyone shows their latest works by reading them aloud or passing them around. They exchange what they see, hear or feel; and give each other their suggestions for improvement.

As a performance and directing major at New York University, Cao Cao, not content to only perform, still wants to try his hand at movie directing and even movie producing if an opportunity arises. In his spare time, he sometimes writes play scripts too. It wouldn't be surprising some day if we see a movie or TV play that is written, performed, directed and even produced by him. The historical Cao Cao was adept with both the pen and sword and the contemporary Cao Cao is gifted in many ways. It should be thought of as a transnational, trans-era cultural inheritance between the two.

The Chinese saying "Live in peace and work with pleasure" is embodied by his life in Beijing. "Every day is a good day," as the lyrics of a song goes, and he is so happy that I doubt if he still misses America. Yes, his life is satisfactory with a happy marriage, a new house and a coming baby. His career is prosperous with performances and hosting TV programs. He frequently appears on screen and is well known among the Chinese. He has not only "lived and worked in peace and contentment" but also convinced his father to purchase a house in China.

The father's house is also located in Panjiayuan area, just within an arm's length of the son's. With the new house, it is not necessary any more to stay in hotels when he travels in China and visits the junior Kos-Read. The senior Mr. Kos-Read, approaching his sixties, has been learning Chinese. Not satisfied with simple phrases like "*ni hao*" (How are you) or "*xie xie*" (Thank you), he hopes that when he meets Li's family, he will be able to talk in Chinese not only about weather but about some other topics. Of course it's not an easy job for him, but he is determined and even asked his son to pick out a Chinese name for him.

"My father is an 'old young man' full of vigor and enthusiasm," said Jonathan with pride. From Jonathan's description, I have in my mind an image of "old naughty boy". Jonathan continued, "He is the kind of guy that would walk into the street to join young people in demonstrations against environmental

damage, war or a government policy. I think he is like a fighter so I have named him "*Doushi*", a homophone for fighter.

It is nothing out of the ordinary for a father to name his son, whether in China or in America. But in the rare situation of the Kos-Read's, the son has named the father. "Like father, like son," as we say in China. In a reverse way, however, we can judge the father's conduct from the son, as well. This is a genetic hypothesis as well as a psychological proposition that might be a fitting research subject for the psychologist Mr. Doushi.

Postscript

On March 8, 2007, Cao Cao's wife gave birth to a baby girl by C-section. The new-born baby, seven pounds in weight and 20 inches long, has inherited the beauty of both the parents. The new father, so happy with "the very cute girl who has long limbs", has named her Roxanne Diana Kos-Read. Roxanne is taken from the Princess of Alexander the Great. Cao Cao hasn't yet decided on a Chinese name for the baby, they're still collecting ideas for that.

Translated by Yang Yaohua

Personal File

Name: Uwechue Emmanuel

Chinese Name: Hao Ge

Nationality: Liberian

Occupation: Singer

Time in China: 4 years

Good Songs

In the year 2003, a young African came to China with nothing but a dream — a life-long dream for music. Four years have gone by since then, and he has built up an enormous reputation as a singer in this country and made his dream come true. How did he do it? When this writer sat down for an interview with this young man, he went back through time to show the colorful footprints he has left along his path of life.

"Star Boulevard", a talent show at the China Central Television Station, is an immensely popular singing contest whose ratings rising rapidly from the weekly preliminaries, to the monthly knock-out, to the annual grand finale. Like all previous annual finales, the 2006 one was once again another feast for the audience's eyes and ears. An African singer from Liberia won zealous fans among the audience with his unique voice during one of them monthly competitions in 2006. At the annual finale, he took TV viewers by storm with his incisive and vivid melodious representation of Chinese songs, winning second place. Many of the viewers, though, felt he deserved a better prize, and even complained online against the unfairness to him.

The singer, Uwechue Emmanuel, has a resounding Chinese name — Hao Ge, which means "good song". All those who are touched by Hao Ge's singing concede that he absolutely deserves that name. As he enjoys ever-increasing popularity, Hao Ge also receives constant invitations to perform on many TV programs and gala events all over the country. To everyone's surprise, this young African has become a focal point and an unusual sight on China's stages, attracting big audiences at grand art festivals. Now, if you search on the Internet for "Hao Ge" (in Chinese, of course), you'll find tens of thousands of related results, and the number swells with each passing day. Many people have enjoyed his songs online and the number of viewers of his video clips has been high.

Popular as he is, Hao Ge assumes no air of celebrity and is still as coy and good-natured as he used to be. Whenever someone compliments him on his outstanding performance, he just blushes a bit and asks for "mercy". He is the exact image of a good child so adored by the Chinese.

A Five–Year–Old Boy Moved His Audience to Tears

The six-foot Hao Ge, strong and sturdy, is in such good shape that he would be "fat if he gained one pound, skinny if lost one pound". Many say he looks like the 1995 World Footballer of the Year George Weah. In fact, black people often look similar to the Chinese, just as Chinese all look identical in the eyes of Westerners. The TV screen has a slight distorting effect on performers' images, and the real Hao Ge appears a little bit more elegant in person than Weah.

Hao Ge has an acknowledged rare voice, a blessing from God. His authentic and scientific method of singing reveals that he has had professional training. When I asked him about his musical education, he said "Choir in church," with a smile. "I started singing as a choirboy when I was only five years old. The priest taught us vocal techniques as well as the Bible." The then five-year-old lad, only slightly higher than an adult's knee, already had the experience of performing for the public. Maybe that's why Hao Ge is always able to touch the emotions of his audience with his singing.

When he was still five, Hao Ge even went onstage as the lead singer on a grand occasion. "I still remember, when my choir performed in a gym for the first time, many adults present were moved to tears." A five-year-old little kid leading a group of children, singing songs with an angel-sweet voice, created an extremely holy, pure and beautiful religious atmosphere in which all present felt their souls purified, and extended with tears their heartfelt thanks to God.

When the little choirboy grew up, he got fairly good grades in school. Although he was someone who ardently loved music, Uwechue was not allowed to choose his own major. "My parents have the absolute final say in my family, and we were left with almost no choice for our majors. Just like many other Africans

from a traditional culture, my father expected that I would work as a doctor, a lawyer, or an engineer after I was out of college." It seems that African parents, like Chinese parents, have a fixed idea of "longing to see their sons become dragons", or hoping their kids have a bright future.

According to his father's arrangements, Uwechue went to Morovia University's Mathematics Department and finished school with his M.S. degree. Even though he had no interest in mathematics, he was smart to get his degree with a pretty decent grade. Then he worked as an airplane engineer, an occupation admirable to many, but since music is his lifelong passion, Uwechue found the job as torture for him. "I majored in science and engineering totally out of compliance with my father's wishes, I have had a deep love of music ever since I was five years old," he said, recalling his student days. "During my college years, I learned to play piano and electronic bass and formed a music band with my buddies. We quickly became well-known and performed at many places. Later I went on a world tour with the band. We went to perform in many countries like Holland, Australia, the United States, Thailand, Japan and so on and received much acclaim. Half a year after I graduated from college, I was determined to leave my engineer job to pursue my musical dreams." Abandoning his career after so many years at college deeply angered his father. His son's choice was completely unfathomable to the indignant father. "I have paid so much for your college education, but you don't even want to work. Do you want to starve to death?" But the son had grown up and wasn't so docile anymore. "I have been working for half a year, I haven't been happy even for a single day, and I feel like I'm suffering from penal labor. It is a waste of life if you only work for food and just goofing around."

If he continued with the engineering job, Uwechue could follow a path as a respectable professional and would have had a well-off life. However, afflicted with his dreams and getting antsy, Hao Ge was determined to strike out on a new path, and this caused a disagreement between father and son so sharp that their opinions were as different as black and white. With such a wide generation gap, as so often happens in China, it is not easy for the old and the young to communicate with and understand each other. However, Chinese audiences should take delight in his persistence. Because of that persistence there is one less melancholy engineer in Liberia, and one more passionate singer in China. Given his gifted voice, many musicians would consider it a reckless waste of talent if he hadn't gone into singing.

Countless Fans in China

A Chinese person from Zhengzhou, who Uwechue met in school, was highly appreciative of his singing. "The kind of tone you have is rare and you could be well received in China. I'd be happy to offer you some help if you want to carve out a career in China." This person left with him his contact information and, more importantly, left him with those words of encouragement, which remained in Uwechue's mind. Recalling it now, years later, Hao Ge still believes that he heard the alluring call of faraway China.

Uwechue was born in England and grew up in Liberia. He traveled with his band to many countries in Europe, America and Australia. Born with a natural sense of being a "citizen of the global village", Hao Ge and his buddies traveled

at will around the planet and took any place they liked as their home. When they stepped into a country they loved, they stayed. The five-member band finally disbanded, with the members now living in five different countries and building their respective careers there. Uwechue ended up in China, which, to his mind, is a country with a mysterious culture.

Hao Ge touched Chinese soil for the first time in 2002. Upon his arrival, he understood nothing of the Chinese language and had no impression of China to speak of. Besides the name "Mao Tse-tung", he knew only that China was "a poor and revolutionary country". Seeing is believing. The country he saw with his own eyes was so different from what he had imagined. "Not the third world," he exclaimed with admiration. "China is a developed country." Obviously, he hadn't taken the UN Human Development Index into account for his judgment.

He felt a bit lonely after a year of hanging out in clubs in different hotels in Zhengzhou. He found the musical atmosphere in the city wasn't suitable for developing a singer's career. Rather than a cultural center, Zhengzhou is a hub of overland transportation. Chinese friends told him that musicians should go to Beijing, which is the real center of culture. He came to Beijing in 2003 and happily discovered that it was a city full of music, with many first-rate musicians. It was indeed the Promised Land he had been looking for. He was struck with awe when he saw the extent of the city's modernization and internationalization. He was even more excited by the numerous art festivals and the appreciative audience in the city.

One day, when he was onstage in a bar, he spotted his idol Liu Huan, a top Chinese singer, in the audience. After being introduced to the big shot, he started chatting with Liu using his recently-learned broken Chinese. Considering Hao's difficulty with Chinese, Liu immediately responded in pure and fluent English. "I was surprised at his perfect English," Hao said. "I would never have guessed he spoke such good English." He was told afterwards that Liu Huan had majored in French at college and had picked up English as his second foreign language. Hao Ge, whose mother tongue is English, was even more amazed.

Liu Huan fully affirmed his talent for music and offered him some valuable

suggestions. "You are good at English songs, but you have to sing Chinese songs if you want to advance in China, and have more Chinese appreciate your music." Liu also made him a promise, "Come to me when you have problems and I will try my best to help you out." Hao Ge didn't quite understand the significance of the Chinese saying "One evening's conversation with a superior man is better than ten years of study", but he somehow had the feeling that Liu's guidance would play a vital role in his future development. Even more unexpectedly, three years later Hao Ge became a regular singer contracted with High View Star Works — Liu Huan's music studio.

Chinese are kind and hospitable, and people from the entertainment business were willing to help this African chap. He still feels in his heart the warmth of so many friends who have offered him help and taken good care of him, though his first freezing winter in Beijing caused the tropical fellow great suffering. When recalling that "frozen" experience, he exaggeratedly mimics trembling with cold. "I almost froze to death. But eventually I have gotten used to it. It's nothing if you put on warmer clothes."

He is in love with Chinese culture, and in love with the country. He has been working hard to learn the Chinese language, Chinese songs and Beijing opera. He even learned paper-cut skills from a folk artist.

Maybe he was born to carry a tune. He has made huge strides in his oral Chinese though he still feels daunted by written Chinese characters. He doesn't miss

any opportunity to practice his oral Chinese and notes down all the good sentences he comes across, whether catch phrases or amusing slang. His friends are happy to "transfer intellectual property" and pledge to give him private tutoring in Chinese. Many TV stations invite Hao Ge to do shows because his sense of humor and wisecracks, expressed in Chinese, usually achieve unexpected effects.

Hao Ge sings Chinese songs clearly enunciated and in a full voice, and his musical talents have been appreciated by many professionals. In September 2005, at the recommendation of a friend, Hao Ge took part in "Star Boulevard", a singing contest at the China Central Television (CCTV) Station. Bi Fujian, the host of the show, didn't take him seriously at first and gave him a routine audition, because there were many foreign participants with great skills in the competition. Bi was immediately surprised by his singing after the audition. My god! Such a good voice! Such an excellent song! No problem. Just go ahead!

Surely, he "hit his mark at the first shot"; surely, he "soared into the sky with one flap of his wings". He won first place in the weekly preliminary, then first place in the monthly knock-out. In the end, he took second place in the annual finale. Mr. Bi said during the show: "In 2005 the first weekly and monthly champion was Abao, and I expected Abao would take the first place at the finale. Sure enough he did. Hao Ge has taken first place both at the weekly and monthly competitions, and I expected that he would be able to take first place in this year's finale. Well, the second place is not so bad." A trace of a pity was detectable in his remarks. Many viewers also felt pity for him, and even questioned in their online postings the fairness of the adjudicators.

After he got first place in the weekly championship of the "Star Boulevard", Hao Ge signed a full membership contract with High View Star Works after being recommended by Liu Huan. "It is my honor to be favored by Mr. Liu. Of course he is farsighted in recommending me." Hao Ge is confident that Liu wouldn't let him down. In the contests that followed, he got a lot of advice from Liu Huan, who went with friends to the contest site to cheer him, and even canvass votes onstage for him at the annual finale.

"He is my teacher and my big brother and has given me so much guidance." He gave a thumbs-up when talking about Liu Huan's songs which, as Hao Ge put it, "are all eternal classics". From the weekly competition to the annual finale, this African chap entered the contest singing songs almost all chosen from Liu Huan's classics, such as "Cannot Live Without You", "Everlasting Sunrise on the Grasslands", "Cherish the Memory of My Battle Companion" and so on. "For example, when I was about to sing 'Cherish the Memory of My Battle Companion', which is the theme song of the movie *Guest From the Ice-Caped Mountains*, Mr. Liu told me the background story to get me emotionally engaged, and so I did it with a lot of emotion." With the elegant way of singing he has learned from Mr. Liu, combined with his R&B style and heartfelt singing, he always touches the soul of his audience.

Hao Ge has won tens of thousands of fans. "An African bro could move us Chinese audience to tears with his Chinese songs!" Many of his audience amazed.

On the stage of the grand finale, host Bi egged him on to present an aria from Peking Opera. Hao Ge, in dead earnest, put on the opera costumes and then played the dark-skinned Judge Bao Gong, a role in *Behead the Emperor's son-in-law*. There was no need for him to put on black-skin makeup; his natural color spared him the process. His remarkable imitative vocal music drew loud applause. With instruction from Ms. Qiu Yun, daughter of later Qiu Shengrong, an outstanding Peking Opera artist, Hao Ge learned this aria in just three days. "He has a marvelous power of understanding," Ms. Qiu Yun said.

When foreigners translate the term *Jing Ju*, a unique form of Chinese theater, into "Peking Opera", they can often end up feeling daunted when they try to study it. But Hao Ge has cooked up "a secret shortcut" in learning folk arts like Peking Opera. He thinks of Peking Opera as Chinese Rap, which removes most of the pressure from the learning process. The shortest distance between the two points is a straight line. Whether it is science or art, the simplest way is usually the superior way in expressing it. Remember that Hao Ge has a masters degree in science; the master has his scientific way of learning.

Hao Ge shakes the age with his great reputation. He was invited by CCTV to perform at the 2007 Chinese New Year Gala with a famous Chinese songstress Han Hong. In singing "In a Faraway Place", a classic love song, the two thrilled the minds and stirred the souls of the audience with their heavenly high ranges. On New Year's Eve, at least 900 million viewers watched the wonderful duo on TV, and more Chinese got to know the young African.

To perform in the event is considered a great honor and a symbol of high standing in show circles, a dream of many Chinese artists. There have been very few foreign artists who have ever performed on this stage. In this enlivening night, Hao Ge stood on the stage of this grand event, and was seen by millions of eyes. It was the biggest success in his career so far.

During the "Star Boulevard" singing contest, his fans heartily applauded for his singing while holding up signs reading "Hao Ge, Good Songs", and this conveyed to him their high expectations. Indeed, Hao Ge didn't let them down. Some think it might better fit with his current status to make a sign reading "Hao Ge, Unceasing Songs".

Stay in China and Sing Good Songs

On March 2, 2007, a group of friends threw a birthday party in a pub in honor of Hao Ge, who hurried back to the party from three successive shows. Many of those present were celebrities of the music industry. Hao Ge was deeply touched by the presence of Mr. and Mrs. Ge Yanping, the chief director of "Star Boulevard", Abao, the first place holder of 2005's finale and Aerfa, a little star shining on the "Star Boulevard". "So many friends came here to celebrate his birthday," the famous musician Li Jie said in his congratulatory speech. "We can see what a good reputation Hao Ge has in our music circle." Besides Liu Huan, Li Jie, and Lao Zai, Hao Ge boasted, Cui Jian, father of China's rock music, composer San Bao, famous singers like Ding Wei, Lin Yilun, Pang Long, Yang Kun and Lu Wei are all his friends.

Hao Ge is popular in show circles and well received by audiences. He is approached with warm smiling faces wherever he goes and will get a helping hand whenever he finds himself in need. Here in China he has realized his music dreams, and here in China he feels as free as a fish swimming in the sea. He is deeply in love with the country that admits him with her openheartedness and blesses him as her own child. He has traveled to many other countries where he suffered so many hardships in life and so many tortures in realizing his dreams; at last he has found the right place with the feeling of being home.

He wants to stay and build up his singing career in China, and even wants

to become a Chinese citizen. Why the Chinese citizenship? "Music is my first priority and I have my music career in China," he said. "Although I have been to many other countries, I have felt that homey warmness and sense of security only in China. In cities in many other countries, no one dares to go outside alone at night. But in Beijing, I could walk around safely even after midnight."

Hao Ge's efforts have been paid off handsomely by his achievements. And finally, his father has begun to understand his decision and even plans to pay a visit to his son. To Hao Ge's delight, the generation gap has been bridged. Ready to settle down in China, he rented an apartment and brought his wife and son over. Although Chinese cuisine is well known all over the world, Hao Ge hasn't completely gotten used to it. He is allergic to seafood so he has to stay away from that, and only enjoys food like steamed dumplings, pepper, curry, etc. Of course his favorite is still the African food cooked by his wife.

But things not always go according to plan. His wife couldn't get used to her new cultural and material life in China. She chose to leave him in the end. Hao Ge has to live alone with his five-year-old son. The boy is clever and cute and all his friends like to take the boy outside to play, and offer to take care of him. So Hao Ge doesn't have to worry too much. Though he is "successful in career but frustrated in love", he feels no regret about his original choice. As usual, he still performs and goes all out in making music.

Maybe because he is a Christian, Hao Ge takes what comes with a peaceful mind and is contented. Whether faced with the frustrations of daily life or great successes in his career, he takes it all with stoic calmness. "The kind of attitude you have toward life is the kind of music you will make." We expect Hao Ge to achieve greater success. As for the dissatisfactions of his daily life, he assumes an attitude of "After the rain comes fair weather". If he had money, of course he would first buy music equipment, which he cannot do without, though an audio mixing console would cost him more than 100,000 *yuan*, and tens of thousands more for a brand microphone.

When talking about music, Hao Ge becomes immediately excited. Not long after arriving in China, he told me, a record company in southern China released his album *Red and Black*. The album had songs both in Chinese and English, including classic Chinese songs such as "How Much Love Could Start Over", "Cannot Leave You", "Doesn't Matter". Now he has been recording his albums at Liu Huan's music studio. "With Liu as my guide I am full of confidence." Hao Ge presented me a CD containing his songs and songs sung by other two singers, all the while crooning "Doesn't Matter" in a different style from the original singer.

Besides music, we also talked about his hobbies. He loves cars — the toy for men — but can't afford one right now. "The traffic is terrible in Beijing. You cannot drive at a decent speed." Sometimes he plays table tennis, and there's no one who can match him in his company. One day after he finished a show at CCTV, he played *ping pong* there with a lady and was defeated. This reminded him that China is the kingdom of table tennis. He also favors football and plays forward in a Chinese Star Team. When penetrating, he has a little bit of Weah's style. One time he fell and broke a finger during training. Two guys from the "Shui Mu Nian Hua" band sent him to the hospital. The next day, he appeared on a Shanghai TV show to sing "Boat Tracker's Love". But this time it was the "beloved brother's broken finger," instead of his love, that "swung around the towing rope".

When we were talking about his injury, Hao Ge's assistant, praised him highly for his hard work. "Yes, sometimes we do see people performing on stage while sick," he said, "but this guy is simply born for the stage. He had a temperature of 39 degrees centigrade and was listless backstage. But he was animated again as soon as he got on stage." As for his performance, Mr. Yang said he is good at live singing on stage, and is not the kind of singer who relies on recording first at the audio studio and then lip-synching on stage. "I believe Hao Ge is the leading figure of live singing in China," Mr. Yang concluded.

Hao Ge's strong work ethic and his musical talents have won him high praise from his colleagues. "When he gets a new song with new lyrics and new music scores, he puts phonetic letters next to the Chinese characters that are new to him. He can memorize them all in just half an hour. What a brain he has!"

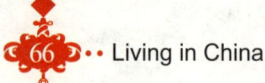

Upon hearing these remarks of praise, instead of being flattered, Hao Ge feels embarrassed at his ignorance of written Chinese. But I am sure it won't be long before he is able to read and write Chinese, since he has already embarked on a course to "eliminate his illiteracy in Chinese".

Translated by Yang Yaohua

Personal File

Name: Antonino Laspina

Chinese Name: Lai Shiping

Nationality: Italian

Occupation: Government Employee

Time in China: 6 years

His Love for Marco Polo

Carrying with him the Mediterranean breeze and 5,000 years of culture, Antonino Laspina traversed Eurasia all the way to this remote, mysterious country in the Far East. Fluent in English, French, Spanish and Portuguese, this Sicilian polyglot regrets only his mediocre Chinese. Besotted with collecting and having read *The Travels of Marco Polo* at a very young age, he never dreamed that he would be attached, for the greater part of his life, to ancient China and the faraway East, and never dreamed he would become the promoter of "the New Marco Polo Program".

As the chief representative of the Italian Government Trading Commission's Beijing Office, Mr. Laspina chose the Chinese name, "Lai Shiping", which was obviously transliterated from his last name. I guess he has "localized" his name for the purpose of "identifying himself with the Chinese people". His localized name, along with his charming smile, is indeed conducive to socializing with Chinese friends and to carrying out Sino-Italian economic and cultural trade.

On the 38th floor of the Jingguang Building, the tallest skyscraper in Beijing, I suddenly realize the profound meaning of his Chinese name as I shake hands with him. What an ideal world it would be if people of different colors on this planet could mingle harmoniously with one another and build a common "global village"! For the peace and prosperity of mankind, we must eliminate war! Any progress made by the human race rests on world peace. He was smart to choose this name, which is an abbreviation of the Chinese phrase "rest on world peace": Lai for "rest on" and Shiping for "world peace".

As the chief representative of the ICE, Mr. Lai has done many valuable things for Sino-Italian economic trade and cultural exchange in the past few years. He has made frequent appearances in the news media and therefore gained a certain reputation among Chinese economic and press circles. When I proposed an interview with him, he readily accepted it. As we sit down for the interview,

he states with a smile that he speaks English, French, Spanish and Portuguese and reads Korean. But he feels "indebted to China", for he knows only "a little bit" of Chinese, though he loves Chinese culture. A brilliant, open-minded talker, he speaks very fast in English, just like an excited football commentator for the Italian A Series. This turns our interview into a pleasant conversation, and a keyed-up recording as well.

Marco Polo, an Idol of His Childhood

It goes without saying that Marco Polo is the most eminent foreign figure in Chinese history. Although not necessarily the first to cross Eurasia into China's central region, he was certainly the first foreigner who made a detailed record of China and introduced it to the West.

The Travels of Marco Polo carries detailed descriptions of different ethnic groups' customs, habits, religions, native products and anecdotes as well as the political, economic and cultural life of China's Yuan Dynasty during the 13th century. *The Travels of Marco Polo* provided foreigners of the medieval age and thereafter with a golden key to understanding China. Now it also provides contemporary Chinese historians with rich references to the Yuan Dynasty

(1271-1368) observed from a "Western angle". The Italian's far-reaching contribution to East-West cultural exchange has earned him great, long-lasting respect in both the West and the East.

Cristoforo Colombo, an Italian navigator of the 15th century, was fascinated by the Oriental World described in *The Travels of Marco Polo* and started sailing the blue seas on his around-the-globe exploration. He discovered the "New World", though he failed to reach the East.

In the West, many people read *The Travels of Marco Polo* as attentively and thoroughly as Colombo did, and yearn for the mysterious East, dreaming of discovering something new. Of course it is impossible for them to discover another geographical "New World". But there is still much to be explored in the cultural "New World". It is the search for their dreams of a "New World" that has made so many people hurry across the planet.

Antonino Laspina was born in Sicily, Italy, at the end of 1950s. He has idolized Marco Polo since he was a little boy. He didn't have the Chinese name "Lai Shiping" then and never thought that someday he would come to live in China. "It was possible to take pleasure trips but I never thought about living in China," he says. He could never have imagined that years later he would be the chief of the ICE Beijing Office, living happily with his family in China.

His hometown Sicily is a scenic island with a long history of 5,000 years. He wears a proud expression when he speaks about his hometown. If the Apennine Peninsula is a boot protruding into the Mediterranean Sea, then the triangular Sicily is the toe of this boot. Situated in the very center of the Mediterranean and influenced by Phoenicia-Punic, Greek and Arabic cultures, it has been the center where different cultures have collided, mingled and merged. Traces of French, Spanish, Portuguese and German cultures can often been seen on the island, that is why it's called "the cradle of European Civilization". Italy, as the German social scientist Friedrich Engels called it, "is the firstborn son of the European Culture". Italy has the status of "the firstborn son", to a great extent, because of the age-old, splendid Sicilian culture. Of the 29 Italian cultural relics on the list of the UN World Heritage Sites, five are on Sicily. Here on the island some Chinese cultural items such as silk and porcelain pieces have been found as well.

When he was five or six years old, Laspina happened to come upon a big archeological excavation. A site of city ruins was found underground near his farmstead. An archeological team led by a Princeton university professor unearthed a city hall, a square, city walls and streets along with a large amount of cultural relics. The little boy was so curious that at first he peeped out from the opening between doors or from the keyhole. Then he walked up close to watch the archeologists working in the field. These archeologists liked the smart kid very much and sometimes they would give him a shard of some relic. He was as happy as if he had found a piece of priceless treasure. That was his first "baptism" in ancient culture.

Born and raised in a place that absorbs and embraces all different cultures, Laspina has had a sense of world citizenship since he was very young. So it was only natural for him to worship his idol Marco Polo. "I even knew to look for *The Travels of Marco Polo* at the library at the age of six or seven. Of course

that was the abridged edition for children. I began reading the original when I was sixteen or seventeen. I have a craving for collecting all different editions of *The Travels* and have so far collected 25 different editions. I was amazed when reading about Kublai Khan and Chinese cities when I was young. They seemed to me simply like fairytales. After I grew up I knew that the things Marco Polo described about China were not fairytales. As a college student, I felt that Marco Polo not only reproduced the sense of those times, but also gave us later generations useful knowledge, and showed us another kind of culture. A great amount of information on China has poured into Western society since China adopted its open-door policy at the end of 1970s. This information proves what Marco Polo said in his book was neither fiction nor myth. You see that the grasslands and the coal mines he mentioned in the book are true. The nonflammable cloth (asbestos cloth) is true too."

Thanks to Marco Polo's book, he has always been full of curiosity and a yearning for the Orient. "I became very much interested in Oriental philosophy when I read about Confucianism at the age of 12. I believe that Greco-Roman philosophy and Oriental philosophy, with Confucianism as its core, can compliment each other. Nothing is impossible if we combine the enterprising spirit of Western culture with the adept restraint of the East, and combine Aristotle with Confucius," he summarizes his experience. "Since I came here I have adopted the method of working to promote my plans in accordance with their natural tendencies, and never imposing things on others. In this way I have achieved pretty good results."

His experience of working in China has provided guidance to Westerners who come to work and live in China. "Once they come to the Orient, Europeans should act like Marco Polo and follow local customs. Try to gain some knowledge of Confucianism, slow the tempo of life, and be good at communicating and mingling with the local people."

This Sicilian boy thought he ought to go to Rome first before proceeding farther to Asia and China. "As a little boy I had big dreams of Rome and thought Rome would be more beautiful than Sicily". And so he chose to go to Rome for his college education. He wanted to prepare himself with enough knowledge to allow him to expand his work and life around the globe. He was always attached to the Orient during his college years, though his activities were limited to Sicily and Rome. "I always thought then that my focus should be on the East," he tells me.

A Young Italian Marches East

As an Occidental saying goes: "All roads lead to Rome." The Sicilian boy realized his dream of Rome, and grew up there. He majored in Political Economics at Catania University and remained at the school after graduation as an assistant to the president. The young man's idol was Marco Polo, however. His dreams would not stop with Rome — he wanted to go farther, in search of bigger dreams.

While working at university, he got his CORCE (professional foreign trade training course) certificate in 1980. He took part in a SIOI course in 1981. In the same year he passed the nationwide exam for government employees and was admitted to the Italian Foreign Trade Committee, beginning work at its headquarters in Rome that October.

In 1982 he married Maria, a girl also born in Sicily. His bride attended the same school he did, in the same major, graduating a few years later. It was 44 degrees Celsius on the day of their wedding, which was an auspicious sign for a life-long happy marriage. That same year the Italian football team won the World Cup. There was nationwide rejoicing on the news. Still immersed in the sweetness of their honeymoon, the young couple had the feeling that the whole world was sending them blessings. It so happened that the Italian team won the World Cup championship again when they celebrated their silver wedding, so they got double congratulations from friends in China.

At last, Antonino Laspina was dispatched to the East in 1985 as a government official. But his road into China was quite tortuous.

He was sent to South Korea when he was 27 and worked in Seoul with his

wife until 1990. His wife became pregnant in South Korea and they went back their hometown in Sicily where their first son, Albert, was born. They returned to South Korea when the boy was six-months old. They went back home in Sicily again in 1987 when they had their second son Augusto, who was named after the founding emperor of the ancient Roman Empire.

He found that South Korea is deeply influenced by Chinese Confucianism. In order to better understand Oriental cultures, he studied the Korean language very hard. He has a passable reading ability in Korean, but his oral Korean still needs to be improved. His pronunciation is pretty good, though. "It's not so easy to learn to pronounce Korean," he said proudly.

He worked for one year in Rome after leaving Korea. Then in 1991 he was dispatched to Kuala Lumpur, Malaysia, and worked there until 1996 as the chief representative of the Italian office there. The Chinese cultural atmosphere is thicker in Malaysia than in Korea since 60 percent of its population is of Chinese origin. During this period he made a lot of friends and established close relations with many Chinese entrepreneurs, businessmen and people from other circles. Most of these employees at the Italian office were Chinese Malaysians. With so many Chinese working under him, he got the false impression that he was working in a Chinese province. He made frequent business trips to Singapore where he found even more Chinese. In Southeast Asian countries, Chinese culture and customs have been well preserved. He took this opportunity to closely observe many Chinese holidays, folk customs and habits such as wedding ceremonies. He tried his best to understand the values of Chinese culture. "I believe Chinese culture and Italian culture, particularly Sicilian culture, have much in common. In both cultures, people value mutual respect, keeping promises and loyalty to family." Precisely because he is good at finding common ground between the two cultures, Laspina got on so well with the local people that they thought this Italian was "very Chinese" and predicted that he would surely "go to China some day".

Finally, in 1996, the day came when he got his assignment to China. But it was to Taipei, instead of Beijing that he had been yearning for. "Maybe the responsibilities in Beijing were too heavy and my boss was afraid that I didn't have enough experience for it. So maybe they sent me first to Taipei for the purpose of training," he said, self-deprecatingly. "Taipei wasn't a bad place for me; after all I was in China anyway." In fact, the work in Taipei was rather heavy for him as chief representative: it was hardly a job just "for training". Many years of working in the areas surrounding China made him very familiar with Chinese culture. During this period he formally took the Chinese name "Lai Shiping". He felt quite comfortable working and living in Taipei and decided that their third child would be born there, instead of traveling thousands of miles back to Sicily.

On April 2, 1997, little Alexander was born. Now Laspinas were a 4-A family: Antonino, Alberto, Augusto and Alexander; all their names began with A except his wife's. We talked about his youngest son's name during the interview. "Is he named after Alexander the Great who marched eastwards in history?" Mr. Lai Shiping nodded. "So there are two great figures in your family now. The historical Alexander the Great didn't reach China during his eastward conquest. The Alexander from your family has completed the eastward conquest in a different way," we joked. "It's a peaceful and friendly eastward conquest," he laughed.

In his mind, China is the center of Asian culture and the center of the Asian economy. It is a developing country with great potential and a great future. The

open China is a tremendous market, and there will be great opportunities for Italy and China to reach win-win agreements in their economic and trade cooperation. He learned a little Chinese when he was in Malaysia and took regular Chinese courses while he was in Taipei. It was a pity that he didn't have enough time to study Chinese full-time as he was busy as the chief of the office, and therefore his Chinese level has never reached that of his other foreign languages. Even now he speaks Chinese like a typewriter, word by word, and never in complete sentences, though his enunciation is clear. He doesn't even speak as well as his wife, and is left far behind by his youngest son who was born in Taipei and studies in Beijing's Yaozhong Bilingual International School.

In 1998 he was recalled back to headquarters in Rome, and since then he has been a member of the I.A.I American-Italian Committee. He has held the position of Promotion and Cooperation director since 2000. During this period, he also held posts in other committees, such as the advisary committee for EU Asian investment projects and the Expo of "2001 Italy in Japan" sponsored by the Italian Government. In 2002 he was included in America's "Who's Who" for his outstanding achievements and global prestige.

A teetotaler and nonsmoker, Mr. Laspina's only hobby is "reading ten thousand books and traveling ten thousand miles". While he was working in Italy he spent all his holidays in other countries, traveling far more than ten thousand miles. In spare time, he finds and buys books and reads like crazy; he's probably already read more than ten thousand books. China and Asia are always on his mind and he pays special attention to any news from the East. Since his Chinese leaves much to be desired, he always feels a bit guilty that he's not reading anything in Chinese. So when he came across any English books on China, he buys them without a moment's hesitation. He not only reads these books but also collects them, such as *A Dream of Red Mansions*, *The Monkey King* and many other masterpieces. People say, "He's a crazy book buyer!"

It's hard to say whether he's crazy or not, but his habits have turned Mr. Laspina into "an old China hand". At present a fashionable saying goes like this: "He who is stubborn and unswerving will succeed." Mr. Laspina's story seemingly bears it out.

Promoter of "The New Marco Polo Program"

Mr. Laspina returned to China in 2003 as the chief representative of the Italian Government Foreign Trade Commission Beijing Office, taking charge like a "duke" who carries considerable authority in the region. "The government gives you the position, but you have to fill the role yourself. The greater your capabilities, the more roles you can play. The position itself is not as important as the role you play. It is what you do, not what position you hold, that decides whether you are successful," he said. "China is a country with great potential for economic development. It's quite challenging working here, but you will have a great sense of achievement if you fulfill your role in this country."

A Chinese saying goes: "Keep thy shop and thy shop will keep thee" and a Western proverb says: "An opportunity favors the prepared head." This is exactly the case with Mr. Laspina who has worked with great enthusiasm and gained rich experience. With his deep understanding of Chinese culture and its economic situation, Mr. Laspina has carried out his ICE career in China as planned, without a hitch.

The year 2003 saw the SARS epidemic, but Mr. Laspina didn't seem to worry about it too much. "Many people from other countries thought China's economic development would slow down as a result. Even some Chinese thought that. I was quite confident that China would get over this difficult period since the Chinese are hard-working people. It turned out just as I expected. Great changes have taken place in China, while the economy has developed at a sustained high speed." He was a bit pleased with himself for his prediction.

"Some thought the work in China would be very hard for me. In fact, the going was very smooth. It was so smooth that it seemed simply extraordinary to other people. But to me it was the natural result of years of efforts. The Italian Foreign Trade Commission, which was established in 1965, has built up a good reputation and broad social connections in China. With such a sound foundation,

it is not hard at all for me to carry out my mission here. Chinese people have much in common with Italians in their values and their ways of conducting themselves in society. If you are open-minded and treat others sincerely, then you will be treated sincerely with open mind, too. Chinese people value faithfulness very highly, just as the Italians do." He has won a lot of friends with his sincerity and faithfulness and has achieved many fruitful results. The Chinese often say, "Good heartedness is always rewarded." It seems that Mr. Laspina has grasped the quintessence of this saying.

China and Italy are both countries with long histories and splendid civilizations. He works hard to advocate East-West cultural exchange and to open up new channels of mutual understanding, trust and mutual benefit. He spares no effort in organizing all kinds of activities to promote friendship and economic cooperation between the two. "I am not a businessman, but a government official who is building a bridge linking the two countries. I introduce China to Italian businessmen and tell them it is the best time to do business here. At the same time I also lobby the Chinese government to pay attention to its economic and trade cooperation with Italy. During these bi-lateral introductions, I never talk big, never exaggerate and try my best to urge them to observe and to learn from their experience. I offer assistance to Chinese doing business in Italy and Italians doing business in China. Sometimes I even use personal connections to help them. Anyway, it is never difficult to solve problems if you make both sides realize that it's meaningful and practical." Mr. Laspina's efforts are even more important at a time when there are frequent trade conflicts between EU and China.

"I always hold the viewpoint that economic trade is simply cultural exchange conducted in the form of currency. China and Italy share a lot in common in their cultures: We esteem family values, treasure friendship and prefer innovation and exploration. Both peoples are adept at creation and like beautiful things. Just as Italians loved Chinese silk and porcelain hundreds of years ago, Chinese people now are fond of fashionable clothing and autos made in Italy. Each country attracts more and more tourists from the other. All these facts show that we appreciate each other's scenery and cultural relics."

He places great importance on the news media and never turns down their requests for interviews. He grasps these good opportunities to promote his Italian way of thinking. His Italian sense of humor and his ability to promote are well received in the Chinese mass media, and thus add impetus to trade and economic connections.

The Italian Association of Printing, Paper-Making and Packing Industry brought four companies to Beijing to seek business opportunities. Speaking at the training course for Chinese technicians from printing industry, Laspina said "The art of printing was introduced into Italy and the rest of Europe between the 13th and 14th centuries. Now we have returned to the mother's home." His warm remarks instantly drew the two sides closer. During a winter sporting goods expo, he told the visitors, "not only does Italy have Formula One auto racing, and the title of world champion of football, it also has outstanding sports technology and equipment. Winter sports, in particular, are very popular in Italy. I would like to invite you to visit the Italian booths." His words made the visitors itch to see. "The 2008 Beijing Olympics will be a great moment, and will give enormous impetus to the development of China's sports industry and to foreign sports industries as well. Some sports goods made in Italy have already been introduced to the games."

ICE has six branches in China and every year it sponsors about one hundred trade-promotion programs. "Like Marco Polo, Italians never lack the pioneer spirit and creativity. When the time is ripe they will come to the market for sure." He was overjoyed when talking about his successful programs.

The 750th birthday anniversary of Marco Polo was held in Beijing's Chaoyang Park on May 31, 2005. During the five-day celebrations, Beijing residents saw and appreciated authentic customs, culture and fashions from Italy. They saw fashion shows put on by Italy's famous companies promoting their latest products, as well as movies and music performances. They also enjoyed Italian wines and gourmet foods prepared on site by Italy's top-notch cuisine schools. They were awed by the fancy cars and motorbikes, interior design by top designers and sports equipment used by world champions. The three famous

brands Valentino, Fendi and Missoni left a deep impression in the visitors' minds. The gondolas sailing on the lakes brought an exotic taste of "Venice Honeymoon" to the 50 couples who had their wedding ceremonies there. A marble statue of Marco Polo sculpted by Italian artists was erected in the center of the park. The grand Italian-theme event climaxed with an Italian-style dinner.

Mr. Laspina named this event "A New Marco Polo Program". He was proud to be its organizer.

Eight thousand students from Tsinghua University attended the "the Night of Italy" party in July 2006. Ferrari, pizza, funny rolling skating and fashion shows vividly heightened the Italian theme. The president of the university believed it was the best activity and Mr. Laspina thought it was a successful "soft education" in Italian culture. An ecological energy-saving building, named "Italy Building", was completed in the Tsinghua Campus. As a guest professor, Laspina gave lectures on the history of Italian garment development at the Tsinghua University Fine Arts College. He took all these occasions as opportunities to introduce Italian culture.

On October 9, 2006, the newly re-named "Jinghe Bell," which means "Competition and Cooperation Bell", sounded 36 times in the Duanmen building of the Forbidden City. A new sort of footwear show was opened inside the gate building. Mr. Laspino had never expected that the show could be held in such a prominent place, and from this he saw China's sincerity in cooperation. "Half of the Italian people wear shoes made in China, and the rate of Italian shoe exports to China increases by 15 percent annually. There are more than one million high-end customers in China, which has created a great market opportunity for Italian shoe makers. Ordinary Italians need medium- and low-grade shoes and that provides a market for shoes made in China. So there is no threat to each other's industry and it is a win-win situation for both of us."

When doing business in China, as he sees it, you should work hard but not push too hard. He appreciates the Chinese attitude of "letting nature take its course". "Chaoyang Park put the Marco Polo statue I presented in an out-of-the-way corner of the park. I thought it was their business where they wanted to put it. It was good enough that they had accepted it, so I didn't take it to heart how they handled it. One day they called. I was a little bit nervous, thinking maybe it was not right for Chinese parks to erect statues of foreigners. To my surprise, they asked me if they could 'put the statue in the center of the park'. 'Of course you can,' I answered without a moment's hesitation. The result was exceptionally good. It was the same with the footwear show. We applied for the footwear show and asked the Chinese side to choose a location for the show. I never dreamed it would proceed so smoothly. They even managed to place the show in the Duan-men building of the Forbidden City! Much better than what I had conceived."

In Beijing, Mr. Laspina, an Italian familiar with Chinese culture, has promoted Sino-Italian economic, trade and cultural exchange with astounding results. With his high-energy efforts, he has filled people with great confidence in the economic prospects between the two countries. "In the next five years, the trade volume between the two countries will double, with an annual increase of up to 20 percent," the self-assured Mr. Laspina said.

Is this merely a fond wish? Or a prediction? Or is it a promise by the promoter of "the New Marco Polo Program"? Let's wait and see!

The 4–A Family's Happy Life

After the experience living in Taipei, the 4-A family heartily enjoys their life in Beijing. "There is no problem with food in Beijing. Everybody likes Chinese food. Sichuan and Guangzhou foods are my favorites. I am pretty good at ordering dishes from menus. One can understand a culture better through its food. Sea slugs, for example, are not really a kind of food for Westerners. But I enjoy trying them. Anyway you have to experience it firsthand. I am used to life here and live the way Chinese people do."

Of course, he doesn't agree that foreigners living China should blindly follow the Chinese way of life. They can continue their familiar lifestyles in China since everything a Westerner might want is available here. "Actually you can find everything you want. You have Western food here in Beijing. You can

enjoy performances by foreign artists. You can take pleasure trips. My family went to Pingyao during the Spring Festival holiday this year. It goes without saying that China has its problems, such as traffic and pollution. I believe it will getting better since China has embarked on its way to internationalization and modernization."

Soon after the interview in his office, we were invited to his 4-A home, with its happy atmosphere. The home consists of two big apartments with the partition wall removed. It is decorated tastefully. Hanging in a prominent place in the sitting room is a picture of "the Priest on the Sea". Vividly depicted are the sea, buildings, a ship, the priest and the people seeing him off. Standing in front of the picture, you can almost feel the sea breeze coming out of it. It is obvious that the host favors this oil painting, because the picture allows him to feel the spirit of "making one's home wherever one is". Could he be an actual cultural priest of modern times?

The sitting room looks like a miniature museum. With all these items on display, the host has vividly and completely expressed his love for Chinese culture and his attachment to his country. Hanged on one wall are many old photos of Chinese maps and buildings of different eras, and portraits of modern life.

Hanging on the other wall are maps of Italy and his hometown of Sicily. He particularly pointed out a map of Sicily with shining gold dots which stand for cities and towns. Homeland is as precious as gold in his mind. We found that high-backed Ming Dynasty wooden chairs exist together with a modern sofa; Buddha statues stand side by side with post-modern sculptures. The display is in great harmony, nothing out of balance. The host couple are truly master-hands at coordinating East-West cultures.

At home, Mr. Laspina is a good father and a good husband. The petite hostess greeted us with a smile. Just as a Chinese saying goes: "There must be a great lady behind every successful man." We were lucky enough to meet the great lady behind Mr. Laspina. To support her husband in his career and to raise their kids in a healthy way, she resolved to give up her own career and stay at home to take care of the husband and the children. His gratitude to his wife shows clearly in his words and manner.

His wife accused him of "heckling" her during an exam, while he was teaching at university and she was his student. "The day before the exam, he asked me what the most difficult part was for me. Then the next day he intentionally gave me a pop quiz on the difficult part. I wouldn't have minded if he didn't give me a preferential treatment. But he shouldn't deliberately embarrass me! Even our friends condemned him…. I was almost ready to say good-bye to him." The whole room rocked with laughter. "That was why I stopped teaching," he said in his defense. "I always stood on principle and displeased almost everyone." The couple, who had just celebrated their silver wedding anniversary, still felt the sweetness when they recalled their dating stories.

They wore expressions of great happiness as they talked about their children. The first A and the second A are at college in Italy, majoring in politics as their parents did. "We have four family members studying politics as their major. Ours is a political family," the oldest A smiled. This is another feature of the 4-A family. "The eldest son likes music. He has formed a band and put out two CDs. Italy is known globally for vocal music. But he likes rock music and he said that he's doing it in order to be famous," the father said, shaking his head. "Some

professionals told me he has a great potential. Well, let him do whatever he likes." Praise is tempered by censure, and this shows the deep feeling between father and son. Mrs. Laspina told us that the second son wanted to be a diplomat. He is fond of electronic gadgets and it is always his duty to take care of the computers when they are down. "It is a free service for us now. But don't know if he'll start charging us in the future." Another burst of laughter.

Only the youngest A is at home. The boy is remarkably cute and a little bit shy, with finely chiseled features, looking like a baby gentleman. He smiles shyly when his parents praise him for his grades at school. "He gets up at six every morning and never cuts class regardless of the weather. He won't let us ask sick leave for him when he's running a temperature. Sometimes I take him as my model," the father proudly said. "The child is father of the man," as the proverb goes. The 10-year-old kid will certainly be somebody when he grows up. When asked what he will do in the future, "A chemist", he answered, speaking with a typical Beijing dialect. He said he likes football and AC Milan is his favorite team. When they got the European Cup, he went out into the street together with father, wearing AC Milan's football jersey. Many Beijing residents thought the

team had come to the city. The mother hopes he will be able to get Chinese citizenship as well, since the boy has such an intense attachment to China. Let's look forward to the day when the citizenship system relaxes.

His wife is fascinated by Chinese culture. She is interested in almost everything: *Taiji* shadow boxing, *guqin* and so on. She even tried a few notes on the musical instrument in her study. Although still in the preliminary stages, her technique is orthodox, with a certain artistic achievement. As for shadow boxing, Mr. Laspina said he was too busy to learn all of it, so he has to have his wife coach him.

Like the Chinese, Sicilians have the strong sense of "roots" in their homeland. From time to time Mr. Laspina goes and stays in Sicily for a while with the family. Getting out of the bustling urban life and back to the quiet countryside of beautiful Sicily, they relax and purify their minds. "My farmstead faces Etna, the biggest active volcano in Europe. When it is quiet, the peaks are covered with snow. But when it erupts, the airport has to be closed. On our farm we grow olives, oranges and other delicious fruits. It's a great feeling when you taste these fruits after coming home tired." But before long, he leaves home again and returns to human society, traveling between Sicily and Rome, or between Rome

and China. Many things are waiting for him to deal with.

Now we call to mind the Marco Polo statue he presented to Chaoyang Park. The name he gave to the statue is "A man who lives in two worlds." In fact, he himself is such a man, because he carries Marco Polo's cultural genes in him.

Translated by Yang Yaohua

Personal File

Name: William Lindesay

Nationality: British

Occupation: Commonweal Affairs

Time in China: 18 years

Standing Guard on the Great Wall

William Lindesay is not a popular name amongst the Chinese people, but the moment it is mentioned he was the first foreigner to volunteer himself to pick up garbage on the Great Wall of China and was the founder of "International Friends of the Great Wall", he is remembered with reverence and fond memories.

Chairman Mao Tse-tung, all along said, "Who are we if we don't reach the Great Wall?" This aroused lofty sentiments and aspirations of numerous people all over ever since.

William Lindesay, a Briton, had a dream ever since he was a little boy. He accomplished his dream in 1987 by finishing a journey of 2,450 kilometers of the Great Wall on foot. After his childhood dream came true, he put himself into a cause of Great Wall protection. In 2001, he registered "International Friends of the Great Wall" in Hong Kong, calling for conservation of the Great Wall. He organized volunteer activities and took people to clean up the environment of the Great Wall several times, and thus became known as "the foreigner picking up garbage on the Great Wall" in China. His unusual contribution to the Great Wall won him the "Friendship Medal" issued by the Chinese government and received interview by Premier Zhu Rongji in 1998. He was later awarded the rank of OBE (Order of the British Empire) granted by Queen Elizabeth II of Britain in Buckingham Palace in 2006.

William Lindesay said, "Who are we if we cannot cherish the Great Wall?" echoing Chairman Mao's saying "Who are we if we don't reach the Great Wall?"

He put his precepts into practice.

A Life with Wall Is Written in the Stars

William Lindesay was born in Wallesay, Liverpool in 1956. As a little boy, he had his own likings. He didn't like to receive the traditional education of a public primary school, and often jumped out of windows to play truant and do "outdoor activities" alone. His parents then sent him to a private school which charged dearly. But teachers there had a new way of teaching. They often took the kids to the field to be close to nature, and made them learn a lot of things in such natural environments. This was just right for little William, and he thought this private school was much better and had much fun than the public school.

His teacher himself was a priest. He told his students that "One must have three books with him at his bedside, one is a prayer book, another is the *Bible*, and the other is an atlas. Prayer books and the *Bible* could not quench thirst of little William's. He liked to study atlas. So the book *Oxford World Atlas for Students* carried him away. From it he learned of the world outside Wallesay, got to know the three islands of Britain, learned about the remote China and the Great Wall there. "I saw China on the map. The Great Wall stretched on the North China. It is so beautiful. I also saw the starting point and the end point of the Great Wall on the map. I dreamed I could walk from one side all the way to the other side." That was when he was 11 years old. Later he was discouraged to make the venture as China was undergoing the Cultural Revolution (1966-1976).

Sometimes one's word can influence a child's whole life. William Lindesay loved running in his early years, perhaps influenced by his two brothers who were marathon runners, and always won the trophies in school. He not only loved to run along the track, but also on highways. His marathon record was two hours and thirty-nine minutes, which showed his physical quality is no less than sports stars. Actually, he loved to run cross-country race. In 1985, he and his elder brother Nick spent 11 hours to finish a 118-kilometer long race of the Hadrian Wall. That is a 118-kilometer long defense wall built in 122 by King Hadrian of the ancient Roman Empire. During the race, Nick said, "the Hadrian

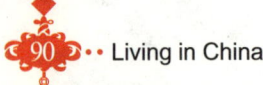

Wall, compared with the Great Wall of China, is just like a toy. You are young and unmarried without a family's burden. Why don't you try to run on the Great Wall? "

That ignited the spark in William, and then there was no looking back.

To accomplish his dream, William Lindesay later went to college and took geography and geology as his major. He liked to go hiking in Wales and Scotland in order to get ready both physically and spiritually. Besides, his mother gave him a roll of film every week to let him practice his photographic skills during the hike in order to record the sceneries of the Great Wall he would see in the future.

After graduation from Liverpool University, he worked in North Sea Oil Field. The drill and production platform on the sea was very small, but he didn't give up his running around it everyday. Later he went to work at a magazine of the Manchester University and never stopped his preparation for the Great Wall. In 1980 when he visited the headquarter of *American National Geographic* in Washington, he bought a globe on which the Great Wall of China was marked. He found no pyramid, no Taj Mahal, nor any other man-made ancient sites marked on it beside the Great Wall. The Great Wall was the only man-made site displayed, which fortified his conviction of "Who are we if we don't reach the Great Wall?"

At last one day his passion and power were released on a great wall and his talents and influence were brought into full play on a larger platform. Because of his destiny, William's life with wall was written in the stars. He was born in Wallesay, grew up under the Hadrian Wall, and shone with dazzling splendor on the Great Wall of China. The three places had one word in common — Wall, while particularly the Great Wall, several thousand kilometers long, was always in his dream, under his feet, in his cameras, and his books.

He firmly believed that he was born for the Great Wall but he never knew that he would have a lifelong tie with the Great Wall.

Travel Alone on the Great Wall 2,450 Kilometers

Growing up in a western world, William knew well how to get sponsors. Outdoor activity needs shoes, clothes, tents, food etc. He got many sponsors like Midland (later merged and purchased by HSBC) to meet expense. Midland had shares in Travelex, the world largest foreign currency exchange corporation. In this way, William became the beneficiary of Thomas Cook. E-traveler's check launched by TMT coincidently had the Great Wall printed on its checks and TMT thought William was the best candidate for advertisement for Thomas Cook.

But William had big problems. As information and books on China, Chinese people, Chinese history and culture were far and few, his knowledge about China was limited to the Great Wall, Mao Tse-tung and chopsticks. In the past very few Westerners visited China and thus not much information was available on the Great Wall except a few pictures. As for language, William could say a few sentences in Cantonese accent "Hello, I am William from Britain" and that too was not understood by the people of northern China where the wall was located as their dialect was different.

Then in 1986, William came to China.

He first visited the imposing Great Wall at Badaling, and then decided to run from Shanhaiguan. But the hot weather knocked him down. The well-trained

William got heat stroke and collapsed. He had to stop. Later, he started from another end of the Great Wall, Jiayuguan Pass. He only ran more than 200 kilometers, then he ran into another frustration. One of his foot bones was broken plus an endless diarrhea, he had to return in the midway.

Being defeated twice didn't make William lose confidence, but gave him two conclusions: One, running on the Great Wall is possible. Two, the Chinese people welcome him. The difficulties on the way were not that terrible and farmers along the Great Wall were very plain and hospitable. No one regarded him as an extraterrestrial being and had a storm in a teacup, but helped him as much as possible. Therefore, William was full of confidence for his future journey. In a word, just as Mao Tse-tung said, the future is bright, but the road is tortuous.

While resting and consolidating in Beijing, William ran into two students on the street of Jianguomenwai he met at Shanhaiguan during his first try on the Great Wall in September 1986. They were looking for a foreigner to practice their oral English. William immediately greeted them with the sentence learned in Liverpool with the Cantonese accent. Both his friends listened to him and got confused. William realized that he should buy a notebook and asked a Chinese to write a paragraph, tell others who he is, what he is doing here. The two students found they could just help each other with William. So they helped William write on the notebook, "Hello, I'm William from Liverpool. I'll run on the Great Wall alone. Please help me! I need water and food." At the end, he put another sentence "Long life to the friendship between China and Britain".

"This is very useful," said William smiling. In farmers' homes along the Great Wall, William showed this notebook to them. Many farmers can't read. He had to wait for their children back from schools. Sometimes he even used body languages, for example, "I'm hungry. I'm tired." That indeed helped to communicate in a basic level.

In 1987, from autumn to winter, William finally reached Shanhaiguan at the seaside in Northeast China from Jiayuguan in the desert in Gansu, west of China. It took him 160 days to finish the journey of 2,450 kilometers. William told us that actually it took him 78 days to tramp on the Great Wall by excluding the time of resting and being interrogated and examined, and expelled out by the police. Many media reported the journey of 2,470 kilometers was not accurate. Some sections of the Great Wall have been gone, some sections are military important places and foreigners are not allowed to approach them. So he had to run off and on for 2,450 kilometers. His English style preciseness and obstinateness won't let him count 20 kilometers more.

But anyway, William is the first foreigner who has walked on the Great Wall. After that he often used of his vacations to make up for the omissions to the Great Wall. Moreover, he earnestly practices what he advocates in protecting the Great Wall, so he has been on the Great Wall for more than 1,200 days in the past 20 years. He is entitled by Xinhua News Agency, the most successful foreigner in exploration of the Great Wall. After tramping on the Great Wall, he wrote down all he saw along the way into a book *Alone on the Great Wall — from Desert to Ocean*, which was published in the UK (Hodder & Stoughton 1989), USA (Fulcrum 1991) and Germany (Sierra/National Geographic Traveler 1997).

Obviously for the 78 days, he endured the hardships of an arduous journey, hunger and tiredness, he even suffered from being chased by wild dogs. While beating dogs, William was so frightened. When he described it afterwards, he

was full of humor, "I nearly became the dogs food". Of course, more memories are warm and nice. The farmers along the Great Wall are plain and friendly. They often took him to their homes and asked him to sit on *kang*, the bricked bed, give him hot water to drink and food to eat. Because they don't know how to communicate with him, they sat there watching him. Some neighbors came to see him and wanted to say something to him so they just shouted at him. "They are testing whether I have any response for they thought I've got hearing problems. Later, they realized that I just couldn't speak Chinese."

It was hard to communicate, but both sides tried very hard. He took out a photo of the Queen to show the farmers. They mistook that to be William's mother. When they found out he was still single, they all showed pity on him and shook heads to him. In Chinese the character "good" is combined with two words woman and son, meaning it's not good unless having both woman and son. After William understood this concept of the Chinese people, he used pictures of his sister-in-law's photo and his nephew's photo and told them they were his wife and son. That reduced his embarrassment of being sympathized.

Farmers treated him whole heartedly. They provided him with food and water and refused to charge any money. William followed the rule and did as the Romans do. He soon won the love of the local people. They made him drink with them and cheered for getting acquainted and for the friendship between China and Britain. William knew clearly that the liquor they drank was very strong, but he was delighted to bottom up with them. In the end, he totally got drunk and fell on the bricked bed for a sweet dream. He really experienced being living with Chinese farmers. He once slept in a huge bed shared with farmers, and learned to get into the quilt naked as they did because farmers thought that sleeping naked is good for health. William's action showed he was fully agreed to that concept.

What made William unhappy is that he was caught by the police on the way for many times. They interrogated him, inspected him, held him up and even asked him to leave within a limited time. At that time China had opened its door to the outside world and practiced economic reform for years, but the inner land in Northwest China was quite backward and out-of-the-way. The sign board "Foreigners are forbidden to enter" could be seen in many places. Some people would be nervous to see foreigners, especially one alone appeared in a somewhat sensitive place taking photos here and there. They were afraid that he would be a spy to collect information. When police saw William, they would interrogate him in order to avoid being blamed for the fault of dereliction of duty. Because of the language barriers, both of them didn't understand each other, so the police would control him and held him up. William was caught nine times on his way to Jiayuguan. Sometimes he was asked and let go. Sometimes he was warned not to go any further. But as soon as he left the police station, he goes his own way, and let others say. Once he was caught by a sandstorm. When everyone was looking for a place to hide, William hastened to run away. Sometimes he was not that lucky. Once he was caught in Dingbian in Shanxi, and was sent to Beijing. While in Yulin he had a bitter experience. He was held up in a hotel for seven days. All his notes, camera, and five rolls of films were confiscated. Fines were raised from 100 *yuan* to 150 *yuan*. Fortunately, most of his films had already been sent back to Beijing and avoid heavy loss. When he walked 1,200 kilometers and it was only one hour's journey to Zhenbeitai, he was stuck. In seven days no matter how hard he tried to persuade the police to let him have a look at Zhenbeitai, which he yearned day and night, but he was refused. He was so disappointed.

However, William was not easy to give up. They didn't let him go, so he sneaked away. When he was expelled from China, William went to Hong Kong and applied for a new passport and returned. Luckily it was not network accessed, the Customs couldn't find William's background. He could continue his journey.

This time, he ran from Dongsheng in the Inner Mongolia toward east. He found the Great Wall was broken off and on in many places, even gone without any trace. He then ran along the railroad making full use of his geographic knowledge learned in college to look for the traces of the Great Wall.

Approaching to Beijing, he saw that the sign board "Foreigners Stop Here" became more and more and he wouldn't want to go turning a blind eye to it. So he visited the Great Wall around this area later in the years.

William finally had his Great Wall dream fulfilled. Though he had some regrets, he had made a great feat anyway. Returning back to Britain, Ji Chaozhu, Chinese Ambassador in Britain gave a high evaluation to his journey of the Great Wall which greatly inspired William. Chinese ambassador's praise was obviously more beneficial to William than police's interrogations and made William realized that China would further open its door to the outside world. As expected, more and more foreigners swamped to China afterwards, like William, carrying backpacks traveling in China alone. And policemen wouldn't keep a close eye on these single travelers, they turned to be nice and friendly and willing to help.

While William Lindesay measured the Great Wall with his feet, he harvested his love as well. During his rest in Beijing, he ran into a beautiful Chinese girl Wu Qi. They got married and Wu Qi bore him two pretty and lovely sons, and became an able assistant to his cause of protecting the Great Wall.

Born in Xi'an and graduated from Northwest University, Wu Qi lived in Longtan Hotel in Beijing at that time. She, like other white-collar young people working in foreign enterprises in Beijing, was always looking for chances to practice oral English. One day at the lobby she met William and started talking with him in English. She asked William what he did in China. William replied, running on the Great Wall. Wu Qi's vocabularies were very limited, so she said with a word, "You are from the desert to the sea then?" Wu Qi couldn't imagine that the word she pumped up with from the desert to the sea later became the subtitle of William's book *Alone on the Great Wall*.

More did Wu Qi think that William would fall in love with her at first sight. When talking about his first impression to Wu Qi, William said, English was very poor, but she was very pretty. As a result, William spent all his energy as he did in super cross-country race of the Great Wall, and started his love chase. He made inquiries everywhere for Wu Qi's information and when he learned that she worked at Daiva Securities Ltd., in the same building with TMT he was advertising, he went directly to her office on the 27th floor from TMT's office on the 11th floor, and invited her to dinner. After he finished the Great Wall journey, his love chase also came to an end. Wu Qi, who is one year younger than William, finally agreed to marry him.

In December 1987, William's brother and sister-in-law flew to Beijing to congratulate his victory of the great journey, and see their younger brother's wife-to-be. What looked a bit ridiculous is that the trip Wu Qi accompanied William's family to climb the Great Wall was her first time, while the British young man William was more qualified to be the tourist guide for this Chinese girl.

Pick Up Litter on the Great Wall

William became famous when he returned to Britain. He went to give lectures everywhere, published articles, made TV programs, and delivered lectures. His book *Alone on the Great Wall* was an instant success. Anyway, it

was incredible for one to tramp on the Great Wall from one end to the other. So people were excited, curious and greatly respected him for his feat.

In 1989 when he was doing a live show at a broadcast station, an old woman listener told William that in the beginning of the 20th century William Gerll had been to the Great Wall and took some photos which she collected at home. She said if William was interested, she would like to give them to him. When William saw those old photos, he was overjoyed. Many places in the photos were as familiar to him as he's been to those places. Some of the photos were taken from the same spot, same angle, but while in the earlier picture a beacon tower was visible, whereas in his picture it was missing.

In the last hundreds of years, the Great Wall had suffered damages caused by erosion of wind and sand and also human elements. William discovered during his journey that at many sections only dilapidated walls remained while at some places the walls were missing altogether. The beacon tower disappeared totally in last few decades.

After William got married and lived for two and a half years in England familiarizing the people about its existence, location and size, he returned to China with his wife and started working as an English polisher at *China Daily*. In 1994 his eldest son Jimmy was born. Thereafter he went along with Wu Qi to her hometown Xi'an, and taught English at University of Technology.

Before William embarked on his journey he had known of the "Long March" of Mao Tse-tung along with his Red Army which was a source of great inspiration for him to get over all hurdles and obstacles enroute. In celebration of Mao Tse-tung's 100th birth anniversary he undertook to traverse the long and arduous journey undertaken many years back by the Red Army, over snow capped mountains and marshlands breaking up the entire route into sections. And covering the entire route in his vacations in 1991 and 1992, he acquired the name "Foreign Red Army" given to him by the veterans of Red Army as a mark of their appreciation and affection.

In 1996, William was invited to work as an English polisher at Xinhua

News Agency, and went to Beijing with his family. To him neither teaching nor his proficiency in English was as important as his love for the Great Wall. It was his passion and dream. He would set off with his bicycle, camera and sleeping bag whenever he got an opportunity and return after two or three days, spending the nights in the hospitality of the farmers or under the cover of becon towers.

With money power improving many Chinese people started outdoor exploration activities and thronged the Great Walls. Some among them became sources of pollution, while others defaced the Great Wall by scribbling and chiseling on the wall surface. William was greatly disappointed. Once when he protested against pollution of environment he was humiliated with remarks: "This is our Chinese matter. It's none of your business."

Having seen the damage of the Great Wall caused by both nature and human beings, and the prospect of greater damage due to development of tourism, William became visibly worried and anxious. The Great Wall was not only the greatest architecture of the world, but also the most precious treasure of the mankind. It was an epitome of man's spirit. He often wondered, "Why these Chinese people don't love their own Great Wall."

He was often depressed and heart-broken as no one seemed to care about the great archeological heritage … once when he mentioned about people's apathy he was snubbed by his wife either to shut up or do something concrete about it and not just grumble. He began an awareness campaign, claiming, "We must learn to walk by this open-air museum quietly, and not scribble our names or words … we want to save the 500-year-old bricks". He wrote in his article, "The Great Wall should be protected not only as a legend, but well protected in physically, including its architecture and surrounding environment."

On April 18 of the same year, he took 120 volunteers to pick up litters on Jinshanling Great Wall, which evoked a great response in the Chinese society. Foreigners picking up litters on the Great Wall forced every Chinese to examine their own conscience and determine the part they needed to play in the great effort.

Five month later in 1999, dustbins were put on the Great Wall and ten sign

boards were erected along the paths leading to the Great Wall in Huairou District, Beijing, "Take nothing but photographs, leave nothing but footprints". In 2000, a project protecting an eight-kilometer stretch of the Great Wall in Huairou started. With this project, William hired six local farmers and founded a Great Wall Environment Station, and set up environmental protection signs on the Great Wall. This project was initially sponsored by Norway Haidlu Corporation, Beijing Office.

Among all environmental protection activities of beautifying the Great Wall organized by William, the one held in September 2000 was the greatest both in strength and momentum. With the motif of "Treasure the Great Wall Under the World Common Cultural Heritage", more than one hundred volunteers from 36 countries gathered at Jinshanling to collect litters.

Among them were government officials of General Office of China National Cultural Relics Bureau and UNESCO Beijing Office. All volunteers raised flags of their countries and marched on the paths leading to the Great Wall. Many volunteers kept the bags used to collect litters as souvenirs, on which were printed the slogan framed by William, such as "If everyone picks up garbage, the Great Wall will be as beautiful as it was in the past." "Who are we

if we cannot cherish the Great Wall? " "Love the Great Wall, Protect the Great Wall." This activity had a great impact both at home and abroad.

Perhaps William didn't expect that collecting litters would greatly increase his popularity in China. He enhanced his reputation "as a foreigner picking up litters on the Great Wall" from "a foreigner tramps on the Great Wall".

Who Are We If We Cannot Cherish the Great Wall?

Almost everyone who knows the Great Wall knows the famous saying of Mao Tse-tung "Who are we if we don't reach the Great Wall?" William well used this saying and changed it into "Who are we if we cannot cherish the Great Wall", which began to find its way deep into the heart of the people.

After the year 2000, William became a full time worker for the maintenance and protection of the Great Wall. In April 2001, he founded and registered "International Friends of the Great Wall" in Hong Kong with objective of assisting China to protect and preserve the ancient monument. William appointed himself as the director and Wu Qi as his assistant. And William's famous quotation, "Who are we if we cannot cherish the Great Wall", has become the keynote of the International Friends of the Great Wall.

Soon after the formation of " International Friends of the Great Wall", William and the Beijing Administrative Bureau for Cultural Relics made a joint plea to the US-based World Monument Fund to have the Great Wall included in the List of World's 100 Most Endangered Sites. After some initial resistance the proposal was accepted. Beijing Municipal framed guidelines for protection and maintenance of the Great Wall as a world heritage site and acknowledged William's contribution as a key factor. Soon after, International Friends of the Great Wall won the "Robert Wilson Heritage Protection Award" issued by the World Cultural Heritage Foundation.

William and his colleagues labored hard to cultivate awareness amongst outdoor activists by constant interactions, reinstalling the broken beacon towers with technical support of experts of Tsinghua University and also to conduct

investigations on the content of steel used in the making of the Great Wall.

The project that gained maximum significance was "The Great Wall Revisited". The inspiration of this project originated from the photos taken by William Gerll a hundred years ago, and an old British woman presenting them to William. Comparing with the old photos, the new ones taken at the same place along the Great Wall showed discernible changes, which triggered thought process on the how best the Great Wall can be if protected from further deterioration and damage.

Sponsored by Shell company in China, William started a series of unusual journeys. He went to Yumenguan at the border of Gansu and Xinjiang in the west, and Laolongtou at Shanhaiguan in the east, and finally enumerated the reasons causing damage to the Great Wall: natural erosion, industrial development, wars, revolution, and tourism development ... all of which have contributed to some degree or other.

In 2007, 20 years after William's journey along the Great Wall, "the International Friends of the Great Wall" in conjunction with some government departments held photographic exhibition. In the Great Wall Re-visited, 72 old and new photos were exhibited, showing people how in a hundred years time the

Great Wall visibly deteriorated. One picture is worth a thousand words. When a British media reported this exhibition, it used such a title, "Two Williams' Great Wall".

In the same year, he wanted to launch an activity program with children and students participation. "They are the future of a country and the world. I hope more young people will be environmentalists. We must look at the Great Wall from a new angle. It's not only an ancient architecture, but also a great sight; it's not only a thing we use today, but also a treasure we must protect well for tomorrow." His message was to preserve the glory of the past for the generations to come.

Receiving Commendations of Both Countries

In 2004 when William visited National Geographic again, he bought another globe from the same shop. He was surprised to find that the Great Wall was no longer appearing on the globe. Returning to Beijing, he read a few articles which mentioned that the Great Wall perished from many of the sites due to natural erosion and wanton human destruction. He realized the reason as to why the Great Wall was no longer shown on the globe. He felt the need for greater vigilance and supervision in the protection of the archaeological monument and soon had a team of more then 50 volunteers between the ages of 21 and 50 who served as loyal watchdogs. Besides his two sons and his wife who always were sources of encouragement, many Chinese and foreigners joined hands, inspired by his indomitable spirit, in the protection and maintenance of the Great Wall.

William was blessed with two sons, Jimmy, the eldest studied at Beijing No. 55 Middle School, and Tommy the youngest son studied at Beijing Fang-caodi Primary School. While in school they were groomed in Chinese, at home they conversed in English. Consequently they grew proficient in both languages. Jimmy inherited his father's sports genes and developed great interests and talents in outdoor sports. His youngest son, though still a minor, participated in many activities for protection of the Great Wall. William groomed his two sons

as his able successors for the noble cause.

In 1998, William received commendation of the State Council for his contribution to the protection of the Great Wall, and also the "Friendship Medal". At the banquet held on the National Day of that year, he and other foreigner volunteers who received citations and awards were received as guests of Premier Zhu Rongji, of the State Council.

William was held in high esteem by the Chinese people for his pursuit of the noble cause of protecting the ancient monument. Foreigner as he was, he came across thousands of miles from his hometown. He was a noble man with noble thoughts. China was not his country of origin yet he labored hard for a great cause. It was not his duty but a great passion.

On July 12, 2006, William Lindesey was honored with "Order of the British Empire" in acknowledgement of his profound contribution toward conservation of the world heritage site. OBE is conferred upon people from different walks of life for outstanding contribution for a great cause. It is somewhat equivalent to "May 1st Labor Medal" in China. In order to receive the medal presented by the British queen, William had to dress in borrowed tuxedo, as he never possessed one. After the ceremony, William, his wife and two sons, Jimmy and Tommy, unfolded flags of China and Britain, and had pictures taken before the Buckingham Palace.

Recollection the words of encouragement by the Queen and his assurance of continuing the work for next 100 years his wife Wu Qi asked him if he would

live that long, William looked at Jimmy and Tommy with a significant smile in silence.

Translated by Li Shujuan
Revised by P. K. Banerjea

Personal File

Name: Marcia Marks

Chinese Name: Ma Xia

Nationality: American

Occupation: Senior Editor

Time in China: 16 years

We Travel Together Forever

She was a devoted Christian and she loved nature. She was a single woman in her fifties when she came to China. Maybe her kindheartedness and devotion touched God and Mother Nature, as an unusual marriage was arranged for her thousands of miles away. That is Marcia, like a tiny flower shining among hundreds of thousands of its kind, had the very character of a mountain flower — insignificant, indomitable and attractive. She nourished beautiful sentiments regarding China. She was deeply in love with China, her family and friends, and nature.

*T*he Chinese Qing Ming (Pure Brightness) Festival is observed to honor the memory of the deceased. In the year 2007, the festival happens to fall on May 5. It is a sunny, warm day. Spring fills the air with its fragrant breath — little birds chirping on tree branches covered in tender shoots, verdant grass coming up in the fields, and bright wild flowers opening in full blossom. On this special day, Tang Xiyang, an environmentalist and environmental writer, has arrived at De Ling Cemetery together with family, friends, and a veteran member of the Green Campers. As in previous years, the group is here to pay their tributes to the memory of Marcia Marks, who was not only a guardian angel of nature but a plain and modest woman, and a noble and great daughter of God. Marcia Marks,

a woman from across the Pacific Ocean, now rests eternally in a flower-covered tomb nestled among green hills. She made light of a thousand-mile journey in order to seek her dreams, and dedicated the latter half of her life to her beloved China. She will remain forever in the land to which she was deeply attached, to be accompanied by her beloved ones and remain in the arms of Mother Nature, who she loved all her life.

First Knowledge of China

Born in the United States, the young Marcia learned fragments of knowledge regarding ancient China from her grandmother, who had had a number of relatives engaged in business and missionary work there. Her home was decorated with furniture and porcelain items from China. During the Christmas season, she would always receive gifts from that faraway country. All these influences created a yearning in her heart to visit that mysterious land, and the desire grew stronger with each passing day. But she couldn't realize her dreams, as Sino-American diplomatic relations had not yet been resumed. After college, Marcia spent a year working in Singapore, a country not very far from China. She made many Chinese friends there, thus stoking her passion for the country. On her return home, Marcia devoted herself to promoting Sino-American friendship. As a member of the American-Sino Friendship Association, she kept herself busy helping to normalize Sino-American relations. She used her savings to attend Harvard University in the advanced studies of the Chinese language. At the same time, she generously helped Chinese living in America by giving them free English classes. After China opened its doors to the USA following the "*Ping Pong Diplomacy*" initiative, and invited then US President Nixon for a visit, Marcia toured China with a delegation of journalists — the first of its kind in China — as an editor and reporter for a women's magazine. In 1980, she was engaged as an educational expert at China's Institute of International Relations. Afterwards, she worked at Peking University, the Foreign Languages Press, and other organizations. She had finally realized the dreams that had been born at an early age.

Nature, the Matchmaker

She was a single woman in her fifties when she came to China. As a devoted Christian, she believed God would arrange everything for her. She loved

nature — the grass, the flowers, the trees, the insects, and the animals — all things belonging to the wilderness. She grasped every opportunity to breathe the fresh air of the wild, and to let nature console her lonely soul. Maybe her kindheartedness and devotion touched God and Mother Nature, as an unusual marriage was arranged for her thousands of miles away.

During a vacation in 1982, Marcia went birdwatching in Xishuangbanna, Yunnan Province. She happened to meet a Mr. Tang Xiyang in her hotel. Mr. Tang, chief editor of *Nature* magazine, who had gone there to observe wild Asian elephants for an article on the environment. Their common pursuits, interests and age linked the two lonely hearts together, and a fated romance quietly began between them. "What's brought you here?" asked Tang. "Bird watching." "Bird watching? Why not go to the zoo? You can see all species there," the surprised Tang asked. "They are not free. I have never seen birds at the zoo." Upon hearing this, Mr. Tang couldn't help feeling a great respect for her unique attitude toward nature. He told Marcia that he was there to observe and study Asian elephants for his book *Living Treasures*. The theme of the new book caught her immediate attention. Marcia liked the book and promised to help publish it. She suggested the book be published not only in Chinese but in English as well. The

joyful Tang jumped at the possibility. With common goals before them, they instantly established a strong rapport, though they had to converse through an interpreter. Their hearts must have communicated directly, untranslated, because even without verbal expression they fully understood each other's feelings. Common ideals and aspirations brought them together. On their very first collaboration they worked side by side, with Tang in charge of writing the book and Marcia in charge of publishing it. They even went together to conduct field surveys. Marcia greatly appreciated Tang's arrangements on these field trips because at that time not all parts of the country were open to foreigners; very often people would come across "Foreigners Not Allowed" signs, even in some areas in Beijing. For instance, when they went to Baiyin'aobao National Park in the Inner Mongolia Autonomous Region, Marcia was denied entrance and had to return to Beijing because the local had not received clearance from above for Marcia's visit, and said that park was not open to foreign visitors. Despite this problem, Marcia was still able to visit many places at that time — seeing many rare birds and animals — all thanks to Tang. Tang, in his capacity as chief editor of *Nature* magazine, managed to get permits from the proper government departments allowing Marcia to accompany him to many national parks, great mountains, and other famous spots that were "out of bounds" for foreigners.

Engagement at Bird Island, Qinghai Lake

In the five short years between 1982 to 1986, the two left their footprints in many well-known national parks and nature reserves. During that same period, the book *Living Treasures*, the fruit of their first collaboration, came out in China along with an English version in the United States and UK. The time was ripe now for something to happen. In 1985, Marcia and Tang went again to watch birds on Bird Island in Qinghai Lake. Strolling along the lake shore, Marcia was carried away by the beautiful wildflowers on the Qinghai Plateau. She had never allowed Tang to take pictures of her. But this time — the only time — she asked him to take her pictures while she was enjoying the flowers and the birds

all around. "Thank you," the excited Marcia said passionately. Marcia's words, which may not seem out of the ordinary, conveyed deep emotion to Tang. Spontaneously, they found themselves holding each other in a tight embrace. On this day, three years after their first meeting, they pledged their love amidst bright-colored flowers under the blue sky and white clouds. Before that day, Marcia had already put out feelers, asking him "what if we were to live together?" Tang had hesitated at the offer. There was a big difference in terms of their income, as Marcia earned more than ten times what Tang did. It is a serious loss of face for a Chinese husband if he makes less than his wife. Marcia hadn't been certain either; she didn't know if Tang was the kind of person who might simply use their marriage as a means to immigrate abroad. But Tang dispelled all misgivings from her mind by saying that China was his home, and he would not immigrate to the States. The two hearts grew closer.

The Simple Life

Marcia had both a cool-head and an iron-will. Although a lady of graceful makings, she humbled herself happily. "At first I observed her only from the point of view of her daily life," Tang recalled. "She gave up a classy life in New

York and abandoned a respectable, high-paying job in order to come to China. She was so deeply in love with China that she dedicated the rest of her life to this country. Later I found how special her feelings toward China were, when I often heard her tell friends that she was "a Chinese without Chinese citizenship".

Marcia was strict with herself in observing admirable professional standards. She went to the office like clockwork and duly finished her work assignments, never procrastinating. Once, she was tardy coming into the office by only fifteen minutes, but made up for it during her lunch break. Marcia had great expertise in editing, familiarity with Chinese phonetic symbols, printing styles, and the translations of special Chinese names for people, places and organizations. More commendable was her strong sense of responsibility. Since her Chinese left much to be desired, she had some difficulties in understanding the language. However, she would carefully examine the relevant references when she had questions — never allowing a mistake to slip through her fingers. She made valuable suggestions with regards to publishing styles, and the binding and layout were arranged in accordance with foreign readers' taste. She gave lectures to Chinese editors and patiently answered their questions. She would accept jobs involving boring and obscure items that were difficult to translate, which other people had avoided. She worked well into the morning in order to finish any work that had been left over from the previous day. Marcia dealt with a work load that was three times that of any other foreign expert. According to the incomplete records kept by Foreign Languages Press, the number of manuscripts that Marcia revised and polished with high efficiency and quality amounted to one million five hundred thousand Chinese characters. Wherever she worked, she got along quite well with her colleagues, never assuming a haughty manner just because she was an expert. She even did some menial jobs like cleaning toilets and fetching drinking water for the office. She was chosen as a model worker and praised as "living Lei Feng" — a deceased model soldier who performed great deeds for the ordinary people. Unlike some other foreign experts who had lived in China for just a couple of years and then wrote books about the country after returning home, Marcia never wrote her own book on the subject. It was not because she lacked the ability; rather, it was because she had dedicated all her time and efforts to putting the finishing touches on other people's works — neglecting her own fame and gain. The Chinese would say that Marcia "sews a wedding gown for another bride to wear." She wore clothes that had long been out of fashion, had only Chinese steamed buns and baked cakes for meals, rode a bicycle, and wore a watch made in China. Marcia led a very simple life, but she lived within

a richly abundant inner world. She was in love with music and nature. She never used her yearly vacation to go to the States. Instead, she traveled around China and was intoxicated with the natural beauty of mountains and rivers.

A Straightforward Character

Marcia was open-minded and straightforward. When asked what most delighted her in China, she answered "being treated like anyone else", without hesitation. "It's a big headache to be treated differently as a foreigner. I believe none of the foreigners working in China is happy to be closed off from Chinese people."

When she first came to China as an English teacher at the Institute of International Relations, she was placed in an exclusive hotel for foreign experts. She was eager to mingle with the ordinary people, however, and felt isolated in the hotel. Later on, the Foreign Languages Press invited her as a foreign expert. "I will certainly not work in the Press if you put me up in the Friendship Hotel," she stated firmly when she discovered that the Press wanted her to stay at the Friendship Hotel, which was for foreigners only. Finally, she had her wish fulfilled by living in an apartment outside the hotel. "Now I live among Chinese people with Chinese neighbors," she said joyfully.

In the early 80s, China had not yet fully opened to the outside world. The authorities — following an out-of-date idea of "treating foreigners differently from natives" — were still stuck to an unseen line that separated ordinary Chinese from foreigners. It was rumored that a ball was cancelled once on account of a certain leader who didn't like his people dancing with foreigners. "The Chinese people are warned not to have contact with foreigners. I hate rules like this," the angry Marcia said. "In some European countries there used to be ghettos for Jews. The Friendship Hotel is like a ghetto in China for foreigners."

She liked riding a bike, a handy tool in China, but as traffic in Beijing became more congested with an incessant stream of vehicles and thus less friendly to bike riders, it was no longer enjoyable to ride a bike. "In most cases, I take buses now," she told people. To Marcia's dismay however, she learned that very few people in Beijing wait to board the bus in single-file line. People often jostled with one another regardless of age or gender in their attempts to get on the bus. Consequently, strong young men made it on first — leaving women and children and the elderly frustrated at the road side. "In America, everybody has to stand in line to board the bus," the disappointed Marcia said. "Although Americans emphasize individuality, it doesn't mean depriving other people of their rights. That is, you have the right to choose your life style, but at the same time you have to respect others' rights. It is an expression of extreme selfishness to jump the line. At home, family members take care of each other, so why don't people do the same in society?"

The Grace of a Mountain Flower

"Marcia, like a tiny flower shining among hundreds of thousands of its kind, had the very character of a mountain flower," Tang said in describing Marcia. "Insignificant as she was, Marcia was indomitable and attractive. She nourished beautiful sentiments regarding China. She was deeply in love with China, her family and friends, and nature." When talking about her love for nature, Tang told me a story. One day after they got married, Tang went to grocery store to buy food for a visitor. He bought some fried sparrows without a second thought. Marcia was very angry when she saw this, and criticized Tang in her mediocre Chinese, "You are a protector of the environment. How could you not know that a sparrow is a member of nature and should not be killed for food?" Tang came to understand his mistake and felt embarrassed. Of course, he dared not put the fried sparrows on the dinner table. This was one of the rare times that cross words were spoken between them. They almost never had verbal quarrels. Instead, they often used a Chinese dictionary to settle their disputes. Once Marcia was really upset and pointed to a Chinese idiom in a dictionary that read "That's going too far," to show her indignation to Tang.

Marcia's love of family left a permanent impression on Tang Hua and Tang

Xiaonan — Tang's daughters from his previous marriage. Marcia had no children of her own, but she showered unlimited affection on the two daughters and their children. Tang Hua, the elder daughter, was sent to live and work in a farming

area in Hunan Province according to a mandatory policy implemented during the Cultural Revolution. Tang Hua sent Zhou Fan, her only daughter, to Beijing and put the little girl under the care of Marcia and Tang in order to give her a better education. Like many parents and grandparents in China, Marcia went to the boarding school every weekend to bring her granddaughter home. She would attentively listen to the child's tales of life and studying at school, and carefully observe her psychological changes. She would sing songs together with the girl. She guessed that Tang Hua, in faraway Hunan, must miss Zhou Fan very much, and sent Tang Hua tapes of the young girl speaking. The younger daughter, Tang Xiaonan, hadn't been able to conceive even after ten years of marriage. Tang Xiaonan had seen many doctors and had taken many different medicines, but all in vain. Marcia was very anxious when she saw that Tang Xiaonan had almost given up hope. Marcia asked friends to search for fertility treatments, and even sent Tang Xiaonan to a specialist in Zhejiang Province. After all these efforts, a long-awaited boy came into the world on May 9, 1997. The adorable baby brought Marcia a warm, pleasant atmosphere of home. She took great care of the baby, looking up a name in a Chinese dictionary for him, and sent the baby's photos to her relatives and friends abroad. She was indeed the best grandma.

Seven Family Members and Fifteen Hamsters

This is the title of an article by Marcia printed in the *Christian Science Monitor*. Tang's daughters told me a moving story in connection to this article.

In 1993, when Mother was in the process of being transferred, she had no residence for a certain period, since her housing was furnished by her work organization. She had to stay temporarily with us daughters. Seven people from three generations were packed in a 600 sq. ft. apartment for three months. We thought it would be pretty awkward for her. In western society, Father told us, families usually do not have so many members living together under one roof. Furthermore, their houses are spacious and usually have at least two bathrooms; we had only one. We had to wait one after another to use the bathroom after we got out of bed in the morning and before we went to bed in the evening. Mother not only got used to it but managed to do well. In order to stagger the bathroom hours, she would be the last to bed and the first to get up. Usually, this meant using the bathroom after midnight and waking up before five. Additionally, in the

morning, she would do everything in the bathroom as quietly as possible and tiptoe out of the room with a flashlight. Walking down the 24-story high-rise, she would go outside for some morning physical exercise. At times, she would walk back up the 24 flights of stairs to get home when it was still too early for the elevator to be in operation. After breakfast, she would start to work at 6:30 when her son-in-law Zhou Jianhui had just gotten up to go to the bathroom, followed by the third, the fourth, and so on. Every day repeated itself the same way. Instead of feeling uncomfortable, Marcia saw great fun in it. So, out came the article "Seven Family Members and Fifteen Hamsters".

Hamsters? Yes, these little creatures were introduced into the family under the guidance of Mother. Using the hamsters, Marcia gave us a vivid education in how to love animals. One day we got a pair of hamsters from the Guanyuan Pet Market for Zhou Fan, who is crazy about little animals. With golden fluffy fur, rounded ears and a stubby tail, the hamster looks like a miniature bear. Hence, it was nicknamed the "Golden Bear". Actually, hamsters are rodents with black eyes and a pointed snout similar to that of a rat. Our little hamsters kept gnawing at their wooden cage in order to wear down their constantly growing incisors. During a break, Mother would always go visit the little creatures on the balcony to say hello and talk with them. When fed, hamsters, like squirrels, hold their food with their front paws while sitting upright on their hind legs. They eat fast and snatch the food left in the feeder as soon as they finish their share. Before long you will notice their cheeks puff out. They're not swallowing the food — as it turns out, hamsters keep a surplus of food in the pouches of their cheeks. What greedy little guys! "We should give them names," Mother said one day. After a long discussion, we unanimously agreed that, since we have seven already, they should be considered the eighth and ninth members of the family, and therefore, we should call them "Little Eight" and "Little Nine" accordingly.

Every day after dinner we would release them from the cage and let them go out into the hallway for some exercise. The little hamsters ran against each other with their rumps rolling which tickled the family immensely. A month later, they gave birth to a litter of tiny bundles. Maybe because they were accustomed

to out-of-cage exercise, and had a strong desire to be free, the hamsters tried very often to open the cage door with their snouts. They even succeeded several times and jumped onto the window sills. One day we were surprised to find that "Little Eight" had disappeared. We searched high and low, but couldn't find it. We later noticed that the floor drain cover was missing. As hamsters are fond of burrowing, we guessed that Little Eight had probably mistaken the drain pipe, which was 50 meters long and ran down to the second floor, for a tunnel. When we looked down, sure enough we could see a little golden thing on a platform on the second floor. The family felt deeply sorry for its death. "We should put it in a box and bury it under a tree," Mother told Zhou Fan. Other people might think it was a little unnecessary to treat a dead hamster like this. Anyway, we did as Mother told us and held a simple, solemn "funeral" for the rodent. By doing so, we expressed our regret for not taking a better care of the little thing. Our hamsters multiplied to "Little Fifteen".

The Green Bible

Tang and Marcia published their first book in 1986, both in China and

abroad. This book drew great attention from all over and made Tang's name known to foreign environmental organizations and environmentalists. With a far-reaching vision in mind, Tang did not stop there. He wanted to visit foreign countries and learn from their experiences in environmental protection. He told Marcia his plan and got a prompt positive response. Marcia, an enthusiastic naturalist, began to make immediate preparations for a world tour. Generously opening her wallet, Marcia contributed 10,000 US dollars from her savings to the plan. At the same time, she sought financial support and assistance from foreign countries and organizations. Thanks to her efforts, the couple was able again to pack their traveling bags and go on a long journey. Within seven months, they visited more than ten countries and focused on national parks and sanctuaries in seven countries: the former Soviet Union, Germany, Switzerland, France, UK, the USA, and Canada. The distance they covered was equivalent to one and half times around the earth. At the end of the journey, they brought home more than one hundred kilograms of printed material. Marcia spent a lot of time concentrating her energy on sorting out the material and arranging for it to be translated into Chinese. When Tang finished the book three years later, Marcia again helped him with translating it into English and polishing the English manuscript. The English version of the book *A Green World Tour* was published in 1999, three years after Marcia had already passed away. This book has established Tang's academic standing as the No. 1 environmental writer in China. The book — the Green Bible as it is called — has been adopted as entrylevel teaching material for environmental protection for many Chinese people. The book, 400,000 Chinese characters long, is the embodiment of many years of painstaking effort by two ordinary people approaching their seventies. Despite the differences in their cultural backgrounds, life experiences, languages and personalities, Mother Nature brought the two together and, after years of nurturing, they became a happily married couple.

Green Camp — A Green Movement Prompted by a Letter

Marcia had a profound understanding of China and had deep feelings of love toward the country. When relatives or friends visited from abroad, she would tell them about China with a great deal of warmth. She never claimed to be an expert on China nor ever harangued them on issues concerning the country. She respected China as she did the USA. The great changes that have taken place in China left a deep impression on her. Everything that happened in China, big or small, would draw her keenest attention. She would concern herself with it, support it, and help it, disregarding all else, even her life. On November 25, 1995, Tang Xiyang got a letter from a reader exposing a plan by the Yunnan Deqin county government to cut down a 100-square-kilometer area of trees in a virgin forest in the Baima Snow Mountain Nature Reserve, as a way of solving its financial problems. What was more serious was the fact that the forest was inhabited by more than 200 snub-nosed golden monkeys. Tang was astonished. How could they be so brazen as to cut down a thousand-year-old virgin dark conifer forest inhabited by rich flora and fauna — especially the rare snub-nosed golden monkey? Tang could not sit still, he had to take action. A great plan popped into

his mind. Rather than going by himself, he thought it would be much better if he could go there with a group of college students to conduct field investigation and training. Marcia quite agreed with this idea and readily handed him a 1,000 *yuan* as funds for the trip. "If it's not enough, I'll give more," Marcia assured him. But to everybody's surprise, just at this point, Marcia came down with an illness. It was diagnosed as cancer of the esophagus, and it had already begun to spread.

After Christmas, Marcia's condition worsened. But she refused to be hospitalized. Instead, she asked a professional member of the Religious Society of Friends from America to treat her illness by praying. The family was unable to change her mind but had to respect her decision. Despite being tortured by cancer, Marcia was calm and steady as usual — reading books, listening to music, doing physical exercise, and sometimes even watching live broadcasts of world tennis games. Marcia never stopped working. Even after the diagnosis of cancer was confirmed, Marcia polished the English versions of five books and numerous manuscripts. Sometimes she would lie in bed or hide herself in the bathroom in silence in order to clean the ooze from her skin ulcers. She never so much as grimaced or groaned over the pain. She was reduced to a skeleton and was so thin that she looked like she could be blown down by a gust of wind, but her will was as sturdy as forged iron.

Even with such bad health, Marcia was still concerned very much for the preparation of the Green Camp's trip to Yunnan. Tang was encountering troubles and difficulties in organizing the trip. When he complained, Marcia advised him "to learn to love others and to love nature and not to be too Maoist."

As the departure day of the Green Camp was approaching, Marcia's condition rapidly deteriorated. The cancer had quickly spread to her liver and had totally shut down her metabolism. Her worn-out body couldn't hold any longer and seemed like it would collapse at any moment. On July 20, to make matters worse, she developed acute enteritis. She went to the restroom five times in one morning. This kind of torment would be hard enough for a healthy person to bear, let alone for the weak Marcia. At last, she was completely exhausted and collapsed.

On that evening, Tang held a family meeting to discuss two questions: the first was whether Marcia should be hospitalized and the second was whether Tang should go to Yunnan as planned. To the family's surprise, Marcia, who had always hated being hospitalized, did not reject the idea that day. Maybe she knew that she had completely lost her ability to take care of herself. Furthermore, she knew that if she didn't go to the hospital, Tang would never go to Yunnan.

"Go!" was Marcia's firm statement regarding Tang's trip to Yunnan.

"I am a human being. A human being has feelings. How can I leave you alone at this moment," Tang exclaimed.

The children were moved to tears. But Tang shed no tears, and neither did Marcia. "You should go since you have made so much preparation. Everything is ready. So you should go. You should go." she calmly repeated.

To respect Mother's wishes, the children told Tang that he should go. Only Xiaonan, the younger daughter, kept silent.

"Xiaonan, what's your opinion?" Tang asked.

"Mom, are you sure you really want Father to go?" Xiaonan said looking at Mother.

"Yes. I would not be happy if he didn't go." Marcia said in a weak but firm voice.

Tang understood his wife very well. He knew she couldn't make herself fully understood in Chinese. He expressed her meaning with a Chinese idiom, saying "she means that she would 'die without closing her eyes' if I did not go."

The departure day was nearing. Marcia, who didn't like being in the limelight, unexpectedly agreed to make a recorded speech for the opening ceremony of the Green Camp. She earnestly prepared the text of the speech.

"I am very proud of all of you. You've all been eager and willing to help and to cooperate with one another. That's the right spirit with which to begin your trip.

"You are off to learn about nature. I hope you won't just admire the grand vistas and spectacular trees and animals. To experience nature you must learn to

know it intimately. That
takes patience and humil-
ity. I remember when I
went on a backpacking trip
into the wilderness of the
Great Smoky Mountains in
North Carolina, our group
guide advised us to learn
the names of all the wild
flowers we saw. He said if
we were to go to a party
and found people there

we'd never seen before, we would be sure to learn their names and something
about them. It should be the same when we go into the wilderness.

"And not just in the wilderness either. One day I was watching the swallows flying back and forth to their nests under our eaves here in Beijing when I
suddenly noticed they had red patches between their tails. I immediately looked
them up in my bird book and discovered they were red-rump swallows, a species
I had never seen before. We shouldn't be content to say, 'Oh, those are swallows;
those are sparrows.' What kind of sparrows? We should honor them with the
same individuality that we want others to see in us.

"So I hope you will not only look through your binoculars at the distant ob-
jects, but turn them around and look through the other end at the tiny flowers and
ferns at your feet. You'll be amazed at the intricate patterns, colors and shapes
you'll see. Some are functional, to attract insects and such, but some we cannot
explain other than as a proof of the enormous diversity of our universe.

"Don't plod on unseeing, unaware. Be quiet and let nature come to you.
Nature has secrets, and so do you. Your own secrets may be unknown even to
you. During your month together you'll learn from each other as well. It can be
a harmonious and expansive experience in terms of human relationship just as
it should be in terms of your finding your place in the grand scheme of nature.

Learn to appreciate one another and you'll learn to appreciate yourself.

"You are young enough to retain a sense of wonder about the world. Actually, we are all young enough, but sometimes we bury this sense of wonder under the care and concerns that we rather needlessly pursue. Wonder goes along with creativity and inspiration, without it we would have no great writers or artists and no great scientists. Nature not only fosters a sense of wonder, but confirms its truth and validity.

"I could say much more, but I don't want to ramble on. My thoughts will be with you constantly, and I shall be anxious to hear all the details of your trip when you return, so keep a journal and keep your hearts open. The more you give during this experience, the more you'll receive."

Bidding Farewell to the Green Camp with Her Life

July 25 was the day when the Green Camp was to embark on its journey to Yunnan. At 6:40 that morning, a telephone call from the hospital brought us grievous news: Marcia had passed away.

When Tang hurried to the hospital, his beloved had already left this world. The four bundles of fresh flowers were still on the window sill. Tang picked up the most beautiful one and laid it by her pillow. "Now you may go with us to Yunnan," he said to her affectionately.

The No. 61 Express Train zipped through to the south. It was a green train laden with great hopes and expectations. Maybe by the arrangement of God, Marcia's heart was there in the train, and she was marching forward together with her loved ones.

Her eternal departure was an extremely grievous event for the Green Campers. And she has become a shining paragon for those nature lovers.

It has been eleven years since Marcia passed away. But she is still alive in Tang's heart. "I have never thought of her in sadness. I always take her as a source of power, a spiritual booster and a philosopher. She has remolded my outlook of life with the legacy of her thoughts and deeds. Indeed Marcia has left in

me much of her image".

I, this writer, was lucky enough to join the couple in the editing and translation of their first book *Living Treasures*. I also took part in Marcia's seminar on editing and helped her with her lecture manuscripts. I will never forget her austerity, enthusiasm, kindheartedness, seriousness, and meticulousness when it came to work. Today I, too, present a bundle of flowers in her honor to express my respectfulness to her. Her family has specially picked out a big bouquet of mountain flowers in full bloom. These brightly colored, graceful flowers of all shapes symbolize her character and morality. I am sure Marcia would love it.

On her tombstone I see this epitaph:

"God is the first; others are the second; I am the third."

Mother Nature is a book. Life is a book. No matter what situation you are in, no matter how rough the road is, no matter what the future will be, you will certainly benefit from it so long as you open and read it.

"God is the first; others are the second; I am the third." That is Marcia's motto. She is just like these mountain flowers, small but great.

The green campers have never discontinued their green movement since their first camp in Baima Snow Mountain in 1996. Their activities include: protecting virgin forests in southeastern Tibet in 1997; protecting the wetland eco-system of the Three-River Plain in Northeast China in 1998; studying the effects of eco-tourism on Hanasi Lake in north Xinjiang in 1999; exploring the desert ecology in Takelamakan Desert in south Xinjiang in 2000; participating in TFAW project of Asian elephant protection in Yunnan's Simao area in 2001; protecting Saunders' Gull and the ecosystem of tide marshlands in Liaoning Province in 2002; protecting the wetlands and respecting social traditions in Sichuan's Nuo'ergai region in 2003; treasuring tropical natural resources and paying attention to the ocean ecosystems in Hainan Island in 2004; exploring the ancient Silk Road in Gansu Province in 2005; and returning to Baima Snow Mountain in 2006. Every time before they embark upon a new activity, the green campers go to Marcia's tomb to "talk" with her and "comfort" her soul. Actually, Marcia never leaves them, just as she said, "My thoughts will be with you constantly."

Yes, the green movement will never cease, and Marcia will travel together with us forever.

By Li Shujuan
Translated by Yang Yaohua

Personal File

Name: David M. Jacobson

Chinese Name: Yang Dawu

Nationality: Canadian

Occupation: Businessman

Time in China: 21 years

A Poetic Courtyard Life

David M. Jacobson was born in Trinidad, West Indies, grew up in Canada, went to college in the USA, and is the foreign son-in-law who came to live with his wife's family in China. Like his mother-in-law Gladys Yang before him, he followed his lover to China. In a small court-yard lying in the heart of Beijing, he expresses his love, runs his company and that enchanting yard, and has determined to spend the rest of his life there.

*T*his Canadian, David Jacobson, has the Chinese name of Yang Dawu. "Dawu" is no doubt a smart transliteration of David. And his wife is surnamed Yang. So this foreign son-in-law, who lives with his wife's family in China, has adopted his wife's surname. The English word "David" is usually transliterated as "Dawei" or "Daiwei". "Dawu" is very rare, but full of connotations and very ingenious. The name of his and his wife's consulting company is "Saiweng". It has the flavor of Oriental philosophy. It was originally created by David, which surprises a lot of people.

David has an easy and successful life, whether in career or day to day affairs. "Saiweng" has grown into one of the largest information consulting companies in Asia. He lives happily in that small courtyard, bought by his wife and father-in-law. He likes to share his happiness with others and invites his friends and colleagues over to chat idly on the roof or sit in the yard. You might even find him busy in the kitchen showing off his cooking skills. His father-in-law is a contemporary celebrity with whom he has at least one thing in common— drinking. Both like to spend the days when "Seats are full of guests and cups are never empty of wine."

One weekend we call on the Yang residence. One reason is to see Yang Xianyi, a famous Chinese translator, well known for his translation of *A Dream of Red Mansions*. The other is to see how this Canadian lives his contented life in China.

Building a Home in a Place Full of People

Traversing the scenic spot of Houhai Lake and the noisy Lotus Market and crisscrossing the "*hutong*" (alleys) of the Houhai district, we suddenly find ourselves in a quiet and secluded spot. The Yang residence sits in Xiaojinsi Alley (The Alley of the Little Gold Thread). One gets the artistic feel here of what Tao Yuanming, the famous Tang poet (618-907), wrote in his poem *Drinking Wine*: "I build my home in a place full of people, but hear no clamor of carts and horses."

We use the round knocker on the door to summon the residents. Yang Zhi, Yang Xiangyi's daughter, opens the door. She grew up in the residential compound of the Foreign Languages Bureau, so we are all casually acquainted. David has gone out shopping for the food he will cook in the evening. It seems that we will have some luck eating something delicious.

On entering the living room, we are delighted to see the hale and hearty Yang Xianyi. At the age of 94, he is still clear minded, quick in word, in sum, really incredible. We tell him that the Foreign Language Bureau has hung the portraits of all the Chinese pioneers who had been engaged in broadcasting and translations in the lobby of the office building. People look on them with reverence. Among them are he and his deceased wife Gladys Yang. He gives a faint smile but says nothing. He has undergone many hardships in his life and thus is used to remaining indifferent to others' opinions. He once mocked himself, "So clever when young, not so when grown, muddled at mid-life, shameless when old." This has long been a classic of humor, widely spread among men of letters.

It is said that the Yang family sold their four-room apartment at Chaoyang-yuan several years ago and bought this courtyard with a loan. Although it is not a standard Beijing courtyard house, it is rich in the flavor of old Beijing. The old-style one-story building faces south. The grey bricks and tiles are plain. But inside it is well furnished, with modern facilities, an open kitchen, reinforced glass in the bathroom, floor heating, and the like. They can live a modern and tasteful life in this old style building, where memories of the past are well preserved. The place is just like the old owner of the house, a typical old Chinese intellectual with rich knowledge of East and West, with the highest level of training, especially in Western culture. "Chinese learning as the core, Western learning for practical use" is well represented in the concept of the house.

Passing by the front of the house is a long passage. A large mural of scribbled "paintings" adorns the courtyard walls. One cannot tell whether it is abstract, impressionist, or fauvist. Anyway, it looks very colorful, with numerous and jumbled content. Yang Zhi says it was an impulse, the collective composition of colleagues who had come to congratulate her on moving into the new residence. The most humorous thing is a word in white, "chai" ("tear down"), drawn at a corner and encircled, very much like the sign meaning to dismantle, commonly seen on old buildings in the streets in Beijing. Such a word on this mural captures the space and time of Beijing. Anyone familiar with the changes in the city would laugh upon seeing it.

The end of the passage leads to a small back yard. Green vines crawl on the wall, adding a wild aspect to it. A shallow pond lies in the center, and you can

see two fat toads coming and going there. David has put some small fish in the pond as well. We are surprised that his big cat has not eaten them as snacks. That cat is very beautiful, but has a strange name, "Stinking Socks". It has many friends that often come to visit by jumping from the walls and roofs of nearby houses. In the mating season of February and August, Stinking Socks' parties with his friends break the quietness. The members of the Yang family, old and young, seem unconcerned with the cats' carnival, regarding this as just a part of nature. Thanks to good sound insulation, they just let the cats go on, the family's simple dreams undisturbed.

Even the birds chirping in the morning and insects calling are enjoyable. It's said there is also a weasel visiting the yard every once in a while. Our hospitable hosts even built a nest for it at the corner of the yard and put some food there irregularly. These are small creatures rarely seen now in the city, so the Yang family consider them as nature's kindness and care for them even more. There are three trees in the yard, one is a date (jujube) tree and two are pear trees, which bear lots of fruit each year. Our hosts share them with their colleagues in the office. However, recently the date tree has died. Luckily the two pear trees still bear fruit and provide a lovely scene in the yard. David likes to change rubbish into fertilizer for flowers. Perhaps he is promoting his concept of a green environment.

The yard is small, but it's big enough for the couple and their friends to chat and enjoy the cool. At the corner of the yard is a spiral staircase, which you can climb to the rooftop deck. Some chairs and one big umbrella make a simple summerhouse. Sitting here, with the breeze blowing gently across your face, you

feel very relaxed. Looking around, you can see the old houses and courtyards that are most typical of the old city. That's because this region is the Shichahai Cultural Reserve laid out by the Beijing Municipal Government. There are no buildings higher than two stories here, except for the Bell and Drum Towers not far away.

The neighbor next door raises pigeons in his yard. It's dusk and the pigeons are back in their coop. They fly back there cooing. What a lively scene! You can imagine what a sight in the early morning when a huge group of pigeons takes off. Pigeon keepers in Beijing like to hang whistles on pigeons' necks, so that when there are flocks of pigeons in the blue sky, one can hear a sweet whistling sound throughout the sky. This is the most characteristically in Beijing. Sitting on the platform of the Yang family's roof, one can enjoy this scene every day. It's said that the owner of the pigeons has a good relationship with David. If Stinking Socks ever attacked the neighbor's pigeons, such a good relationship might deteriorate. It seems that the Yang family also has a good method of educating cats.

While we were discussing the "peaceful coexistence" between cat and pigeon, David climbs to the platform. A middle-aged strong-looking man of six feet, with graying beard and attractive smile, appears in front of us. This was the first impression the Canadian gave to us. He told us that this platform was the best place to watch holiday fireworks. On National Day, they watch the rocketing fireworks let off on Tian'anmen Square and those set off by people during the Spring Festival. After a seven-year ban on fireworks, the ban was finally lifted on the Spring Festival in 2007. Beijing residents set off fireworks as much as they could from the eve of the Chinese New Year to the fifteenth day of the first month. Firecrackers could be heard all night long, and the night sky was brightened and the air permeated with smoke. One gets the sense of a battle for the alley. Of course, it is a war of happiness.

The lifting of the ban on holiday fireworks has been a controversial issue among the Beijingers. There are two different opinions among the Yang family. Yang Zhi thinks the ban shouldn't have been lifted, while David disagrees. But he doesn't set some off himself, but climbs to the deck to watch, putting a pillow over his head as a shield. Their younger son, 17-year-old Yang Yi'an is certainly a supporter. Even without a holiday, he likes experiment at his home, mixing black powder himself. Usually Chinese parents intervene in this kind of dangerous activity, but Yang Yi'an's parents are quite democratic and are not afraid that their son may blow up the yard. His father, who likes to watch the fun, once discovered how his son's experimentation might go wrong. One of Yi'an's explosives blow up and hit David's stomach. Luckily neither he nor his son's face got hurt. Speaking of this thing, Yang Zhi is still irritated, at the same time laughing at the event.

A Long Trip Around the World

David's cooking skills are really excellent, especially his roast chicken breasts, which were quickly appropriated and consumed. Two of his colleagues who had dropped in his family, and we all highly praise his cooking skills and feel that if he hadn't opened an information company but a restaurant, he wouldn't have to worry about earning a living. He works outside at his career and cooks at home — a Canadian edition of the Chinese concept of the new good man.

After dinner, we begin chatting aimlessly in the living room. When night falls, David takes us to the small yard. He has lit several pieces of wood and has a small "campfire party". David tends the fire while recounting his experiences. Yang Zhi adds some supplements now and then, and his two colleagues chip in, making impromptu comic gestures and remarks. Gradually, the story of how a Canadian traveled such a long distance to China becomes clearer and clearer.

David was born in Trinidad, West Indies in 1952, with Canadian national-ity. At the age of eight, he went back to Canada for primary school. When he first saw written Chinese he felt it to be quite intriguing. Of course he couldn't imagine that later on he would forge an indissoluble bond with China. At that time, he only knew that Chinese food was delicious. So he would ask his parents on his birthday to take him to satisfy his craving for this delicious food in a Chinese restaurant. Because of moving about in his early years, David doesn't have a deep impression of Canada. He migrated to the United States at the age of twelve and stayed there till he grew up. Even so, David doesn't have a sense of belonging to the United States. His father died in 1973 when David was 21. His brother and sister also died in their prime. The early withering of the family left him almost have no relatives to turn to and even harder to find a sense of home.

In 1981, David met Yang Zhi, who also was studying in the Department of Near Eastern Languages and Civilizations at the University of Chicago, and fell in love with her. Perhaps it was Yang Zhi's diligence and easiness, or her inher-ent elegance from a family of scholars, that attracted David. They finally mar-ried.

During the ten years of the Cultural Revolution, Yang Zhi went through many hardships. Before her, her father, Yang Xianyi, had gone abroad to study

at Oxford in his early years. There he received an advanced degree and married a British girl. They came back to China and eventually translated *A Dream of Red Mansions* into English, revealing to the world China's number one classic masterpiece. Thereby arose a much-told romantic story of a talented scholar and a beautiful lady. They had a son and two daughters, a perfect and happy family. But during the Cultural Revolution, Yang Xiangyi's honest and frank character turned him into a target of class struggle. He was criticized and jailed. His wife Gladys Yang was accused falsely of being a British spy and taken into custody and put under investigation. Yang Zhi's elder brother died and all were separated. As the youngest daughter in the family, Yang Zhi seemed to be treated the best, but her "foreign doll" face betrayed her family background and she was discriminated against. The Yang parents were liberated after the Cultural Revolution. Yang Zhi and her sister went to the United States to study. Her sister finally settled down in the States, but she decided to return to China in order to work. On top of this she felt that the American way of life was boring.

At that time Yang Zhi was studying Assyriology for her doctorate, while David was studying Arabic and getting ready to go to the Middle East. In 1983, he went to Jordan, but in 1985 returned to Chicago to marry Yang Zhi. He returned to Jordan thereafter for another year. During this period, Yang Zhi received her degree. David then came back to a thriving China with Yang Zhi. Originally, David was a "stateless" rover. After marriage, where his wife went became his home. In fact, coming to China was not only to settle down, but China's thirst for talented people was also a factor.

As early as 1984, the Ministry of Education had decided to establish a

Chinese Institute for the History of Ancient Civilizations (IHAC) in Northeast Normal University, and had allocated special funds to buy books and magazines in Assyriology, Hittitology, Egyptian and Western Classics (Greek and Roman). Three or four European and American experts could be hired to teach these courses every year. Classes for the study of the history of ancient civilizations were set up and senior students from key universities of China were enrolled, including graduate students with master's and doctor's degrees. In 1986, IHAC founded the *Journal of Ancient Civilizations* (JAC), the only international annual in China in a foreign language dealing with the science of history.

David and Yang Zhi were just the talents the Northeast Normal University needed urgently. Yang Zhi's teacher had tried to persuade Yang Zhi to come back and establish IHAC. In addition it would be great if she could come back with David. So at the end of 1986, Yang Zhi came back and became the Vice-Director of IHAC. David went with her, and taught English and historiography, besides polishing articles for JAC. The couple spent four years of a busy and enriched life there.

However, David's teaching concept was different from the university, and Yang Zhi felt it was hard to deal with some people. Moreover, she wanted to take care of her parents, so the couple decided to give up their work in Northeast China and returned to Beijing to work in the Chinese Academy of Social Sciences. David worked as an English editor and polisher, while Yang Zhi worked as a translator and polisher. They worked like this for another three years. Yang Zhi says wryly, "I just worked to get by."

The Wind Blows in the Right Direction

When people reach middle age, they have to think how to live out their life in retirement. Although David was prepared to live the rest of his life in China, his situation could not be compared with Yang Zhi's mother Gladys Yang's generation of experts. That generation had come to China in the most difficult of times. They had passed through countries that hadn't set up foreign relations

with China or were even hostile to China. They had shared the happiness and woes of the Chinese people. For them, the Chinese people were obligated to look after them in the sunset of their lives and give them a proper burial after they died. David was not part of that generation, even though he loved China and was willing to share in the happiness and woes of Chinese people. The couple, therefore, decided to start their own business.

They had discovered that when China went to the outside world after the open-door policy, the world also came to China. However, an imbalance of information often hindered foreign enterprises and international investors from doing business in China. They decided to help those international corporations and foreigners to remove the barrier to information caused by language. At first, they provided English articles containing information translated from 20 newspapers and magazines to *The Washington Post*. At that time there was no Internet, so they had to send faxes. *The Washington Post* was very satisfied and urged them again and again privately not to sell their work to the *New York Times*. From 1992 to 1995, they developed their business simply by sending faxes to their customers and potential customers.

Their first try was very successful and achieved good results. They realized their press clipping company could grow quickly. Such a way of providing information was the first in China and relatively new abroad. Many companies from abroad encouraged them that there was a bright future for this business. Their company subsequently grew from only the couple in 1992, to five, fifteen, and to over 100 at present. It has developed into a qualified, well-established media monitoring and analysis service. Their customers are not limited to the media, but to clients outside China, such as Fortune 500 companies. Besides inspecting news reports for their clients and client's competitors, they also provide English summaries of news from China every day. They write news reviews, industry analyses, and media circulation reports for clients. All this is done in English.

David says proudly, "We track and inspect the Chinese market and Chinese industry information for more than one hundred international companies, and our clients include world Fortune 500 companies, such as Boeing, Intel,

Motorola, Nokia, General Motors, GE, and Microsoft. And our list of international clients grows longer year after year." David tells us that they inspect national newspapers, magazines and other journals, altogether over 700. "That almost covers all of the mainstream media in China," we exclaim. David smiles, "Now our inspection range has expanded to television and the Internet. At least 20 television stations and 400 websites are under our oversight."

As David talks, at the height of his enthusiasm a look of disappointment suddenly appears. "However, my historical study had to stop completely. I have gotten lazier too, and write less. And my Arabic is almost completely forgotten." Actually, David is not lazy. He spends all his time and energy in registering the company and running it. Doing business is not an easy job. If he hadn't put aside his historical study of the Middle East, his company, "Saiweng", would have bombed. He has forgotten his Arabic, but he has mastered Chinese instead by self-study. "Yes, I can console myself with the Chinese saying, 'When the old man on the frontier ("Saiweng") lost his mare, who could have guessed it was a blessing in disguise.' "

As David mentions this Chinese literary quotation, he praises the dialectic involved. He liked the idea so much that he named his company with the expression in Chinese — Beijing Saiweng Information Services, which in English is Beijing SinoFile Information Services. If you look at the logo of his company, you can easily find two small characters "Saiweng" under the English "Sino-

File", with a portrait of a Chinese old man drawn in Chinese style beside it. David tells us that the painting of this old man is a self-portrait by Weng Tonghe, tutor to Emperor Guangxu of the Qing Dynasty (1644-1911). The painting was in his father-in-law Yang Xianyi's collection. Such a logo displays the cultural detail of his company. It shows that a scholar who runs a business will surely promote the cultural quality of the company. One of his employees evaluates David and his wife, "The couple are not businessmen at all, but scholars."

David's company has over a hundred employees and many are young people returned from overseas study. It also has four foreign polishers. In the office, they communicate in both English and Chinese, and both bosses don't act like bosses at all. They keep a harmonious working atmosphere and treat each other equally. Everyone works hard, but is not tied to fussy regulations. Employees can bring their pet cats and dogs to work, and at four o'clock in the afternoon, David often takes the lead calling out, "It's time to play!" Then a badminton match might begin. It might continue till the end of office hours, when everyone returns home feeling content.

Outsiders may consider the company "overly democratic" because of things like "playing badminton during office hours". Whenever David is asked, "How can your people play ball during office hours?" he shrugs and says nothing. He thinks efficiency is more important than form. Actually, he has instituted the standard management of a Western company — everyone is responsible for their work and must keep a strict and orderly pace. At the same time, he also pays attention to a harmonious atmosphere in the company, trying to making everyone work hard and have a good spirit so that the company is vigorous. One young employee told us, "Working here is a delight."

That's why all young workers in the company don't regard David and Yang Zhi as bosses, but as elder brother and sister. They often call them "Teacher Yang" or "Boss" once in a while as a joke. They come to the Yang home just as if it is their own and say "Hello" to Yang Xianyi

as they would to their own fathers, and they ask David's younger son about his studies and hobbies when they see him. Those with babies often bring them to show the family, while single people often come to discuss courting strategies. At meals, they sit and eat like family members, and seeing something that they can help out with in the small yard, they spare no energy to give a hand. Sometimes, a group of people swarms here, sitting around chatting after eating and drinking. At this moment, David looks much younger. He laughs with them and complains now and then that, "What you said is nonsense!"

With this kind of boss, a group of young people, and a team with such cohesiveness, how can SinoFile not be successful?!

In 1996, in order to meet the needs of the growing company, they set their eyes on an old Anglican church close to the west gate of the Xinhua News Agency and decided to renovate it as their office. "It had nothing except mice," Yang Zhi says. In 1997, SinoFile got rid of the mice and moved into the old church. Now the company has a technical research team composed of a dozen or so people to support it in information transformation with new and high technology. Everything is on track with good prospects. "We don't have many difficulties, so we dare to play ping pong, badminton and so on," says a vice president of the company proudly. We ask David if he approves of his words. David smiles and shrugs as usual.

They've got few competitors at home and none from abroad. Beijing Sino-File Information Service has entered into the most pleasant of stages: "The shores are broad when the tide is calm. And the wind is blowing in the right direction." (From a poem, "Moored Under North Fort Hill", by Wang Wan, a poet of the Tang Dynasty.)

Natural and Unrestrained in the Moonlight

David found an end in China. His family and his career are all here. His lifestyle and mode of thinking are "localized". When he first arrived in China in 1986, China had already opened its door to the outside world, but the economy still lagged behind. He also experienced the time when goods were in short supply. However, in the past 20 years, China has changed dramatically and its GDP has leapt to third in the world. But since the Chinese population is so large, its average GDP is still very low. China is still a developing country, but its potential is there for all to see. David is full of confidence about China, a feeling that has never changed, even in 1989 and SARS of 2003.

In 1989, when the Canadian Embassy informed David to withdraw from China, he said, "Why would I leave? I'm safe here. There is no need to worry." Besides, he hardly regards himself as a real Canadian. He loves China and looks at everything from "Chinese" perspective. In recent years he's been trying to get a Chinese green card. But it's so complicated to go through all the procedures. "First, I need to have a certificate issued by the Canadian side to identify me as this kind of person or not that kind of person, then a marriage certificate issued in Chicago, and at last a certificate issued by the Ministry of Public Security to prove that I have no criminal record. Sigh, I am accustomed to the bureaucracies of the world."

David's eldest son is now studying in the United States. He plans to come back to China after making some money after school. His youngest son, Yang Yi'an, has finished junior high school in China and is receiving distance education for senior high school over the Internet. This is a kind of overseas study at home. In his spare time, this 17-year-old handsome young man loves music. In his room you can find a drum kit and musical instruments. He often exchanges views with his friends on art. Anyway, he has got enough space and democracy at home for him to fully develop his own interests. As many other children with international family backgrounds, he was born to be a translator. Sometimes,

David and Yang Zhi ask him to translate something to earn some pocket money on one side, while getting social experience on the other. "He does well in translations from Chinese into English, but not very well from English into Chinese," says Yang Zhi. In fact, his authentic Beijing dialect and English, both inherited from his family, are excellent.

David looks very content with his sons and with his family of three generations living in their small courtyard. We can't think of anything with which he is dissatisfied.

David is used to the four seasons of Beijing and likes every one of them. After the Waking of Insects in the spring, a seasonal point which usually falls on the 5th or 6th of March, he begins to worry about whether his little creatures in the small yard have come to life after hibernation. After a rain in the summer, he may fold some paper boats and put them on the pond in the rear yard. In an autumn evening, he may sit on the deck enjoying the moon, while every snowfall in winter is a festival in his courtyard. He is like a child and makes a snowman with his son. David doesn't like the "concrete forests" of the modern city, "especially the high-rises with balconies all wrapped up. You can't keep in touch with nature by living there. What's the difference between living in that kind of building from living in a casket?" he says.

What he likes the best is a rainy day. Every time it rains, he likes to open the big umbrella in the small yard, listening to the rhythm of the rain. Is this romantic behavior caused by so many memories of drought left him while he studied the history of the Middle East in Jordan? Or has he got the heart of a poet under his scholarly appearance? The rain in Beijing sometimes lingers on, and sometimes it's wild, but it's all aggressive. If you stand longer outside, you'll get wet for sure. David doesn't care at all, for he loves to experience that poetic feel. How can he get that without getting soaked?

Translated by Li Shujuan

Personal File

Name: Anneli Kilpelainen

Chinese Name: Jiang Enli

Nationality: Finn

Occupation: Charity Worker

Time in China: 7 years

A Finnish Mother

There is a large family, comprised of nine kids, living in Lijiang, an ancient town in Yunnan Province. The kids are not related to each other by blood and have only one parent — Jiang Enli, who is not their biological mother. This mother is from a faraway country on the other side of the world, and she settled down in the small town seven years ago.

*F*olks in town all know this unique family, but have no idea why a lady from Finland would come to this remote area and take on responsibility as the children's adoptive mother. What is the tender story behind her decision?

The story is a long one, which goes back to the beginning of 2000.

Looking for Orphans

Jiang Enli had never imagined she would come here to work, and take this old city as her second home. Seven year ago, when she first visited, the charity foundation she was affiliated with asked her to foster some orphans there. Her Finnish name is Anneli Kilpelainen, and she only took a Chinese name after arriving at Lijiang. She was fascinated by its beautiful scenery and named herself Jiang Enli. Within this name is her first impression of Lijiang — that it was God's blessing which led her to Lijiang.

In May 2000, Jiang and her friend He Mei, a Malaysian lady, arrived at Baoshan, a remote town under Lijiang city's jurisdiction.

This is an extremely secluded area with only one run-down highway that ends at the town office. From the office, the two ladies had to walk another 30 rugged miles to their destination — a mountain village of the Pumi ethnic group. It was already May, but the air was still quite chilly with heavy fog due

to the high elevation. After a whole day's journey on foot, Jiang and He finally reached Zhugu Village at dusk. The fifty-year-old Jiang Enli was still in high spirits despite the fact that she still suffered from a leg injury sustained in a traffic accident years ago.

The village is scattered widely because it is very hard for locals to find a big enough place in the craggy terrain to build their homes close together. Instead of setting up their houses in clusters like typical Chinese villages, the villagers have to build their houses on small lots miles apart. The shortest distance between any two homes is three to four miles. The area where the village office sits is the most populated, with about ten households, and the village's only primary school is located here.

The school has less than 50 students. Most of the students have to hike for more than an hour along zigzagging paths in the mountains to get to school. These kids become experienced hiking in and around mountains before they even reach school age. Not all children in the village go to school; it depends entirely on their families' financial situation. There are many dropouts mostly because their parents cannot afford the 50 US dollars annual tuition. The amount may be insignificant elsewhere, but for Zhugu villagers it is still a rather heavy burden.

At the village office, Jiang met the first orphan and adored him at first glance. Seven-year-old He Yuan from the Pumi ethnic group, dressed in rags. His father had died two years ago and his mother had disappeared. Now he was under the care of his frail grandparents.

The boy, with black sparkling eyes, clung to his grandma and was a little shy standing in front of the foreigners, who looked so different from the villagers. Eventually Jiang's amiability shortened the distance between the strangers. He Yuan was a second grader and had some reading skills. Cuddling the little boy affectionately, Jiang asked him to try writing some Chinese and to draw a simple picture. The closeness created a warm feeling between the two. Two hours later, when Jiang asked the boy if he would like to go to school and live with her in Lijiang City, the smiling boy nodded shyly. "He wants to go! He

would like to stay with us," Jiang said joyfully. Actually the boy had never been away from his grandmother, never left the deep mountains, and never seen the outside world in his eight years of life.

As night fell, Jiang went to He Yuan's home, nestled at the foot of a mountain. Once inside the humble log house, Jiang was surprised to see there was nothing there but a fire pan and an adobe platform to sleep on. No furniture whatsoever. No electricity. In a metal frame hanging on a pillar a burning pine torch was the only source of light. It was a totally alien world to her. The room was dim, yet full of warmth. She could tell that the family, with no one to provide for them, was completely destitute. She could also tell that they also led their life with gratification and dignity, though their situation was desperate. They were very hospitable, though they were shy and reserved. Cherishing a deep love for the boy, the frail grandparents had tried their very best to support him at school ever since his parents passed away. As usual in mountain villages, when children like He Yuan reach the age of seven, they are supposed to help their families with herding cattle and sheep or collecting firewood as cooking fuel. The possibility for them to continue their schooling becomes very slim. As her understanding of the family deepened, Jiang made the decision to adopt the child on her way back to the village office.

Jiang also met He Huiqin, a little girl from the same primary school. Just like most kids from the deep mountains, Huiqin always wore a sunny smile and a pure expression. The girl had lost her parents during a violent earthquake in 1996, when she was still too young to understand the world. So most of the memories she had enshrined in her heart were related to her school teachers. She sang Jiang a song, "We are under the loving care of our teachers, though we have no more hugs from mothers…." Deeply moved, Jiang came up and gave Huiqin a big hug. The girl had been left in the care of her uncle since the earthquake. Her uncle's home was far from the school and she had to struggle for two days along the mountainous path to get to school. Since she wouldn't be able to go back to her uncle's very often, she had to live at school. The girl regarded the school as her second home. "Would you like to live together with us in Lijiang?"

Jiang asked Huiqin. The bashful girl only smiled and gave no answer. This made Jiang a bit worried. "We will have nine children in the family. You will be their big sister and teach them how to write. Is that okay?" Jiang asked again. This time the girl smiled with a nod. This delighted Jiang very much. Very soon these kids would become the lights of her eyes.

Like He Yuan and Huiqin, all the kids Jiang brought "home" were from these isolated villages in the deep mountains. These young simple souls, just like their mountain folks, didn't know anything of the outside world. They didn't know either what a kind of life they would have in future. With the help from the charity foundation and friends, Jiang Enli rented a house with a courtyard in Lijiang and started her new life in China.

New Home

Jiang Enli has another big family back in her home country. Originally one of nine siblings, Jiang got along well with the family. She had never thought she would spend her life in an unknown country together with nine unfamiliar kids. Already in her fifties, she was a little bit reluctant at first to leave her sweet home for a new life in Lijiang. But her strong maternal love for the kids chased away her hesitation. She was deeply concerned about all the hapless kids, ranging in age from 5 to 13, and each with different heartbreaking stories of their young lives. She was determined to stay. But no one was sure what the Finnish mother of nine might encounter.

The nine children were all from different families and had diverse personalities. They spoke different dialects since they were from different ethnic groups such as Yi, Pumi, Naxi and Bai. They were accustomed to life in their particular groups before they joined the family. But the disparity between the mother and the kids was even bigger than that between the kids themselves. Jiang took these differences not as barriers between them but rather as opportunities to learn more about the ethnic cultures. Her deep maternal love for the kids has knitted strong ties in the family.

Six months slipped by. Immersed in the loving care of their Mom, the once shy and lonely children grew into cheerful angels. Besides Mom, they also had grandparents from New Zealand to take care of them. The two grandparents worked as volunteers in the family, which is named "Rainbow Home of Hopes" by the charity foundation.

Under the arrangement of Mom, the children have regular physical check-ups and proper medical treatment if necessary. Before long they were all in great health. But one day a boy, Guiyou by name, had a medical emergency and was hospitalized for surgery in Lijiang Hospital. After Guiyou was rushed to the operating room on a gurney, Mom and the grandparents kept praying outside until the boy woke up from surgery. They took turns keeping watch by the little patient's bedside 24 hours a day and devoted painstaking care to him. Ward mates and the hospital staff were amazed and totally touched by their dedication.

Little Guiyou made a quick recovery with the meticulous care of Mommy and grandparents. A week later, Guiyou called Mommy when he was ready to be discharged. Jiang Enli put aside her chores at hand and rushed to the hospital immediately. Bringing the child home safe and sound made her happier than

anything. She gave him a toy rabbit as a welcome-home gift, which was really exciting for the boy, and also prepared a big dinner to celebrate his complete recovery. This unexpected episode brought the kids even closer to their Mom.

Spring Outing

Four years elapsed, and Jiang and the kids, now a harmonious whole, welcomed the spring of 2004. As they had in previous years, the family made a cross-country excursion one weekend, to enjoy the fresh air of spring.

Idyllic in the springtime, Naxi villages are decorated with brilliant colors — pear trees flaunting snow white blossom, peach trees bursting into bloom with pink flowers, honey bees dancing among flower clusters. Laughter accompanied the cheerful family as they wandered through the beautiful fields.

To Jiang's delight, the family enjoys good health and happiness and is never without hearty laughter. After four years of sharing a common life with her children, Jiang couldn't live without her kids. That is really beyond her own expectation. At the same time, these kids are also very attached to their mother. As these little village children grew up into lively youngsters, Jiang has gradually assimilated into the local society.

At the end of the excursion, Jiang took her children to Mr. He, a well-known Naxi doctor of traditional Chinese medicine. She hoped to further improve the kids' health with Chinese food therapy. Now, as the kids were sitting around the doctor, she was concerned the most about He Xiaojun, a chronic bed-wetter.

"He often suffers from bed-wetting," she told the doctor. "The boy is pretty nervous about that and I don't know what's wrong with him."

The doctor conducted a physical examination on the boy. "Nothing wrong," the doctor said. "He is lacking *Yuanqi* (vitality), that's it."

"What is *Yuanqi*?" Jiang Enli asked, struck by these esoteric words. *Yuanqi*, a concept from Chinese Taoism, is not heard in western society. Looking at the perplexed Mom, the kids burst into giggles.

"Don't laugh at me, kids. Tell me what *Yuanqi* is," Mommy insisted. Not knowing how to explain to her in plain Chinese, the doctor assured her it was an easy, curable problem.

Next it was the turn of He Yuan, the shy little boy she had taken home from Zhugu Village four year before, now the closest to her.

"He Yuan suffers from laziness," the kids uttered simultaneously.

"Yes, he does. He Yuan, you are lazy, so you suffer from laziness disease, right?" she joked with the boy. Lying in Mom's arms and acting spoiled, He Yuan grinned with delight. The taciturn boy, fond of reading and composition, was always among the list of top scorers in his class.

"He always complains of dizziness," she told the doctor.

"It is nothing serious. It will be fine once he's taken some medicine," the doctor assured her after he finished the checkup. Jiang felt at great ease upon hearing this.

In the past four years, in order to better understand her kids, Jiang had developed a great interest in learning Chinese culture and the Chinese language. Now she can speak fluent Chinese with a Lijiang accent. To Jiang Enli, this was the only real obstacle to bringing up the nine kids. She had to understand and take care of nine children from nine different backgrounds with different personalities. Therefore nothing was trivial with regard to her children. They became the most important part of her life. The loving care from their adoptive mother had helped the children clear up the shadows that hung over their early childhood. The loving care had bound the youngsters closely with Mom. The kids always kept their hearts open to Mom and there was nothing the kids would keep secret from her.

365 Days a Year

All year round for the last four years, Jiang got up very early every morning, prepared the kids for breakfast, and then saw them off to school. It is the most bustling time of the day: Mom hugs each of them and says goodbye and

the kids, with the warmth of Mom's body, go to school in high spirits.

"Be careful!" She never forgets to exhort the kids to be cautious when crossing the street. She will linger outside until the kids are out of the lane and out of her sight. Then she will tidy up the rooms with Little Zhang, the family cook. The two-story building is located in a residential community in the north part of the small city. On the first floor are the children's bedrooms, and on the second are study rooms with books and musical instruments like a piano and violin, donated by her friends and charity organizations.

At lunch, children come home again for a meal. Jiang would mingle with them after lunch, teaching them handicrafts, or telling them stories. She has many hobbies and has gradually passed them on to the kids. Knitting, for example, is her consummate skill and, in her opinion, a good way to build up dexterity.

With the kids all asking Mommy for tutoring, like little birds chirping together, the short break is a sweet and happy moment for her. In the family, all the children, boys and girls, have to take part in D.I.Y. handicrafts in order to strengthen their physical coordination.

"That's not right. Do it like this," Jiang patiently advises Xiaojun, who seems to be all thumbs in knitting. Of the four boys, He Yuan is the most adroit, as he is in most subjects. When he has already finished a small piece, his brothers are still tinkering with their knitting needles. Every day the family will do some activities for a little while before the kids go back school.

The busiest time of day is when the kids come back from school. The courtyard is always filled with laughter and excitement. Over the last four years, Jiang has passed most of her days like this. Busy as she is, she derives a great deal of enjoyment from helping kids reading and doing homework.

Cheerful Zhuzhu, the youngest daughter who joined with Mom at the age of four, is in first grade. "We shall strive to be stronger and rely on ourselves; we shall master all skills needed in serving the people." Zhuzhu is reading aloud.

"Wow, you understand this big piece now!" the delighted Mom gives her a kiss on the cheek.

The little girl gazes at Mom with deep feeling, and smiles with great pride.

Besides supervising the kids while they do their homework and household chores, Jiang, like all mothers, has a lot of more to mind, like stitching and sewing. It goes without saying that it is strenuous to raise so many kids at the same time. But each and every day she learns something surprising from the kids. Day after day, she uses her love, hard work and patience to bring up the new family, which, in return, makes her life full and happy. "God sent me here, gave me nine children and brought me a happy life," she often says.

Friends

In the last four years, Jiang has gotten to know many neighbors. She chats with them when they drop in on occasionally. This morning, after the kids have left for school, two friends she made not long ago have dropped by for a chat.

"I have a big family in Finland and my mother gave birth to nine children. You see, I have nine children too," Jiang said proudly. "My mother would be very happy to know this if she is still alive."

"I think our Mom needs to find a Dad for the family," said Ms. He, the family tutor, smiling.

"Yes, why not," the friends chimed in with the tutor.

"I feel more free being single," she answered. "If I was married I would have to go with my husband and wouldn't be able to be here with these kids."

"Yes, our kids need a Dad. Ms. He is going to get married and they will be the parents," Jiang rejoiced.

"Anyway, you have to have a Dad for the kids," her friends emphasized.

"Let God decide for me." Jiang, though approaching her sixties, still remains single. She has dedicated most of her life to philanthropy and will dedicate the rest of her life to the Chinese children.

"My mind will be at rest when the kids grow up, get jobs and can rely on themselves." She tells her friends that she will stay in Lijiang for the rest of her life if nothing goes wrong.

Through frequent contact with the local residents, Jiang has quickly immersed herself in the local life, becoming, in her words, "a true member" of the local Naxi ethnic group.

A friend from Finland paid her a visit a little while ago. Visits from old friends has more or less relieved her of her homesickness. Over the last four years, stitch by stitch, Jiang has embedded her love for her country into a piece of embroidery, a national flag of Finland. The visit from a fellow countryman has brought the warmth of home back into her mind again. She joyfully displayed to her friend the embroidered national flag and some old photos. "This one was taken when I was three," she told her friend, pointing to a time-weathered photo. "My parents have nine children. By God's blessing, I have nine kids too."

The friend has specially brought some tree twigs from Finland. Holding the twigs, she could almost smell the fragrance of her hometown. Jiang uses these twigs for massage in a Finnish-style sauna she has set up at home. This traditional Finnish bathing method is effective in alleviating her pressure when she feels

unwell.

Family Parties

The family would hold occasional parties with different themes. At today's evening party the kids act out small skits. They are encouraged to give free rein to their imagination for an impromptu performance. Now the kids are confident and a little older, quite different from what they used to be. Their performance is full of surprising wit and humor. He Yuan plays the role of a pregnant woman. He uses a napkin as a scarf, puts on a lady's blouse for a costume and stuffs a cushion in front of his belly. Everybody is laughing their head off even before he's begun. He Yuan, now a lively, cheerful youngster, is no longer the sheepish and shy boy from Zhugu Village.

After the party, the children sit around Mommy and tell her their dreams for the future.

"I want to make tons of money and buy a camera and record all these plays," Huiqin dreams.

"Mom, I want to buy you a fancy car," Xiaojun boasts.

"I want to buy you a house," Yingying says. "And I also want to be a professional hairdresser and make Mommy look like a princess."

These words give Jiang a great sense of pride, and drive away all her fatigue. The kids are the most cherished treasures in her life. She told children, she needed no presents but to see them grow up in good health and become useful people. There is a close bond between her and the children, and her love has led them toward their bright future.

Postscript

Jiang Enli was my neighbor in Lijiang. She is not interested in interviews with journalists. I was allowed to take some snapshots of the family only after I had known her for a long period of time. As a close friend, I finally persuaded her to sit down for an interview. She promised that she would allow me to record the everyday life of these kids with my video camera until they are fully grown. For the sake of her children, she had turned down many requests for news coverage. Asked why, she said she didn't want her children to feel they were different from others, and she hoped they would grow up like other kids did. Since I had mingled with them for quite a long time, the kids never regarded me as a stranger and they looked very natural when facing my camera. After I was transferred to Kunming, I didn't see them as often. Fortunately my mother is also a friend of Jiang's, so when I was not there, my Mom would drop by the house on my behalf. In fact, my mother loves this family too. I will continue with this story to the very end.

By Feng Xiaohua
Translated by Yang Yaohua
Photographs provided by Feng Xiaohua

Personal File

Name: David Noel Tool

Chinese Name: Du Dawei

Nationality: American

Occupation: Professor

Time in China: 10 years

The Number One "Signage Police"

Du Dawei, an affable American going grey at the temples and bearing an ardent love for traditional Chinese attire and culture, is the epitome of scholarly demeanor and soldierly bearing. Since forming his ties with China he has never regarded himself as an outsider, and he never tires of "nit-picking" English signage around Beijing. Recently it has been rumored that this "old chap" has conceived a "secret plan" that will make his Beijing life more enjoyable, and probably make him forget to return to his American home.

$\mathcal{D}$avid Noel Tool is his real name, which is easily transliterated into Chinese as Du Dawei. Local folks call him "Lao Du", or "Old Du". This elderly gentleman prefers to be addressed as "Lao Du". "Lao" is a specific form of address that shows intimacy and informality, making him feel warm and pleased. Lao Du feels a bit humbled by his chosen surname because of the respect he has for the great poet Du Fu of the Tang Dynasty (618-907), who is also referred to as "Lao Du". "I like Du Fu's disposition, a poet's disposition of always being concerned about the fate of the nation." Our Lao Du is also concerned about a nation — China.

Recently, Lao Du's popularity has shot up due to his frequent appearances in Beijing's major news media. Almost everyone has noticed that, from the bathrooms in five-star hotels to the roadside restrooms, the English signs reading "W.C." have been changed and standardized to "Toilet". It is known to many that the American Du Dawei advocates the standardization of English signage. But of course, his merits are not limited to this.

Since he started teaching — his first love — at Beijing International Studies University in 2001, Du Dawei has been voluntarily correcting mangled public English signs throughout Beijing, and at the same time working as an advisor to the Organizing Committee of Beijing Speaks Foreign Languages Program. On January 12, 2006, he was honored with the "Great Wall Friendship Reward" for his outstanding contributions to "Beijing's economic and social development". On March 28, 2007, he was chosen, through public acclaim on the Internet, as one of the "Top Ten Volunteers", the only foreigner to receive the honor. He has done a great deal to improve Beijing's image and thus has won the great esteem of the Chinese people. He never regards himself as an outsider, and the Chinese always regard him as one of their own.

Attached to Oriental Culture

We came to interview him at his home in the living quarters for foreign teachers at the Beijing International Studies University. Once inside his home, we found ourself standing in the middle of a miniature museum of Chinese culture. On the walls, doors, and anywhere where something could be hung, you can see face masks painted with theatrical makeup or traditional Chinese calligraphy and paintings. One wall of the sitting room is covered with a set of four picture plaques done in a theme of the four seasons. The home, full of an air of antiquity, is furnished with old-fashioned Chinese furniture: an eight-immortal square table and wooden armchairs, curio cabinets, a long narrow table and bookshelves. Piled on tables and in cabinets and bookshelves are books along with a variety of antiques and cultural relics — figurines of Lord Guan, Bao

Gong, Buddha and Guanyin, theatrical headgear, and other bric-a-brac. Even the doorways and bathrooms are decorated with a dazzling array of knick-knacks.

When speaking of Bao Gong, a well-known historical official who fought against corruption, Lao Du shows deep admiration. "He is the paragon of a civil servant." As for Lord Guan, the retired US army colonel says: "He is the sage of war, the god of soldiers." Of course it is a must to have a Buddha to worship, as Du Dawei has converted to Buddhism.

The hale and hearty Lao Du has great affection for traditional Chinese clothes. Hanging in his closets are many beautiful "Tang Zhuang". The six-foot-one professor, with his scholarly bearing and stalwart body tempered by army training, looks especially "cool" and even classier than most natives would attired in these traditional Chinese garments. It seems that the suits are specially conceived for him.

During the interview Lao Du, sitting in an old-fashioned wooden armchair, talks cheerfully and humorously and intermingles English with Chinese. Starting on the subject of his attachment to Chinese culture, he recalls memories of Chinese-themed movies he saw as a child: the Four Heavenly Kings, the King of Hell and his two constables, Ox Head and Horse Face, and the bloodcurdling scenes of cruel tortures in Hell. "I don't know why I was scared stiff then." His brows knitted and a strange expression on his face, he seems to have returned to his childhood. I can somewhat tell from his expression the tremendous fear struck in his young heart by that version of Chinese culture. However that couldn't count as a real understanding of Chinese culture. His real, close contact with it came many years later.

Lao Du majored in German at college and wanted to carve out a career teaching German history after graduation. Who would have thought that fate would dispatch him to Vietnam in 1966, and put him through a life-and-death ordeal? The sensation of visiting that country was so exotic to him he felt it was like "walking on the Moon". However, while there he also experienced danger as grave as the hells he had seen in books and movies. "In a single day, eighteen of my fellow soldiers fell in battle and laid down their lives in a foreign country. I sadly and keenly felt how fragile and precious human life was and how helpless we often seemed to be." Christian doctrine couldn't help him ease his vexation and bewilderment. Therefore, he had a crisis of religious belief between 1966 and 1991.

He returned from the Vietnamese theater intending to further his learning, and attended Southern California University as an reserve serviceman. He had come into first-hand contact with Vietnamese culture during his years there and had become interested in its religion, history, herbal medicine and folk customs. At first he wanted to study the Vietnamese culture. It happened that his wife's aunt was the friend of Prof. H. E. Chen, who explained to him that Vietnamese culture has its roots in China and advised him to take Chinese culture as his study subject, which would naturally enable him to grasp the essence of other Asian cultures. He then took Chinese cultural geography as his study subject, with Professor Chen, who had been the president of China's Fujian University, as his tutor. He got his Master's degree with a thesis entitled "The Huanghe (Yellow River): Problems and Solutions". After graduation, he remained at the school teaching Chinese cultural geography. "I learned to read and write Chinese characters in their original complex form," he says proudly. Nowadays, students in

China are only required to read, not to write, the traditional complex style characters; thus, many young Chinese have more trouble writing the old style characters than he.

In 1983, he received a doctoral degree in education. He held several posts simultaneously and kept himself busy every day. He was not so happy, though, maybe because of his religious vacuity, or maybe because he did not feel fulfilled. He felt a particular sense of loss in 2000 when, after having retired from the Army with a pension as a 30-year veteran, he thought "I could enjoy an easy sort of life using my green thumb in my backyard garden or making furniture in my basement workshop. But that is not the life I want. I thought it'd be really intolerably wasteful if I were worthless to society. I wanted to be a useful old fellow."

The great poet Li Bai of the Chinese Tang Dynasty says in his poem: "Heaven gave me the talent, let it be employed." With such rich experience, ample knowledge of history and firm grounding in Chinese culture, how could he live out his days insipidly in his back yard, planting tomatoes? In September 1990, he was recommended as a guest professor at China's Lanzhou University and as an advisor to the school's management. His main job was to give lectures to college teachers on how to write English academic theses for international publication.

During his three years working in Lanzhou, he made many Chinese friends and gained a deeper understanding of Chinese culture. Here he found his greatest pleasure in *Qinqiang*, a local opera style, and the Yellow River. He would go to a *Qinqiang* theater five times a week, and go to sit and watch the river twice a week. *Qinqiang*'s vigorous staging and ardent vocals was much to his liking; it could enrapt and intoxicate him. He would sit quietly on the bank of the turbulent river, the mother of Chinese civilization, and think of the eternity of limitless Heaven and the endless Earth. His soul would feel purified and at ease. Don't forget his master's dissertation was on the "Yellow River" when he was majoring in Chinese cultural geography in college.

This three-year period was an important part of his life, not only because he gained a deeper understanding of Chinese culture but also because he found his spiritual foundations. Before leaving China, a British friend gave him a book entitled *Buddhism* by the British writer Christmas Humphries. Enlightened by Buddhist philosophy, he seemed to find all the answers to the many unsolved questions long buried in his mind. "I find the Greater Vehicle of Buddhism is similar to Christianity but the Lesser Vehicle has helped me clear up all the suspicions clouding my mind." Since then he has become a devout Buddhist. He was startled when a fortune teller told him that he had "come home" to China. Life here is so appealing and he really feels at home. "I am so interested in calligraphy, the *guqin* (seven-stringed plucked instrument similar to zither), Confucianism and many other aspects of Chinese culture. He feels he must have been a Chinese Buddhist monk in his previous life.

His attachment to Oriental culture began in Vietnam and strengthened in China. He was promoted to the rank of colonel in 1993 and had to go back to the States.

In 2001, maybe because he was longing for traditional Chinese culture and wanted to do something meaningful for that country, he wanted to "go home". Just at this point, he got a call from Beijing. When he was teaching in Lanzhou University, he and the geology department chairman had become bosom friends. They were attached to each other like brothers. "I call him 'big brother'. His

three sons call me uncle. I would go to his home every weekend, just like one family. 'I've retired and live in Beijing now so you come to see me in Beijing', he told me in a letter that year. One of his in-laws was the Dean of the College of International Economics and Trade of Beijing International Studies University and they needed language teachers like me. So I was invited to Beijing by a single letter." On August 28, 2001, Lao Du "returned home" as a guest professor at that school.

"Back home" now, he spends almost all his time in China, except that for two short trips in the States to take care of family affairs, and occasional visits to the International Buddhist Academy in Sri Lanka, where he used to work as an educational administrator. He keeps trying to entice his wife and children to join him in China where he is "too happy to return to American life".

Correct English Signs

He came to Beijing on August 28, 2001, and, soon after that, he encountered an embarrassment that left a deep impression on his mind. Lao Du, a rapt fan of *Qinqiang* Opera, now became a devotee of Peking Opera. One day in October, he was attending a Peking Opera performance in the Chang'an Theater. Many foreigners in the audience burst into laughter at one point, which made him feel uneasy and the Chinese audience feel puzzled. The theater, in order to help foreign audience understand the plot better, offered a running translation in English. To his dismay, it was full of errors that turned the opera into a laughingstock. When the Monkey King supposedly rode clouds on to the stage, an accompanying line that should have said "auspicious clouds" read "auspicious clods" instead, which made the foreigners laugh their heads off. Standing on the Chinese side, he was overcome with shame by the bad English translations while, standing on the side of the foreigners, he was offended by the ridicule of the foreign audience.

Lao Du said: "I felt that caption incident brought shame to both the Chinese and the foreigners. And that made me, a lover of Chinese culture, feel doubly

ashamed. They made these oversights in translation because they didn't have a sincere attitude toward their culture. We have to bear in mind that even a single wrong word could result in foreign visitors misunderstanding this 5,000-year old civilization.

It's not hard to imagine that, when describing their trips to China, these foreign visitors would tell their friends and families about the loopy translations, along with what they have seen and heard in the country. Actually some websites exist that specialize in collecting Beijing's bad English signs. It's said that the click rates on these websites is pretty high. Lao Du heard a friend once speak admiringly of China's profound and rich culture, while simultaneously pouring ridicule on mangled English translations. On the very same night the opera performance ended, Lao Du wrote a letter to China's Ministry of Culture earnestly appealing that they allow him, as a volunteer, to clean up the bad English signage in Beijing. "The English signage is aimed to help foreigners to better understand China," he said in the letter. "But some of these English signs are too Chinese and will have effects counter to their true purpose." His opinions and efforts has been highly valued by the city government.

In 2002, the Organizing Committee of Beijing Speaks Foreign Languages Program was established. The Committee's purpose is to help realize the concept of "New Beijing, Great Olympics", to promote Beijing's image as a capital, a cultural and livable city and an international metropolis, and to raise its level of modernization and internationalization. South Korea did the same years ago. Before the 1988 Olympic Games in Seoul, the Korean Government took the Olympics as a turning point to improve its citizens' English, standardize English signs, and train volunteers for the games. After 14 years of effort, from 1988 until 2002 when South Korea hosted the FIFA World Cup, the country finally cleaned up and standardized its public English signs.

Upon its establishment, the Organizing Committee invited Du Dawei to be its advisor, and Lao Du gladly accepted the offer. His first job was to remove bad English translations from traffic signs. For example, the English sign warning of slippery roads after snowfall was "Black Spot', and Lao Du changed it to "Icy Road". The traffic sign warning against driving while drowsy read "Don't Drive Tiredly". Du said it should be "Don't Drive When Tired". For a passage crossing beneath a road, he changed "Tunnel" to "Underpass". He replaced "Protect circumstance begins with me" with "Protecting the environment begins with me".

His second assignment was to polish the English versions of commentaries on scenic and cultural spots. He revised the English captions at the Forbidden City, Beihai, the Temple of Heaven and many other locations including the Anti-Japanese War museums, the English guide at the Simatai Section of the Great Wall, and the English descriptions on the display boards at many other places. In early 2004, Dawei and the committee finished the translation and proofreading of "A Corpus of Descriptive Captions for Traffic, Parks and Scenic Spots in Beijing". Then, the Organizing Committee assigned him to revise the commentaries for 40 museums and culture sites and then 40 other smaller exhibition halls.

Every Friday from 2003 to 2005, Du Dawei shuttled between Beijing's museums, carrying his computer printouts of English museum signage. He would input the English descriptive captions on his laptop and correct them at home. Then he would send the polished versions to the Committee office or directly to the museums. Du Dawei found great pleasure in it, though it was hard work. The museums were very cooperative and, in order to ensure accuracy, would even permit Lao Du to touch the treasures of various dynasties, allowing not only visual admiration but also tactile enjoyment. He couldn't hold back his excitement when recalling his feelings as he touched those priceless relics. "It was great!" "It was gorgeous!" "It was inconceivable for a Lao Wai to have this chance!"

By helping the museums, he fulfilled his long-cherished wish. When he was at Lanzhou University, he visited the city museum and found there were no English captions at all. He volunteered to write for these museums but, to his regret, his offer was not appreciated and the museum officials told him that they "didn't need it". "Maybe they felt there were too few foreign visitors there," he guessed. After his offer was turned down, he tried every means to make Chinese people understand that "Foreigners are especially interested in museums. Usually they get their first knowledge of a country from its museums. But in China at that time, people didn't give due attention to museums".

He always held a nearly religious devotion to Chinese culture. In museums, when he sees a guide explaining the sights to tourists in English, he often listens to the guide for a while, then comes up to tell him or her honestly: "Your English is good, but in some cases it cannot be easily understood by foreigners. I suggest you say…."

He encountered quite a number of English signs that he couldn't make sense of, not even to guess their meaning. He had to ask his graduate students to retranslate them first. After revising them, he would send the improved versions to the committee and Professor Chen Lin to check their cultural accuracy. Professor Chen is well-known among translators and enthusiasts of the English language. His collaboration with Chen ensured the quality of the translations. That's why Chinese and foreign friends call the two the "signage police".

Michael Cook is another friend who works with him on the committee. Michael, a Briton who grew up in China, speaks Chinese as fluently as his native tongue. Because of the differences between British English and American English, the "signage police" often have disputes regarding translations. Sometimes

they compromise with each other on their disagreements or, if compromise was impossible, they would ask Mr. Liu Yang, Chairman of the Organizing Committee, for arbitration. Thinking that Michael's Chinese is too good, but Lao Du's opinion should be respected, Mr. Liu would say jokingly: "If Lao Du understands it; anybody can understand it," or, "If Lao Du's happy, I'm happy." Luckily, Michael could accept Mr. Liu's "partiality" and of course Lao Du is amiable. So they let it pass. But the committee also decided in their first meetings to use American English rather than British English in Beijing signage.

Lao Du became famous for his English sign corrections and became familiar to more and more locals. When walking down the street, he would be greeted by many strangers. "Hi, Lao Du. You missed a sign at…. Go take a look." Or "Hi, Lao Du, why haven't you corrected the English mistakes in Xiushui Street?" Not long ago, a TV correspondent from NBC came to tell him that there were three English mistakes on street signs that he had missed and offered to go with him to inspect.

The letter "L" was missing from the sign of "the Temple of the Sun"; "the Crescent Moon Spring" was translated as the "Curved Poo"; the English commentary for the Zhihua Temple contained a serious error that turned the temple into an unknown fairytale. What was farthest off the beam was the English name for the sign of a proctology hospital in Chaoyang District: "Hospital for Anus and Intestine Disease." This indecent sign always provoked explosive laughter from foreign visitors. They would grab their cameras and have their pictures taken standing in front of the sign. I can imagine that we would laugh our heads off if we were abroad and saw a Chinese sign reading "Anus Hospital"; for sure we would have our picture taken with the sign. But Lao Du did not think it was funny at all, because this was the picture the *lao wai* were taking home as a reminder of their visit to China. Lao Du wanted them taking home pictures of them standing at the Great Wall, the Forbidden City, or the Temple of Heaven, showing the greatness of China, not these silly signs. The next day he went to the hospital and suggested they change the sign. The hospital changed it within two weeks at a cost of 30,000 *yuan*.

He keeps two computers in his study, one in English and the other in Chinese. For years, Du Dawei has corrected, proofread, and compiled materials in English. The 6-volume "Handbook of Translations", for example, bears his painstaking efforts and those of the entire committee on each and every page. The handbooks have been published, the mangled English signage will soon be gone from view. Bathrooms or restrooms have been standardized to "toilet", with men's as "Gents/Men" and women's as "Ladies/Women". The sign for restricted entry is "Staff Only". The sign of "Show Mercy to Grass" now reads "Please Keep Off the Grass." "Danger! High Voltage" has replaced "Be careful of being electrified".

In order to standardize "W.C." to "Toilet", the committee sought the advice of the British Embassy in Beijing. They found out that "W.C." was actually a British euphemism which doesn't make any sense to Americans. "Toilet", which is derived from Latin, is obvious to British, Americans, Italians, or Spanish, etc. A great sense of accomplishment arose in his mind when he saw that "Toilet" had finally replaced "W.C." throughout the city.

He has developed a yen for finding and correcting English errors. Whether on business or pleasure trips, he always keeps his eyes open for loopy English signs. Once he finds such signs, he never gives up.

Some say that Lao Du cannot "stand a grain of sand in his eye", which means he can't tolerate the existence of a single bad English sign. Others say that he "loves well and beats soundly". In a word, he goes "nit-picking" in Beijing's streets and has won unanimous appreciation from Chinese people and foreigners. One fine example has a boundless attractive power. There are many people who want to be enlisted in this "nit-picking army". Many of his students have joined him in this clean-up activity. Some from the States, Singapore, and Hong Kong discuss with him standard translations of names of places. Now, the city has already replaced 6,300 English signs, his contribution to which cannot be left unrecognized. He responds modestly to the commendations of the people and the government award: "In fact I am only your 'face'. It should be attributed to many other people who do the real work; I only accept the reward on your

The Number One "Signage Police" ·· 171

behalf."

The applause was especially loud when this foreign face appeared among Beijing's "Top Ten Volunteers".

Translation of Chinese Menus

In addition to the assignments from the Organizing Committee, in the past few years Du Dawei has been paying great attention to another long-neglected translation — English menus in restaurants. In China's restaurants, there is either no English menu or there is a menu in Chinglish, that is, Chinese-style English. With regard to menu translations, Du Dawei joked: "The variety of translations is greater than that of dishes themselves."

Lao Du admits that it is a most difficult task to translate Chinese menus. To more than 31,000 foreign residents in Beijing, the English menu is the "business card" of Chinese cuisine. Actually many of them have been attracted to China by its reputation for fine food. But an unintelligible English menu full of nonsense often renders them at a complete loss as to what to choose. In some restaurants, "Wanton", for example, is translated as "to swallow the clouds". Egg drop soup turns into "The Sun Rising over Dongting Lake". Sliced cold chicken in the Sichuan style is named "Slobbering Chicken". "Hot Candied Sweet Potato" becomes "Wire Pulled Sweet Potato". I doubt that foreign diners would be able to understand the connection between the sweet potato and wire pulling.

The Chinese cuisine usually embraces a great number of cultural elements. But it is difficult to put it into a foreign language if the name of a common dish carries too much cultural content. In translating menus, it would just be fine to "call a spade a spade". Take the egg drop soup for example. If calling it fried egg in soup is clear to everyone, why call it "The Sun Rising over Dongting Lake?" Even Chinese customers are often unable to make head or tails of it before seeing the soup, let alone foreigners. For some dishes, it is better to use the translations accepted through common practice. It would be excessive to impose "cultural content" on ordinary dishes. Fortunately Lao Du is working with the

Committee to standardize menu translations.

Lao Du showed me a piece of paper bearing the following names:

中文标识 (Chinese)	错误译法（Wrong Translation）
生鱼块 sashimi (sliced raw fish)	Chop the strange fish
童子鸡 pullet (spring chicken)	Chicken without sexual life
驴打滚 soybean cake (sprinkled with soybean meal)	Rolling donkey
四喜丸子 quadruple-happiness meatballs	Four glad meatballs

Such translations make us laugh. It's really quite a tough job to correct such absurdities, because it's not easy to maintain the Chinese meaning while also maintaining a correct, concise translation. "*Tong Zi* chicken", which means young hen, can be literally listed as "pullet" or "spring chicken". As for "Sliced raw fish", we don't know how they came up with "chop" and "strange." The soybean cake, called "*Lü Da Gun*" or "Donkey taking a dust bath" in Chinese, is a hard nut to crack. Probably "*Si Xi* meatballs" is another difficult one, because there are so many cultural elements in it and you cannot attach a long explanation to its English name on a menu.

It seems Lao Du encountered quite a headache in translating "*Si Xi* meatballs". When he asked us the meaning of "*Si Xi*", I dared not to give him careless answer without first checking the references. I looked in a Chinese dictionary and found its meaning. "*Si Xi*" refers to the four biggest felicities in Chinese people's lives: refreshing rain after a long drought; meeting an old friend from a distant land; one's wedding night in the red-candle-lit nuptial chamber; and success in an imperial examination. There is so much meaning contained in the four big meatballs that I couldn't imagine how Lao Du could choose a proper name for it.

He will have plenty of hard nuts to crack. But Lao Du is so fond of Chinese food that he wouldn't allow the well-known Chinese cuisine to be ruined by rubbish translations.

Advocating the "Ask Me Program"

Lao Du has proposed an "Ask Me Program" to the Beijing Volunteer Association and the Foreign Affairs Office. He has done so because he has found that many foreigners in Beijing are not as comfortable as he. Many foreign visitors who don't speak Chinese will lose their "sense of direction". Almost every time he is out in the streets, he is stopped and asked by a worried foreigner with map in hand and a lost look in their eyes, "Can you help me?"

"I know some seniors," he tells me. "They speak rather good English. An old lady started learning English in 2001, when she was 79, and speaks better English than many of my students now. Another, named Jason, is 74 and he works as a volunteer guide in the Forbidden City. The oldest person I know hoping to be a volunteer is 84. Many of the old folks I know in the volunteer program have an English level higher than some university students. To be frank, these old folks won't have equal opportunities with the young people in serving as volunteers at the Olympic games. But they can provide services in their communities and other public places." Du Dawei suggests that they be arranged to work in twos and threes as volunteer docents in museums to meet foreigners' needs for Chinese knowledge, and as information sources, wearing colorful tee shirts reading "Ask Me", to help foreign visitors in scenic spots and shopping areas.

Lao Du's life experiences have proven that accomplishments achieved at an advanced age can bring about happiness. He believes his volunteer work has set an example for other senior people. "I am 65 years old but I feel that I am still of use to society, so I am very happy about that," he said. "Happiness brings me good health, and the good health will bring me longevity. I sincerely want other old people to be happy, healthy volunteers like me."

He plans to recommend "Ask Me" volunteer activities at the Dashilan Business Area and Wangfujing Shopping Street as well as Tian'anmen, Liulichang, Xiushui Street, Panjiayuan and at the museums. He wants to offer training to

some Beijing natives and let them work in pairs to provide volunteer services in these places. They can escort foreigners to speciality stores and give foreign visitors directions to particular scenic spots. By doing so, the volunteers will improve their English and the foreign visitors will get help they need. At the same time this will help business get customers. Isn't that a win-win-win situation?

Strive for Obstacle–Free Access" for the Disabled

Listed on his business card are several titles. From those titles, you see that he has been engaged as an advisor to many organizations, proving that he really is a useful person. He is a person not only "of use", but, I have to add, a person "of great talents". It is interesting to note that the most prominent title on the card is "Consultant for Access Unlimited in China" for the disabled.

Lao Du is dedicated to the welfare of the disabled. He has made a loud appeal on news media to society at large to offer better services for the disabled. His article, "Obstacle-Free Access for the Disabled in Museums and Cultural Scenic Spots", which was published in the *Weekly China's Cultural Relics*, has attracted wide-spread attention. The 2008 Paralympics, to be held in Beijing soon after the 2008 Olympic Games, is a challenge as well as an opportunity. Lao Du's article has been a timely edification and reference for the departments concerned. As the advisor to the Association of the Disabled of Beijing, Du Dawei has conducted surveys at these tourist attractions and made his suggestions. His appeal has resulted in special access being provided for Tuancheng in Beijing's Beihai Park. At the entrance of the Forbidden City the high thresholds of the gates are being modified to allow entrance for the disabled. Lao Du is very happy about these improvements.

He emphasizes that, as a special group of people, the disabled should be provided with more convenient, conscientious travel services by society. Particularly, hotels and restaurants should set up green access for them. Unfortunately, "many hotels and restaurants don't want to do that. They are afraid the service would be too expensive. That's wrong. Each year in America a great number of

handicapped people take leisure trips". According to statistics , the annual travel expenses of the American disabled outside the US amounts to US$3.7 billion. Their major destinations are Canada and Mexico; then Thailand. "They are eager to come to China but the country hasn't built up adequate facilities for them, so they can't come. I think we should take the Paralympic Games as an opportunity to quicken the pace of green access construction for foreign disabled tourists. What I most want to say is that the Chinese disabled will also be the beneficiaries of this improvement." In fact, there are many wealthy people among the disabled who have great purchasing power. But "a single step can stop them from spending money. Taking good care of the disabled in this case is not a government responsibility but a matter of morality and the social consciousness of the commercial, hotel and tourism industry." he says.

Lao Du points to a report in the *China Daily* which notes that during the Olympic Games in Beijing, 40 percent of TV programs will be focused on local culture. Through the news media he wants to remind the commercial hotel and tourism industries that they should take this excellent opportunity to show the rest of the world the "Culture-Enriched Olympics" we have promised. At present Du Dawei has been compiling a handbook called *Beijing Culture — a Guide Book*, which will make it easier for foreign visitors to understand China. He has two employees to help him with the handbook and one of them is a young disabled man.

China needs "access" to the rest of the world, and the world needs "access" to China. The disabled need access, and cultural exchange needs access too. He has put all his efforts into the establishment of access between the East and the West.

Conceiving a New Life Plan

Du Dawei has found religious belief and new sense of life's significance in China. He plans to work in China to his last day. He even has the idea to "scatter his cremated ashes in the Yellow River". Maybe because of the infernal torture of

the Vietnam war, or maybe because of the Buddhist philosophy he has studied, he has a peaceful, happy, and auspicious mind. When he sees someone scared or irritated about a lost key, a cat's death or a small fire in a house, he calmly asks, "Any casualties?" "Since everybody is fine, why are you worried so much?" Nothing in the world is more important than life. You will have much less worries and troubles if you see the world with an open mind and take things as they come.

Despite all of Lao Du's involvement in these volunteer activities, his greatest love, and what he feels is his greatest service to China, is helping his international trade and finance students and his translation students better prepare themselves for their role in Chinese society. Though he has great respect for the historic role of the traditional education system, he sees the need for change now in order for China to take its deserved position on the world stage. He says the Chinese people are too intelligent and have so much to offer. They can no longer just be viewed as the factory labor force of the world.

The Chinese education system must do a better job in developing analytical, innovative thinkers so as to meet the competition and to make a contribution

to solving the world's many problems. He holds up Zhang Ruimin, the CEO of Haier, as a good role model, not only for doing business, but for thinking and action. Zhang's call for every employee to be a "strategic business partner" is a call that Lao Du wants all Chinese students to answer, not only in commercial enterprises but in all fields of science, of technology, of the economy and the humanities.

China is far too important a nation and its people far too intelligent to just be a labor force for the world. There are great social and environmental problems that need the attention of this great intelligent nation. In China we must overcome the traditional reluctance of students to open their mouths and participate in class. He tells his students that "every moment is a rehearsal for the rest of your lives", and that they must begin now to adopt the skills and ways of thinking that will make them more successful people in this competitive world.

It goes without saying that sometimes he feels a bit lonely. After all, he is living far from his family. "You were a Chinese monk in your previous life and a monk again in your present life," I joke with him. "It's no problem. I have been trying to talk my wife and children into coming over. I plan to buy a house with courtyard in the suburbs and have them over. Then I'll set up a shop for them to make jewelry and pottery. My wife likes to make jewelry and my son is a ceramic artist teaching at Berkeley University. I hope they can't resist the temptation," he says with a sly smile.

May he succeed in carrying out his "tricks"! May he and his family soon be reunited in China!

Translated by Yang Yaohua
Photo graphs provided by Huang Jie

A Western Student of Chinese Painting

His lifestyle is almost exactly that of an authentic Chinese person: he eats Chinese food, drinks Chinese tea, has Chinese friends, discusses Chinese historical figures and practices *Taiji*. He takes pleasure in Chinese music and painting. He is an artist who understands western art thoroughly, but his works — both his free-hand brushwork and the parts carefully left blank — are made in China. This artist is the French painter Francois Bossiere.

"Amphibious Human"

Among all the Westerners who are good at Chinese painting, one artist is particularly well known to the Chinese people: Giuseppe Gastiglione, who lived in China for 52 years, from the reign of Emperor Kangxi to Qianlong (1662-1736) of the Qing Dynasty (1644-1911). He was a favored minister of the Chinese Emperor, and the royal painter. He brought Western theories of art into China and practiced Chinese painting himself. However, Gastigloine's painting is still painted with Western skills. He respected reality, and his eyes were like camera lenses. His thoughts and methods never strayed from the style of copying reality mechanically.

Starting with a French artist named Francois Bossiere, the Oriental sensibility began to sneak into the Western art world. As if a fairy from the East ere holding this Western painter's hand while he worked, his free-hand brushworks and blank spaces are one hundred percent "made in China".

Coming out of the Xizhimen subway station and walking about 200 meters to the south, there is a Granville Italian style café. French painter Francois stood there. He was wearing a checked shirt, was tall and thin with blue eyes and light-colored hair. He looked like a basketball player. The way he shakes hands with people shows that he has been part of the Oriental culture for a long time, and you can feel that he must deeply understand the theories of Chinese painting —

where your thought reaches, your brush follows.

Francois's house in Beijing is not big, but is quite artistic. On his shelves is his vast collection of various Chinese books, from *Chronological Category of Ba Da Shan Ren* to *My Name Is Red*. Around the house are his paintings, mostly Chinese-style ink paintings.

Seated for a while, Francois stood up with a cigarette between his fingers and turned up the speakers. Suddenly the entire house was filled with the sound of *guqin* (seven-stringed plucked instrument) music. It feels like the music was composed for the paintings. He not only likes the *guqin*, but also the *pipa* (a plucked string instrument with a fretted fingerboard), another traditional Chinese instrument. When he was teaching in Xi'an, one of his students played for him. The moment she started, he immediately fell in love with the music and thought it resembles Spanish Flamenco music very much. Although it is not that refined, it is so pure that it can move anyone.

Francois was born in Paris in 1956. He loved painting when he was just a small boy. His mother was from a small town in southern France and the mountains there were big and bleak. People could easily find shell fossils in the mountains. His mother who knew so much about prehistoric culture reminded him: Don't copy others' works. You should not copy. She wanted him to express his own style. As a Westerner who behaves as his spirit moves him, he knew the importance of being outside the normal world when he was just a small boy.

Xizhimen is one of Beijing's prosperous spots. It is definitely not an easy thing to maintain a calm mood while painting in such a noisy place. But from Francois's works, you can tell that he has already grasped the ability to keep his mind in nature while in the midst of the crowd.

In July 2007, his series of works *Ancient Jars Major Suites* were exhibited in Beijing. Many of his new works were shown. His excellent Chinese ink paintings attracted the attention of many Chinese senior painters and critics.

It is said that Eastern culture and Western culture are like two mountain

peaks standing and facing each other. When the two communicate, they can do so only in the valley at the feet of the mountains. But when people see Francois's Chinese paintings and the ideal scenery outlined there, it makes them think that this saying might be worth reconsidering. From Francois's paintings, Chinese authorities of art concluded that Westerners not only understand Chinese spirit, but are also able to draw upon its soul.

Before I met Francois, I heard that he is an artist who deeply understands Western art. When he was young, he saw almost no Chinese artworks. The works that left profound marks in his memory and also affected his future painting were the ones he saw before he was 30 years old. This means that the art formality that Francois follows is generally Western.

The content of our talks varied from the East to the West and then from the West to the East. Francois was talking back and forth, showing no difficulties. Looking at the mature Chinese style paintings, I couldn't help asking myself, how could a European person who grew up in Western culture became such an amphibious artist who knows the Eastern image so well? The answer does not seem to be complicated. As Francois said, no matter what the tradition is, the ultimate goal that art pursues is always the same.

When he was nearly 20 years old, he traveled to Greece. On Crete, in the HertsReese Museum, he saw pottery jars, chops, and wall paintings for the first time. He was completely into the paintings and patterns on them, he says: "Really, I did not drink any alcohol, but for three days I was in a state of drunkenness."

One day, about 20 years later, Francois suddenly had the impulse to try painting on a large canvas. When the first sets of canvas were ready, he decided to go to Madrid. That was the first time he had been there. In the Museo Nacional Del Prado, he saw the Flemish artist Bosch's works, they were exaggerated and weird. They immediately attracted his attention. At the same time, he also indulges in Goya's world. From Goya's painting in the Ermita de San Antonio de La Florida, he sensed the Chinese style, although the content of the painting was typically Western.

The journey to Spain made Francois a real painter. A door had opened for

him, and it connected the West to the East.

Twenty years later, in 2007, one of the collections from the Prado Museum — "From Tiziano to Goya" — came to Beijing. Standing on the foreign land, facing his early piece, Francois again felt the happiness of painting. His feeling led his spirit. In the China National Museum of Fine Arts, Francois saw the masterpieces once again, and tears burst from his eyes. He really hopes that the Chinese people can also find such happiness, which can only be found in the most classical art.

Chinese Art: Calm and Harmonious

Why does he love Chinese art so much? When asked, Francois looked like an innocent child and answered: "I don't know."

In 1983, he started to learn the *Book of Changes*; in 1984, he started reading *Words of Monk Bitter Melon* (the work of painter Shi Tao, who lived in the 1600s at the end of the Ming Dynasty and early Qing Dynasty). When he started to touch Chinese culture, first he read Chinese ancient masterpieces; that was 25 years ago.

Everything comes from the simplest drawn line. He understands Shi Tao's words deeply, that freedom and spirit are hard to find in Western culture.

In 1994, Francois first came to China. For the first time, Eastern culture pulled aside her veil in front of this Western painter. Francois realized that the Chinese people are really different from Westerners, for example, the Chinese people like to ask questions, while the Westerners focus more on answers. In Qu Yuan's *Heaven Asks*, he threw 170 heavy questions at readers. The Westerners worked harder on answering questions. For example, in the *Bible*, laws are set down about how people should behave.

His lifestyle is almost exactly that of an authentic Chinese person: he eats Chinese food, drinks Chinese tea, has Chinese friends, discusses Chinese historical figures and practices *Taiji*. "Chinese aesthetics give me a kind of confidence."

"I like Ba Da and Xu Wei," this slender Frenchman said, word by word. He

likes the simple feeling they convey, he feels the eternal in an instant. Truly, in Francois works, you can see Ba Da Shan Ren's style; only this Ba Da Shan Ren is wearing a Western suit and possesses French elegance.

When asked the difference between the Chinese brush and the oil painting brush, Francois said directly: one is soft, the other is hard. He looks for brushes all over Beijing, from Panjiayuan to Liulichang to an eight-square-meter shop next to Guozijian.

Chinese painting uses rice paper, and paintings are made very quickly. The painters have to compose their works first in their mind, because there is no way to make corrections after you finish painting. Chinese painting also saves a lot of room, only a few strokes can collect all kinds of elements and bring them together. Francois believes that Chinese painting provides him with a kind of spiritual freedom, and he said: "Chinese art is hailed as the acme of perfection. It displays so much imagination, and satisfies people's pursuit of wisdom, tranquil and harmony."

At the end of 1989, Francois met Chinese anthropologist Yu Shuo. Later this anthropologist from Beijing Normal University became his wife. In the

past, in Paris, when Yu Shuo saw Francois's paintings for the first time, her first impression was that they were beautiful, a kind of beauty filled with wildness and mystery. It was just like the feeling she had when she saw Spanish or Gypsy girls.

After they were married, Yu Shuo found out that Francois performs a "Holly Ceremony" every morning. One morning, when he finished washing, he suddenly told his wife, using the Chinese words he just learned: "I am going to find my head." His wife immediately understood that he was going out for some fresh air.

Waking up headless and gradually finding his head again has become Francois's Holly Ceremony. Francois's ceremony has three parts: drinking a cup of coffee, reading three poems, and painting three ink paintings. Before he's finished this, nothing his wife says to him actually enters his brain.

When Francois accompanied his wife to Alps to do anthropological research, he discovered a mysterious valley with more than 100,000 rock paintings. Every day he walked on small paths in the mountain and found the quietness that can only be found in his studio. Francois suddenly realized that people actually did not know anything about the creation of nature.

"The Westerners don't paint mountains, but oceans." Francois said, because in the eyes of Western painters "The still mountains cannot show one's painting skills, but flowing water can."

Maybe it is the habit of Chinese painters to love painting mountains. Francois said that he would rather leave the oceans to the philosophers and go to observe the mountains. According to him, a tradition needs to be maintained and transferred, but to his surprise, nowadays, painters all love to live in big cities, and don't choose to stay in the mountains.

Times have changed. It is really hard to grasp the spirit that the ancients once had. "I want to paint mountains, but after seeing Huangshan Mountain or Huashan Mountain, where can I find my uniqueness?" Francois admitted that he couldn't see through the eyes of Fan Kuan, Ju Ran or Guo Xi unless he could ride donkeys, live in wild shelters, and hide in the forest for a couple of weeks.

Late this spring, Francois went to Qinling with a few students from the Xi'an Academy of Fine Arts. It is a wild place with almost no visitors. Suddenly, he seemed to be able to feel what the ancients felt before. Modern people live in the concrete forests, running around on the highways, and their ears are filled with commercials; the image of the virtual world is much larger than the real one. Francois said: "How could we ever have the sense that the ancients had?"

The famous painter Zeng Laide once said that among all the Western artists who practice both Western and Eastern art, Francois is the only one who combines the two so well. It is hard to say that his paintings are purely Western or Eastern. Both styles exist in his paintings at the same time, sometimes one is stronger and sometimes the other is stronger. They support each other mutually and naturally. He controls the two styles freely with no difficulty.

According to Francois, the distance between Chinese culture and Western culture is not really far. For example, the thoughts of Paul Klee are really close to Shi Tao's. The time is different, their languages are different, and their styles of paintings are different, one is oil painting, the other is ink painting, but they are so similar in theories and thoughts.

From the works of jazz musician Thelonius Monk, Francois found the finest expression of the combination of the abstract and the practical. Monk is an African-American musician, now people don't say jazz is American music, but describe it as American-African music. It is multi-cultural.

From Jan Vermeer's works, Francois saw the Chinese style "leaving blank". This Dutch painter's works displayed the essence of oil painting, but more importantly, and surprisingly, they contain the style of "leaving blank" — which is completely Eastern. Francois said: "We could never expect anything like this from a 17th century painter."

"I saw the 'blank' part in his works. Through the exact details, we can feel that uncertainty is everywhere. We don't know what the young girl is doing, or what her clothes are made of. We will have to guess. There is an oil painting hanging behind her, but there is only half of it and the image is blurred, we cannot tell the content of that painting … the observers have to complete it themselves, and this is exactly the feeling I have when I see Ba Da's paintings."

From Jan Vermeer to Ba Da, Francois's thought leaped dramatically. He has always been interested in the practice of Chinese philosophical ideas in art. For more than 20 years, he has loved using bamboo sticks to lay the patterns of *bagua* (Eight Trigrams), then finding the answers in the *Book of Changes*. When he is doing so, he has never thought that this is a Chinese thing. Chinese aesthetics enable him to directly sense and understand western art pieces without wasting time in reading mountains of documents.

Yu Shuo said: "Francois has more than 100 little sketching booklets within his reach. He draws every day, as though it was a religious ceremony, he never stops."

The blue color that Francois uses in his painting reminds the guest professor from the Central Academy of Art, Jin Zhilin, of the Chinese *Qinghua* porcelain vase. Francois's inspiration actually comes from the houses of Andalusia. One night, Francois was looking at the art collection of Ba Da Shan Ren. Sensing the uninhibited spirit of the painter, Francois suddenly realized that Dadaism from the early 20th century actually contains deeply holy and sacred characteristics. It was just expressed in a cynical form. Francois feelings and senses have always swung back and forth from the West to the East.

The Strength of Culture Is in Mixing

One year, one of Francois' friends in America received a post card. On it was painted a black Spanish bull, and the image of the bull reminded his friend of the paintings of Qi Baishi, but he wondered how Qi Baishi could ever have seen bull-fighting. When he turned the post card over, he realized the painter was actually Francois.

Francois loves talking about the combination of cultures and civilization. For example, Hugo was exiled. He wrote a famous article criticizing the burning of China's Old Summer Palace. Louis the 14th's royal painter Nicolas Poussin insisted on staying in Italy and refused to go back to France no matter how the French King tried to get him to go back to France. As for Francois himself, he decided to devote himself to art after visiting the Scotland highlands, and became a real painter in Spain.

Francois said: "I am interested in everything that Chinese philosophy discusses. I use the discussions as the proof of my own existence and memory. When I just came to China, I was really happy. It seems that all the thoughts I had about China were correct and China also accepted me. As for me, I don't need to become a Chinese person first to be accepted and absorb the nourishment of Chinese thoughts and ideas."

Another thing that Francois cherishes very much is Chinese folk art.

In May 2004, Francois was preparing his exhibition in Beijing, and encountered professor Jin Zhilin from the Central Academy of Art. It seemed that he was fated to meet Professor Jin. Jin Zhilin told Francois that he worked with peasants artists and invited Francois to visit the villages in northern Shaanxi. He built a museum there and exhibited art pieces made by peasants.

Francois accepted the invitation because he had never been to the rural area of China to know another part of China and its art there. His visit proved worthwhile: Francois found another world.

Jin Zhilin's hometown of Yanchuan is a very remote and bleak place, but the style of the paper-cut art pieces by peasants are extremely real and honest. Francois was excited and loved their works immediately.

At that time, a TV crew was also doing interviews in that village. One of the young cameramen told Francois: "I have been here for three days, and I strongly feel that I am not a true Chinese person." His words touched Francois. Compared to the cameraman, he felt moved in two ways: not only within China but also within different provinces, there are so many different worlds coexisting, and they all function in different ways. It may be just because of the existence of different worlds that Francois believes that the Chinese paintings can stand out so obviously and contain so much information.

"In China, the people who come to my exhibitions are always more obviously moved by my work than they are in France. People here observe carefully, they feel and think. No matter their method or angle in understanding my pieces, they take my paintings very seriously, although they cannot always express this feeling in language."

Francois soon realized that there was a wide gap between Chinese philosophy as he understood it and the realities of contemporary China.

China now is developing at a rapid pace, and its new concepts of time and space are very close to those of America. Francois thinks the modern structure of Chinese cities is more Western than those of Europe. It is really hard for people to leave them, and stay away long enough to think clearly. Therefore, the phenomenon is awkward: China is going really fast while Europe is slow; China is really noisy while Europe is comparatively quiet.

Francois said that this might mean that living in modern China, people were not able to paint a mountain according to the traditional concepts. Everything around the world is spinning so fast, and we are not living in a space suitable for painting.

The misunderstanding of Francois' pieces now appears in his exhibitions. Many people pay sympathy to him and think that he cannot understand Chinese philosophical concepts because of his Chinese language. In fact, it is not the original content of that philosophy — such as the unity of heaven and humanity, or how the Way begets one and one begets two — which confuses Francois, it is the modern explanations that confuse him.

The question is that, the closer you are to something, the less you can understand it. Francois said that it is just like looking at an oil painting. In order to completely appreciate it, you will have to move back and forth.

Francois senses some caution in many contemporary paintings done in the Chinese traditional style, just like the caution he can see in the European academic paintings of the 19th century. He thinks the images of Chinese painters' works are too full. It does not embody the concept of "resembling yet not resembling", but instead becomes purely "resembles". Perhaps, after almost one century of self-denial, China needs to acknowledge herself and be acknowledged by others. A calm criticism hasn't really started yet.

Painter Zeng Laide came to all three of Francois' exhibitions. He is moved by Francois' changes every time. He feels that Francois is becoming closer and closer to the Chinese people. But he does not want Francois to become a Chinese

person completely. He hopes that Francois can maintain his view as an outsider to examine and absorb Chinese civilization from a different angle, all the while shaping himself.

By Zhang Hong
Translated by Ma Dongxiao

Personal File

Name: Junko Haraguchi

Chinese Name: Yuan Kou Chun Zi

Nationality: Japanese

Occupation: Senior Editor

Time in China: 14 years

The Pleasure of "Discovery"

Junko Haraguchi, a petite Japanese lady who embodies both the traditional and the modern, has lived for the most opportune period of 14 years in China. Over the years, she has observed fast-changing China from her unique point of view, and dispatched to Japan numerous articles on everything that has taken place, big or small, in her adopted country. Seemingly tame but full of the charm of daily life, these articles have proven to possess a fascinating appeal for her readers. This free-lance writer who loves Chinese-style fried potato shreds, has become a de facto people-to-people ambassador. Today I am on my way to visit the ambassador at her Beijing "residence".

$\mathscr{I}$ follow her directions and make one brief turn after getting off the subway at Dawanglu Station, and instantly find myself in SOHO Modern City, a well-known condo community in the capital. It is just a few steps from the subway station! No wonder Junko told me that it only takes a minute to walk to her home. When she told me "one minute" I thought I'd misheard her, and she'd actually said "seven minutes". I feel a moment of admiration for the punctuality of the Japanese.

A "Three–Park" Home

Haraguchi already stands in the doorway as I reach for the doorbell. Startled by the stranger, two kittens whiz onto an armchair and stare at me with watchful eyes, prepare to flee at any moment. "I am sorry. The cats shed and spread their hair everywhere," Haraguchi apologizes while cleaning a chair for me. "It doesn't matter. I love cats too," I assure her. "Really?" This seems to put her more at ease, and she makes tea for me.

Too impatient to take a seat, I start looking around the apartment. To my surprise, it looks no different from a typical Chinese home, furnished with European style furniture but no tatami. Maybe the only trace of the Japanese way of life that lingers in this home is that everyone walks barefoot on the floor. "People

of my generation are no longer used to kneeling on tatami. Yes, my mother's generation still does that. I have no tatami even in my home in Tokyo." Haraguchi tells me that she likes simple décor. The landlord put flowers here and there and curtains on all the windows. It was too much furnishing for her. Haraguchi kept only a few simple items of furniture and asked the landlord to remove the rest when she moved in. Now I notice that the SOHO Modern City's beautiful silhouette is fully visible through the big French window without blinds.

Haraguchi has rented this apartment solely due to her deep involvement with the Beijing 2008 Olympic Games. July 13, 2001 was the day when the International Olympic Committee was to choose by ballot the host of the 2008 Olympic Games. There was a big rooftop party at SOHO Modern City that night, as everyone waited for the final result of the vote. Like all others present, Junko Haraguchi was so happy and so excited that she was moved to tears when the big news came that China had won. Standing on top of the building, Haraguchi saw a grand, unforgettable spectacle — hundreds of thousands of excited Beijing residents rushing onto the Chang'an Avenue thoroughfare to join the stream of people flowing into Tian'anmen Square for the celebration carnival. Later she wanted to rent an apartment in this area because of its convenient public transit system. She paid the rent deposit without a moment's hesitation when she saw the huge French windows facing SOHO Modern City. Through the window, you can make out the rooftop where the party was held. "When I moved in," Haraguchi says, "it was all open fields around the building. Great changes have taken place in the area in the last few years, with quite a number of high-rises popping up to the north of here. My apartment is on the 29th floor and nothing obscures the view. Colorful neon lights gorgeously dot the skyline of SOHO

Modern City at night. Every time I see the rooftop from the sitting room, my thoughts return to that night's celebration party."

In the sitting room is a big round table with books piled on top. Her study is filled with books too. "It's so cluttered here. You can't keep it tidy with the cats always messing it up," she explains, slightly embarrassed. "It's much better here. It was even worse in my Panjiayuan apartment. It was so messy that there wasn't even space for visitors to sit." To be honest, the "messiness" in her home reveals a kind of unintentional gracefulness and elegance, a home décor similar to that of the cultural workers introduced in Japanese lifestyle magazines.

Haraguchi bought a 70-square-meter apartment in the Panjianyuan area in 1998. It was expensive because those apartments were on the market for foreign buyers only. Later on the government annulled this "for-foreigner-only" policy and now foreigners are on an equal footing with Chinese in purchasing houses. "I bought it too early and paid too much," says Haraguchi, still regretful. Not only did she miss the right time, but she also chose a location that is inconvenient transportation-wise. Anyhow, there was one benefit for her: the apartment was close to the Panjiayuan antique market. Haraguchi loves to collect antiques, glassware in particular. She would go browsing the market whenever she had time, and would always take something home. That's why her home is decorated with such a variety of bric-a-brac, most of which was bought at the antique market. She visits the market so often that all the vendors know her well and fervently try to sell to her when she shows up.

In addition to handicrafts, Haraguchi also loves little animals. She kept three little pet birds when she lived in her Panjiayuan apartment. She even erected an artificial tree just inside the door for the birds to play on. Visitors would see the birds jumping and flying around the tree when they stepped inside. Some friends jokingly labeled her apartment as "a three-park home"—Beijing Zoo Park, Beijing Botanical Park and Panjiayuan Park. "It is hard for a journalist to keep a tidy home," Haraguchi said by way of excusing herself. "When friends visited, I greeted them with 'have a seat' and they would ask me, perplexedly, 'where'? So I had to make room for them." I cannot but laugh upon hearing her

story. Anyway it is rare for a foreigner to display the essence of Beijing's three parks inside a single apartment.

Using public transportation when she was living in Panjiayuan was terribly inconvenient, since her home was far from any subway station. Wanting a better location, Haraguchi rented out the old apartment for 3,500 *yuan* a month and moved into her present apartment at SOHO Modern City. Here in her new home, you can still see glimpses of Panjiayuan Park, with an artistic glass vase here and a pair of stone-carved fu dogs there. She still keeps the "zoo", symbolized by the cats. She had to give up "the botanical park", however, since the two naughty cats destroy any plant that she tries to grow.

The two female cats, Mimi and Tuola (Tiger in Japanese), have been living with Haraguchi for more than a year. Naming a female cat Tiger is a little strange — it sounds too fierce for a cute cat. "Tuola has colorfully striped fur and looks like a tiger," Haraguchi explains. "And of course there are female tigers anyway." Mimi, in heat, cries constantly while I talk with Haraguchi. "I want to have them spayed. But I can't make my mind because I think it would be too cruel to them." Mimi, more active than Tiger, now sniffs at our shoes and then jumps on to the armchair. Haraguchi says Mimi is not only active but also "scholarly". "She likes watching TV and will stand upright when she sees something

exciting on the screen." Haraguchi loves Mimi so much that she has managed to put her photo in *LuLuBu Beijing* magazine. "The photo has nothing to do with my article and the magazine was reluctant to carry it. I didn't have any other reason either. In the end my excuse was that she was born in Beijing." She shows me the photo in a copy of the magazine, and looks very pleased.

Born in the 60s, Haraguchi doesn't have any children of her own. Asked about her future plans for having children, she says that she has no plan in particular. "No special plans to have children or not. I am busy every day and feel happy enough to the kittens with me." It seems that Haraguchi truly regards the cats as her kids.

Timeliness, Favorable Location and Good Relations

During our two-hour interview, Haraguchi frequently refers to the topic of "Timeliness, favorable location and harmony." (The concept is taken from a well-known Chinese classic: Heaven's favorable weather is less important than Earth's advantageous terrain, and Earth's advantageous terrain is less important than human unity.)

Junko Haraguchi and her husband Ari Haraguchi were schoolmates at Japan's Keio University. After graduation in 1985, Junko worked as an editor in a Tokyo publishing house and later worked as a publicity agent in a film distribution company. As a member of the first generation of female professionals, she didn't have other women's experiences to learn from, and had to forge her own way and rely on herself for everything. It was a life unavoidably full of sorrows as well as joys. Luckily enough, she enjoyed relative equality with her male colleagues in terms of personal growth. During her work assignments abroad, she met many foreign female professionals, particularly in Paris. She found that many middle-aged French women in mass media had had outstanding careers and at the same time led colorful lives. But Japanese women at that age usually quit their jobs and stay at home as housewives, doing nothing but taking care of their husbands and kids, even if they are highly educated. At most, they

perform sado, or tea ceremonies, as a pastime. "It's a pity!" sighs Haraguchi. The independence of European women has greatly touched her and opened her eyes: "They can lead such a wonderful lives, why can't I?"

Junko Haraguchi came to Beijing with her husband in 1993. At that time, the Japanese public media didn't carry much news about Beijing. You would find that most news reports, if there were any at all, would be on political and economical topics, nothing about everyday life in Beijing. "To be frank, I had a fearful image of Beijing in my mind before I came!"

Since she settled down in Beijing, Haraguchi has been surprised to find so many amazing things in the ancient Chinese capital: delicious foods, delightful places and other splendid things, all of them new to her. Life in Beijing is without doubt a great enjoyment for Haraguchi, who is fond of architecture, good food, fashion and travel. Gradually, she has fostered an intense aspiration to introduce life in Beijing to her Japanese readers. Starting with small columns in Japanese magazines, she dispatched articles one after another depicting what she saw in the Chinese capital. No one else was doing this at that time, because many thought that it would be out of the question that Beijing's everyday life might appear in fashion magazines.

Since the year 2000, the content of Japanese magazines has gradually changed. Friends in the Japanese news media have asked Haraguchi for articles on daily life in China. Nowadays, all Japanese fashion magazines carry slice-of-life news from Beijing, along with similar reports from New York, Paris, London and Milan. As a freelancer, every year Haraguchi contributes between 50 to 100 articles to Japanese magazines, newspapers and websites about China's public figures, travel, architecture, interior design, fashion, cuisine and so on. She has also written books, such as "Smart Chinese Kitchen" and "Anecdotes from the Streets of Beijing and Shanghai", which are well received in Japan.

One day, she met a Japanese "grandpa" at a dumpling restaurant she had recommended in a Japanese magazine. The grandpa asked her if she too had found it after reading Junko Haraguchi's article. "I am Haraguchi herself," she answered. Her surprised country fellow was so excited that he insisted on having

a picture taken with her, and remained in contact with Haraguchi even after he returned to Japan. This gave Junko great gratification.

During a chat with an American correspondent, she learned that the American news media mainly concentrates on political and economic life, with very few articles on daily life. It was all quite colorless and boring, the admiring correspondent told her, adding "I would like to write about such daily-life stuff and Chinese dumplings too when I am retired." I can see Haraguchi feels a sense of accomplishment as she says "There are more news reports on China's daily life in Japan then in the USA, and I think Japan must be No.1 in this respect".

Haraguchi attributes her accomplishments mostly to her "timely" arrival in Beijing. "It wouldn't have worked if I came here ten years earlier or ten years later. Coming in 1983 would have been too early, I wouldn't have had much to do because Japanese press circles weren't paying much attention to China. And it would have been too late if I came after 2003, when there was already a great deal of news reports on Beijing's daily life — there wouldn't have been much

elbowroom left for me. If I hadn't come at the right time, I wouldn't have been able to see the sharp-contrast changes and to write on so many interesting subjects. The Chinese people talk a lot about 'Timeliness, favorable location and good relations'. I think I have grasped the advantage of 'Timeliness'."

Speaking pure, fluent Mandarin, Haraguchi amazes me with her frequent quotes of recondite Chinese classics. Occasionally during the interview, she comes across a word or two that's not easy for her to pronounce perfectly. Then she earnestly asks me to help her with the pronunciation. Nobody would believe that she spoke no Chinese when she came more than ten years ago.

Her husband Ari Haraguchi came to China in 1989 and spent a year studying Chinese at Beijing Normal University. He sent his wife to the same school to take the same course after she joined him in Beijing. So the couple became alumni in Beijing. "I like Beijing because of its artistic atmosphere," she tells me. "At the beginning, when China adopted its reform and open-door policy, people here didn't work so hard to keep pace with the tempo of modern life like Japanese people." Haraguchi recalls. "At that time, there were many salons for different circles of cultural life. You had salons for painters, sculptors, musicians, etc. Members would frequently get together, chatting and enjoying music, and then go to restaurants for quick-boiled lamb. It was all very interesting." Before long she'd made many friends, improving her Chinese in the process. "Chatting is very important and beneficial and should be taken as part of the work. I have talked with entrepreneurs, farmers and cultural workers. They all have their own special words and expressions. I have learned most of my Chinese from them."

In 1999, at the recommendation of a friend, Haraguchi took a job as a language expert at *People's China*, a monthly Japanese-language periodical. There she experienced firsthand the institutional culture of Chinese organizations, broadened her knowledge of the country, and greatly improved her Chinese. Sometimes she would go with other reporters to cover events. By doing so, Haraguchi gained a thorough understanding of the changing country. Now, though no longer a full-timer, she still carries out her duties as an expert, writing articles, opening columns and creating ideas for the magazine.

Haraguchi has greatly bettered her Chinese over the years. Full of a sense of humor, she often amuses her Chinese colleagues with witty remarks and even the latest slang. Her co-workers call her "Junko Sang", or Ms. Junko, and she likes this intimate form of Japanese address. When she sees others working overtime, she would blithely calls out "Comrades, thank you for working hard!" a pet phrase commonly spoken by Chinese leaders, which makes her colleagues bubble with laughter.

Working for a Beijing magazine aimed at native Japanese readers, Haraguchi has access to the latest information on China's reforms. That should be considered one of the advantages of "favorable location". While working in China, she has made many Chinese friends and friends from other countries. And this, to her mind, is the advantage of "good relations'.

Haraguchi, so to speak, has all the advantages of "timeliness, favorable location and good relations". That's why she is in her element working in Beijing and enjoys a successful career and a smooth life here.

Beijing, a Place Worthy of Exploring

As a well-known connoisseur of fine food, Haraguchi always surprises her friends at the dining table with the delicacies she orders and obscure dish names that trip off her tongue.

Haraguchi used to eat Chinese food in Japan. Most of those dishes belonged to Shanghai or Guangzhou cuisine, more or less Japanized to suit local tastes and deprived much of their Chinese flavors. She has found so many "authentic delicacies" in Beijing that she never had in Japan. Her favorites are crispy potato shreds and other vegetables, which have strong temptations to her with their simple tastes and bright green color. To Haraguchi, the finest food should be cooked with the freshest ingredients and the simplest method, like fried shredded potatoes. At the time when she first came to Beijing, many Japanese people never heard of fried shredded potatoes. So starting from shredded potatoes, she has introduced many home-made dishes to her Japanese readers, such as stewed

eggplant and shredded pork with thick soy sauce. Many readers tried her recipes and fell in love with Beijing cuisine.

With a good palate for food, Haraguchi has tasted almost all Beijing's delicacies, even Madoufu, Beijing's most typical Muslim snack with a very strong lamb smell. It is prepared with lamb tallow and green beans. I have never dared touched it, myself, but Haraguchi loves it. I find that really amazing. She is a frequent guest at many specialized restaurants which even natives have never heard of.

What has made me most envious is that she never gains weight no matter what she eats or how much of it.

During her work as a reviser for *People's China*, she found that most of the articles carried in the magazine were related to economy. There were very few on Beijing's daily life. So she started a special column called "China's Grocery Store" and wrote about many commonplace things, like thermos flasks and old style tea pots. These items, much ignored by the Chinese themselves, have aroused keen interest among the Japanese readers. Her Chinese colleagues were

really blown away and of course admired her unique observations.

Haraguchi didn't pay much attention to these small items at first. Since she started the column, she has developed the habit of carefully observing everything around her. She always finds something new when she browses along the streetsides. "Beijing is a place worth exploring." As she puts it, usually she doesn't have anything special in mind and just finds something new "unintentionally". She works and plays, leading

a routine life the same as everyone else. It is in the course of this routine life that she finds some interesting stuff and then describes them in her articles.

In the spring of 2002, her article "Discoveries in the *Hutongs*" was published in *FIGARO JAPAN*, a widely-known fashion magazine in Japan. She told the readers about her discoveries, such as special restaurants and hotels, in Beijing's *hutongs*, which are narrow alleys very characteristic of the capital. The concept of the *hutong* made its first appearance in Japanese fashion magazines thanks to Haraguchi, and it's now not uncommon to find articles on *hutongs* in Japan. Particularly amazing is that a restaurant in Tokyo is named after *hutongs*.

Along with "Discoveries in the *Hutongs*" was a photo: In a narrow *hutong*, people walk amid dense willow catkin-floss hovering in a gentle breeze, a really charming scene. A reader even called to ask the best time to see the willow floss. No one would have imagined that this most common willow floss, a regular annoyance for Beijing residents, could become so charming and poetic in her articles. Many readers wrote to the magazine requesting to know the exact time when willow floss would come out, as they planned to come to Beijing especially to see it. "It's not that life lacks beauty," the great artist Auguste Rodin said. "It is because our eyes cannot discover the beauty." I am again amazed at her talent for keen observation. Haraguchi is indeed a person with artistic vision.

Haraguchi prefers the Beijing she saw more than ten years ago to the Beijing of today. "Do you think Beijing is getting Europeanized?" once she asked us. Yes, indeed Beijing is changing fast, looking more like a metropolis and starting to lose many of its charming elements. She is shifting her sight to other cities while still keeping an eye on the changes in Beijing. She started a new column called "China's Refined Tastes" with her interesting discoveries. However, she has found that Chinese cities are becoming more and more identical, causing a sense of déjà vu, all with wide thoroughfares like Changan Avenue, impressive office buildings and CBD areas.

Of course, Haraguchi still admires the great changes that have taken place in China. "America is very much developed but changes slowly; the same is true of Japan. China changes so rapidly that you can't catch up with it. It is quite challenging to work as a journalist in China."

The Dual–Responsibility of a People-to-People Ambassador

She believes that, as a worker in mass media, she represents her country with what she says or does. She has interviewed Chinese people from all walks of life. She respects their opinions and tries to exchange views in hope they might change their negative attitudes toward Japan.

Not long ago, Haraguchi went to cover a remote village. A surprised villager asked her if "Japanese ladies need to work". She realized that she was the first Japanese woman they had seen. While she was in the village, she was the representative of Japan and was responsible for conveying the friendship of her people to the locals.

When Japanese friends come to visit, she shows them around. Her friends are always content with the sightseeing. "Likewise, if I were to tell them all the many shortcomings of Beijing, they would come away feeling that Beijing was a terrible place. I feel at the bottom of my heart that I have a dual responsibility to convey good will between both groups of people."

Her husband Ari Haraguchi has taken on the same responsibility. In 1989, Ari, a businessman, was transferred to China by his company. Later on, he set up a cyber school in his Alma Mater, Beijing Normal University. Japanese people can now access Chinese learning courses via the Internet. Mr. Haraguchi spends half of his time in China while Mrs. Haraguchi stays in Beijing most of the time.

There is a funny story behind the name "Ari". Mr. Haraguchi's father was an idealist and gave a lot of thought to Japanese social classes. Deeply influenced by Chairman Mao Tse-tung's ideology, the senior Haraguchi had long dreamed of becoming a socialist. But "unfortunately" he was from a "landlord" family. He named his two sons "Kou" (Public) and "Yu" (Owned) respectively, in hope that he would "rectify" his social class status through the younger generation. This respectable old gentleman has nourished deep and positive feelings toward China. Today he continues learning Chinese even though he is already in

his mid-seventies.

The Sino-Japanese relationship has been advanced mainly by non-governmental sectors. There would be greater harmony and fewer disputes in the world if there were more people-to-people ambassadors like Junko Haraguchi. I really have a strong urge to say to her, loudly: "Comrade Haraguchi, you have done a great job!" I guess she would probably reply with "Serve the people!"

By Zhang Chunxia
Translated by Yang Yaohua

Personal File

Name: Jin Ho Jun

Nationality: Korean

Occupation: Student

Time in China: 8 years

A Korean Doctor Sir Named "China"

Jin Ho Jun, a 34-year-old Korean, has stayed in China for more than eight years because of his love for Chinese medicine; he now regards China as his home. He led a simple and austere student life for most of that time. His college life, a time when most Chinese students are enjoying themselves, this "ascetic" was immersed in traditional Chinese medicine and spent more than fifteen hours every day "meeting the ancients in spirit".

Traditional Chinese Medicine Fever in Korea

When we met Jin Ho Jun at the gate of the Beijing University of Chinese Medicine, the Korean student in front of us didn't look nerdy, which was our impression of most students of traditional Chinese medicine, but more like the handsome boy from our neighborhood, with sharp eyes behind red glasses.

We started our talk with the once-popular Korean TV series *The Great Jang Geum*. Jin Ho Jun said with a smile, "Jang Geum is the first Korean who brought milk vetch root from China to Korea."

At that time, milk vetch root was called Bai Ben and was not available in Korea. Thanks to Jang Geom it was introduced to Korea from China and spread among the common people. Now it has become one of the indispensable tonics good for reinforcing "*qi*" (the Chinese word for vital energy).

Jin Ho Jun explained that traditional Chinese medicine is quite popular in Korea and traditional doctors' income is even higher than that of doctors of Western medicine. The Korean magazine *Career* (a monthly employment periodical), once took a survey of "the most popular professions in Korea for 2010", and the result showed that the most popular profession in Korea in 2010 was a doctor of traditional Chinese medicine.

Koreans edited the Chinese book *The Medical Classic of the Yellow Emperor* into a work as interesting as a novel, and so the book is quite popular

in Korea. Recently Koreans are also preparing to use the name Korean Medicine for Chinese medicine and apply for World Heritage status. This action has aroused opposition among traditional Chinese medicine doctors in China.

"Most Koreans drink a decoction of medicinal ingredients since childhood", Jin Ho Jun said. Traditional Chinese Medicine is regarded as a superior major in Korea and the entrance examination is as difficult as that to enter Tsinghua University or Peking University in China. Moreover, the income after graduation is quite high. There are eleven universities in Korea for traditional Chinese medicine and it is rather competitive for students to apply for their bachelor programs. Every year, a majority of freshmen entering traditional Chinese medicine universities are people who have already had great career achievements, such as correspondents, university professors, leaders of big corporations, etc.

Four Hours of Sleep Every Day

Jin Ho Jun, together with two other Korean students, paid 3,200 *yuan* each per month to rent an apartment near the school. It takes him only five minutes to walk from home to school. Meanwhile he spends an additional 1,600 *yuan* per month to rent a study room in the school, and studies as hard as the ancient Chinese.

Getting up at seven for class at eight, Jin Ho Jun studies late until around ten each night and then leaves the study room. Jin Ho Jun spends around fifteen hours each day in the study room and has no time even for physical exercises.

The study room is surrounded by Korean atmosphere: on the shelf there stand books in Korean, such as *Treatise on Febrile Caused by Cold*, and *The Theory of Prescriptions and Herbal Formula*; on the wall there hang two Korean characters for "quiet"; on the table are scattered snacks in Korean packaging.

Weak since childhood, Jin Ho Jun had a fever four to five times each year, therefore he has taken a lot of medicine and has a close link with traditional Chinese medicine.

Jin Ho Jun came to China in 1999 and studied at the Changchun Institute

for Chinese Medicine for two years. At the beginning of his stay in China, he did not understand Chinese and had difficulty keeping up in class, as the courses were taught in Chinese. Therefore, he spent half a year learning Chinese. He studied very hard, spent most of his time reading books and slept only four hours a day. He asked four Chinese students to be his Chinese teachers so that he could study Chinese every minute. After one year, he had basically mastered speaking and reading in Chinese and could handle 80% of the vocabulary related to traditional Chinese medicine.

One day, a young man of around 20 was sent to the hospital; he was pale, sweating and having a fever. Jin Ho Jun diagnosed his illness as "stagnation of food". It was his first time practicing acupuncture, but he immediately developed an "acupuncture sense". The patient's symptoms disappeared twenty minutes after his treatment, and Jin Ho Jun became more confident of traditional Chinese medicine.

Jin Ho Jun was accepted by the Beijing University of Chinese Medicine in 2002. He has studied there for five years and was awarded his diploma this July. He finished more than forty courses in traditional Chinese medicine and Western medicine during this period and armed himself from head to toe in knowledge.

Books such as *The Medical Classic of the Yellow Emperor* and *Treatise on Febrile Caused by Cold* by Zhang Zhongjing are all essential and important books. Worried about inaccurate translation from Chinese to Korean, Jin Ho Jun read these books directly in Chinese. However all these books were written in blunt prose in the classical Chinese literary style, and it is not possible to understand the books without some knowledge of the classical Chinese literary style. Therefore Jin Ho Jun started to study classical Chinese literature and even exceeded the common Chinese in terms of understanding classical Chinese.

Though his major is traditional Chinese medicine, Jin Ho Jun is reluctant to practice what he has learned in hospitals. He has his own plan, which is to establish a good foundation in college, and then to pass a doctor's certificate next year. Although this doctor's certificate is not recognized in Korea, Jin Ho Jun is taking this examination quite seriously. After all, in his opinion the family name of traditional Chinese medicine is "China". He will be a trainee at the Chinese Medicine Hospital in Kuanjie after the exam.

After eight years in China, Jin Ho Jun is quite used to life in a foreign country. "When I first came from Korea to China, I was not used to things there; however, it feels like I am a traveler when I go back to Korea now." His roots in Beijing are so deep that he did not return to Korea even during the period when SARS spread and most foreigners left Beijing.

Based on his experience, Jin Ho Jun often prescribes cures for himself and his classmates. Many foreign students suffer from weak lungs and spleen, diarrhea, and poor eating habits. In such cases, Jin Ho Jun prescribes a herbal formula, getting the herbs in nearby stores, and the symptoms normally clear up after the patient takes his decoction.

Traditional Chinese Medicine Should Not Be Linked with Western Medicine

Jin Ho Jun is quite familiar with traditional Chinese medicine works popular on the market, such as *Thinking of Traditional Chinese Medicine* written by Liu Lihong. He liked this book when he read it, because he felt that it follows

the traditions of Chinese medicine.

"Traditional Chinese medicine should not be linked with Western medicine", Jin Ho Jun said. In his opinion, Chinese medicine should not be adulterated. "However, it is difficult to find a school which only teaches Chinese medicine. All schools for traditional Chinese medicine teach both Chinese medicine and Western medicine. I don't think this is right, however."

In Korea, Korean traditional doctors are not allowed to diagnose patients with the help of Western medical equipment, such as ultrasound or hematological examinations; therefore Korean traditional doctors must undertake a thorough study of the human body. In his opinion, the study of traditional Chinese medicine is a slow and painstaking process, and it is difficult to master the rudimentary knowledge within five years. The ideal way is to start out only studying Chinese medicine, and then starting to learn Western medicine after mastering the fundamentals. "If I were the Minister for the Ministry of Health, I would consider students' opinions and would undertake reform based on the particular case of each major." Jin Ho Jun explained quite seriously. However, he also acknowledges that there is a dilemma in that a student wouldn't be able to find a job if he only studied Chinese medicine alone.

"It is a pity that there are no pure traditional Chinese doctors now in China. They are all practicing a mixture of both Chinese and Western medicines." But Jin Ho Jun insists, "The purpose of learning Western medicine is to learn Chinese medicine better, while the opposite is not true."

In his opinion, Chinese medicine and Western medicine are suitable for treating different diseases. For instance, bacterial infections are within the range of Western medicine treatment, while sterility and irregular menstruation are within the range by Chinese medicine treatment and should be adjusted by Chinese herbs. Western medicine has no good solution for those problems.

Jin Ho Jun majors in gynecology, and he feels that women are more likely to be endangered by disease than men, because women have wombs and more complicated internal processes than men. However these female symptoms are better adjusted by traditional Chinese medicine, which has much more effective results than Western medicine.

"All in all", Jin Ho Jun summarized, "Western medicine is good for treatment of acute symptoms, while Chinese medicine is good for the treatment of chronic disease; Western medicine is quick and effective, but often has many side-effects; Chinese medicine doesn't act so quickly, but it can cure the root of the disease."

At the Chinese Medicine Hospital in Kuanjie, Jin Ho Jun became acquainted with Zhang Dawei, a pure traditional Chinese medicine doctor whose ancestors have been Chinese medicine doctors for seven generations. Jin Ho Jun attaches much importance to this type of family tradition and regards it as evidence of authenticity. The best Chinese medicine doctor at the Chinese Medicine Hospital in Kuanjie left behind 150 cures, but only half of them can be applied to patients at this time, as doctors do not know how to apply the other half. "If this situation continues, there will be fewer and fewer traditional secret recipes that can be handed down."

Because of his love for Chinese medicine, Jin Ho Jun volunteered to teach Korean students. During our interview, he was presenting an anatomy course to the students. He emphasized again and again that this course was concerned with fundamentals. "The better the doctor, the more importance he attaches to the structure of the human body," he explained. "In ancient China, dissection was performed secretly, with only the teacher and student present."

Jin Ho Jun's teaching methods are quite special. He sets up rules at the beginning of the class and students must complete a recitation for each class. Moreover those who cannot recite their lesson from memory receive punishment. In his opinion, the stronger the stimulation, the deeper the memory is laid. In fact, his punishment is nothing more than a light slap on the hand or other painless place. A girl nearby snickers, the teacher's rules have resulted in excellent memory among the students.

Discussing his post-graduation plans, Jin Ho Jun said that he was planning to travel around China for two or three years, paying visits to folk Chinese medicine doctors. When I ask about acknowledging folk Chinese medicine doctors as

his teachers, Jin Ho Jun said modestly that he has not reached that level yet, and "the most important thing at this moment is to master the fundamentals."

Asked whether he plans to make a living as a doctor of traditional Chinese medicine, Jin Ho Jun nodded vigorously. He plans to move to London and be a doctor. His younger sister married a British man who can provide some funds. Jin Ho Jun hopes to open a clinic for Chinese medicine treatment in London and introduce this Eastern treasure to the West.

It seems that London would provide a vast space for career development and he could apply his medical skills for the benefit of the people of that land.

By Zhang Hong
Translated by Huang Junmei

Personal File

Name: M. Rizwan

Chinese Name: Li Zewan

Nationality: Indian

Occupation: Professional Trainer,
                Cultural Consultant

Time in China: 8 years

Toward an Open Future

He has an honest, brave and kind heart, just like Raj, the main character in an Indian movie *Awara*. He is versatile and has many hobbies. He is expert at everything from singing and acting, to cooking. But his favorite thing to do is Sino-Indian culture exchange. He was the first to introduce Indian TV dramas to Chinese audiences, and he helped to strengthen academic and friendly relations between the two nations' highest drama institutes — China's Central Academy of Drama and India's National School of Drama. He definitely deserves the title of an ambassador for modern Sino-India cultural exchange. He is M. Rizwan, a handsome young man from India.

$\mathcal{P}$eople always sigh that time flies. That's absolutely true, because time is always sneaking by without anyone noticing.

I don't know when the little girl living next door to me grew up or entered college, neither do I know when she brought back a brown-skinned, sturdy young Indian man with big eyes and black hair. Since then, whenever I pass by her door, I always hear Indian music coming from her home, and smell the mouth-watering fragrance of curry floating out of the kitchen. It always sparks my curiosity, and even my imagination….

So one day, I just knocked on the door and went in to see my neighbor girl and her mysterious Indian boy.

The Road to Knowledge

There is a Chinese saying which goes, "A waterfront pavilion gets the moonlight first." It means the advantage of being in a favored position. Although I'm his neighbor, I wasn't the first to interview him. Both of us were busy and couldn't find time. The deadline was just around the corner, and we finally settled the interview time on one weekend evening in August.

It was time for the interview. I stood in front of his door and knocked. The door opened, a handsome young man in an orange tank top and casual shorts

appeared before me — curled black hair, big eyes and bushy brows, well-built muscles — sending out a spark of youthful vigor, vitality and intelligence. No doubt, this was M. Rizwan, a young man from India bearing the Chinese name Li Zewan.

Through the hall, I entered a bigger room, laid out exactly the same as my home. Though we are neighbors we don't visit each other, and this was my first time to his home. Today was the day to uncover the veil of mystery. We sat down, and began to talk.

M. Rizwan was born in a small village in Dhanbad District in India. India is a major agricultural country, and seventy percent of its population are farmers. He lived in countryside, but he was born and brought up in an intellectual family. His father is an electrician. His grandfathers should be considered landlords as they own a large piece of land. He is from a big family clan, who all make their living off the land left by their forefathers. There are four people in his family, and he is the second child, with one brother. His family is neither very rich, nor very poor, and belongs to the middle class. His family pays great attention to education, and is very strict with the children as far as family education is concerned, so he was well brought up and has developed good habits of abiding the law, following the rules, being polite, and conducting himself well with people in society.

M. Rizwan speaks very authentic Chinese. Everyone meeting him is surprised by his fluency.

"When did you study Chinese? And why?" I asked.

"I passed the entrance exam to Jawaharlal Nehru University, the best university in India, in 1993, and my major was Chinese," said Rizwan. "At that time, I had only heard of China because Premier Jawaharlal Nehru had a very good relationship with Chinese Premier Zhou Enlai. Nehru advocated maintaining friendly relations with China, and said, 'Indian people and Chinese people are sisters and brothers.' This phrase was well known among all Indians at the time. I didn't fully understand it then, but it gave me a very deep impression."

"That's why you wanted to study Chinese, is it?"

"Yes, but my real inspiration came from the principal of my senior high school. When I prepared for the college entrance exam, I got the highest marks in my grade, which immediately attracted the principal's attention. He asked about my future academic plans. I don't like science and engineering, but have a deep interest in literature and the arts, and I also wanted to study a foreign language. The problem was I didn't know which one to choose. So the principal said, 'You should study Chinese because China is developing very quickly. Studying Chinese will surely benefit you in the future. Moreover, China is a country full of hope.' Thinking of his words now, what he said was quite right. He was a far-sighted person. I have no doubt, the Chinese language may benefit everyone."

During his study in Jawaharlal Nehru University, Rizwan not only studied Chinese, but also learned almost everything related to China, including Chinese literature, culture, and history, as well as computer science, advanced English, and international history. In 1998, Rizwan finished his post graduate degree and passed the overseas study scholarship test, sponsored by the Indian government. This is an India-China cultural exchange program organized by the Chinese Scholarship Council in collaboration with the Indian Department of Education. The next year, Rizwan came to China and studied Advance Chinese Language at Beijing Language and Culture University. Actually, Rizwan had already mastered Chinese quite well in listening, reading and writing during his five years of study in India. His only shortcoming was his speaking ability. But one year at Beijing Language and Cultural University helped him to make great progress in speaking.

"To tell you the truth, when I first came to Beijing, I most wanted to study theater and acting at the Central Academy of Drama," said Rizwan smiling. "After half a year of study at Beijing Language and Culture University, the Indian Embassy asked me, 'Would you like to have your scholarship extended and continue studying?' I said yes. I wanted to study theatre and acting at the Central Academy of Drama, but the scholarship didn't include studying drama. I tried several times with them, but it was useless."

Disappointed, Rizwan decided to return home after finishing a year of study at Beijing Language and Cultural University. He thought his "five-plus-one years" of study had made him an expert in Chinese, and it was unnecessary to waste the precious scholarship. They should keep the money for those who needed more to come to study in China. As he was getting ready to go home, a chance opportunity befell him. Once, an Indian cultural fair was going to be held in China. The Indian embassy asked Rizwan to give a performance. It was a chance to show off his talents, and so he made full use of the performing skills he had learned and practiced at the Drama Club of Jawaharlal Nehru University and performed part of a play in cooperation with a painter friend who had no performing background. His performance was highly praised by the Indian Ambassador Mr. Vijay Nambiar, who is now the first assistant to Mr. Ban Ki-Moon, the Secretary of the United Nations. The Ambassador's wife also liked his performance. The smart Rizwan didn't let the opportunity slip through his fingers, and expressed his desire to study at the Central Academy of Drama, and explained the practical difficulties he had encountered. Hearing this, the ambassador said, "But it is such a little thing. Why can't it be solved? Judging from your performance skills and interests, I think you deserve to study at the Central Academy of Drama." Furthermore, he personally wrote a recommendation letter to the relevant departments of the Indian government. With the help of the ambassador, Rizwan received the special permission of the Indian government. This is the only oversea study item which has ever received special approval. "Ambassador Nambia was great. A nice person like him is very hard to find. I'll pray for him forever," said Rizwan with deep admiration. He eventually entered the Central Academy of Drama and studied performing arts with 26 Chinese students in a class in the Department of Acting. "I'm like their elder brother. I still keep in touch with them now," said Rizwan proudly.

Rizwan is a talented and unusually bright lad. He may be young, but he has many smart ideas. One year later, he came up with a new plan. He wanted to learn more at the Academy. He turned his eyes to the directing department. So he jumped to a third year directing class to study directing. Half year later,

he again transferred to a newly established television art department to study for another half a year. In two years' time, he hopped three departments and studied three major with two years' tuition. Even his classmates and teachers said with admiration, "Almost no one is able to study three majors, let alone to accomplish three majors in two years. You are the first one to do this at the Central Academy of Drama."

In 2002, Rizwan went back to India with his new bounty of knowledge, planning to study for a PhD at Jawaharlal Nehru University in New Delhi, the capital of India. But five years of living in China had left him a little unaccustomed to life in Delhi. Since he first left his country town at the age of 16 to attend senior high, university, and then to study abroad in China, his eyes have obviously been opened wide. He is the only one in his family clan who has left home — let alone gone abroad — for school and not returned. As he grew older, his heart soared higher and higher. In his eyes, Delhi seems too small for him. Although he's got many friends there, his heart seems to be held by an invisible thread, pulled back to Beijing by a strong power. According to regulations, all returned overseas students must stay in the country at least for six months before going out again. Rizwan waited patiently for his next trip.

Wandering Days in Beijing

In March 2003, Rizwan came to China, again to Beijing, hoping to find a job here. Unfortunately, not long after his arrival, he encountered an unprecedented disaster — SARS. Schools were closed. Office workers worked from home and became SOHO (Small office, Home office) people. At this time, no company or enterprise hired new workers. The SARS hit Rizwan as a terrible blow. For more than three months, he could find no job. The money he brought with him was nearly exhausted. But the question of a job was still unsettled.

"Where were you living at the time? Did you rent a house?" I asked.

"Luckily, I had somewhere to live, at a friend's place," he grinned, "at the foreign students' dorms in Beijing Language and Cultural University."

"How clever you are! There are plenty of empty beds and conditions are good," I praised him. I am familiar with the situation there because I used to study there.

Just when he was on the verge of being broke, someone provided a timely help and introduced a job to him. Through a friend's recommendation, he went to see a Canadian who was looking for a Hindi speaker to help his company with Hindi mobile software testing. At first he told Rizwan that it was only a two- or three-day job and the pay was 2,000 *yuan*, but in the end it took Rizwan more than two months. He not only had to translate, but also had to type Hindi. He never typed Hindi before (even a good Hindi typist would need a month to finish). Poor Rizwan had to study typing from the very beginning. After the job was finished he went to the Canadian and asked him to raise the payment, but was told that "we had a deal, and it is impossible for the company to pay more". This taught Rizwan a good lesson — why didn't I sign a contract with him at the beginning? From then on, whenever anyone asks him to do something, he insists

on signing a contract first. That is "first stupid, then smart".

Rizwan's life in Beijing was less than smooth at first, but his luck came around. SARS soon passed. In July everything in Beijing was back on track. He found a job in a joint venture set up by the Beida Jade Bird and Indian APTECH companies, engaged in IT training. Because he can speak very good Chinese, he was assigned to be in charge of enrolling new students.

"How was the salary? It could at least cover your basic expenses, right?" I joked.

"At the beginning, the salary was not high," Rizwan said. "I didn't care much. I wanted to show them my ability. Actually, neither of us knew each other's strength. After working a period of time, they thought I was pretty good, and doubled my salary. Pretty good."

He looked very confident. He worked there for more than three and a half years. During this period, he also did part-time jobs. He helped to give more than 150 senior employees of CISCO China computer training. "The pay there was high, and they paid in dollars, sent from abroad."

"Do you still work there?" I asked.

"No, in September 2006, we planned to have a child, so I wanted to switch to a job related to children."

"A child?" I said surprised. "Hold on…. Oh, your wife gave a birth to a child in May," I suddenly remembered. I once made an appointment to interview him in May, but his wife was in hospital for delivery, and then he was busy taking care of his wife and child, so our date of interview kept being postponed.

Love in China

"When did you meet your wife?"

"I met her when I was studying at the Central Academy of Drama. Her home is just near the school. When I saw her in Kentucky Fried Chicken, I felt she was the woman I wanted for the rest of my life," said Rizwan, looking somewhat embarrassed. "I'm not a casual person. I never had any love affairs while I was studying either at Jawaharlal Nehru University or at Beijing Language and Culture University." He looked at me. His eyes were crystal clear, as if I could see his heart in them. "I'm a sensitive person. I can feel how others treat me, who is watching me, what people mean by what they say. I could sense the moment I laid eyes on her that she was the one I was going to marry. She had the same feeling for me. We fell in love at first sight. So I began to invite her out for dinner and we dated."

Oh, so that's the real reason why, when he meant to return home to study for his PhD in 2002, he went back to Beijing after only six months?! He missed her, his lovely Beijing girl.

"You wanted to marry her, but what did her parents think?"

"Her parents are not the stubborn kind. She is the only child of the family, but her parents never spoil her. However, this was their daughter's marriage, an event of lifelong significance, so her father was of course a little worried. Then she asked me to see her parents and talk with them," Rizwan said softly.

"I'm bold and brave, and fear nothing on earth. When I met her parents, they told me that they'd never expected their daughter would marry a foreigner,

and they thought a foreigner was unsuitable for her. Never mind her parents' hesistations — even my parents in India had such worries. You might not know this, but Indian parents care much more for their children than Chinese parents. I'm the only one who left home. They also had doubts about the one I wanted to marry, not only because of cultural differences. In their opinion, foreigners are foreigners. They were mostly worried that one day my wife would divorce me and leave me. I explained to her parents, 'You want her to marry a Chinese, but can you guarantee she will be happy?' Of course, they can't guarantee. I went on, 'You care about your daughter's happiness, don't you? Now your daughter and I have the same attitude toward this — I won't marry anyone except her, and she won't marry anyone but me.' I poured all my thoughts out without hesitation, and had no fear."

After listening to Rizwan's frank, sincere confession of faithful love, the girl's parents finally agreed to the marriage. The two young lovers registered for marriage in Beijing on August 17, 2004 and received their marriage certificates. Two months later, they held a wedding ceremony in India. Rizwan meant to fulfill the wishes of his entire clan in India, and at the same time get the approval of his family members and society.

Two years later, in preparation for bringing up his own child, Rizwan switched jobs to work as a teacher at KindyROO, an Australian company specializing in child training in Beijing. "Don't think this kind of training is only a job for women," Rizwan reminded me, "It's a physical work, too. You have to act and dance. I end up each day totally exhausted.

Owing to his excellent work and his advantage in languages, Rizwan was quickly promoted to be teaching supervisor. His ability in Chinese and English, dancing and performing have brought him opportunities and popularity. He is also the supporter of the family, a good husband. He often goes to the kitchen to cook some delicious food for his wife. At those times the special fragrance of the ingredients and food will drift over from his kitchen window, making my mouth water. Poor me, I have to smell it, but can never taste it. I couldn't help praising his outstanding cooking skills, and he smiled guilelessly and said, "My wife loves to eat Indian food, but she can't cook. Nobody in my family can do it except me. What can I do!"

A Volunteer "Ambassador"

His years in China have taught Rizwan a pure and authentic Chinese. The language has brought him many advantages — passing the exam to go abroad to study in China, choosing the courses he liked, looking for jobs, being promoted, courting, and marrying a Chinese girl. In a word, his Chinese has given him advantages in everything. But he sometimes has troubles or problems, too.

"I'm a person who plays by the rules, and I point out any bad behavior or conduct that I see. I'm just the frank and outspoken type. I think that as a citizen I should contribute to society, not only work to make money. Sometimes, when I see someone smoking in public area, spitting or littering, I will go to them and tell them they shouldn't do that. Some people are good and accept my suggestion or opinion. But others sometimes retort by saying, 'What are you doing here? It's not your business.' I think the Beijing Municipal Government has done a lot of good things for us — constructing so many beautiful buildings, streets, and gardens at street intersections, and each one of us has a responsibility to take good care of public property and the environment. This has a lot to do with people's habits. Someone might not notice that their conducts hurts others or affects society. Take dog ownership as an example. According to real estate regulations, if someone rides an elevator with a dog, they must hold the dog and keep it from touching others. Some people do carry their dogs or leash them so that they don't bother others, but others don't have that consciousness. You know that Muslims can't touch dogs unless they are working in a special field in which they are required to touch them. Moreover, dog owners should clean up their dogs' messes properly, and not let them affect our city's beautiful environment and image."

He went on to say, "One day, I took a walk carrying my three-month-old son. As we approached a small park at the side of the street, a big dog suddenly ran at us. It ran in front of me and stood on its hind legs to lick my poor son. I

was very angry. I don't like dogs, but I can bear it if the dog bites me. If it bites my 3-month-old baby, however, it might cause serious problems. So I said to the female owner of the dog, 'You should understand that there are people in this society who don't like dogs.' She replied, 'People who don't like dogs shouldn't walk here!' That's ridiculous. I know she was wrong. It was a public place, but I didn't want to quarrel with her, and only said to her, 'You should read the "Administration Regulation on Dog Ownership in Beijing" carefully. I'm certainly not against people raising dogs, but they must understand not everyone likes dogs as they do. We at least have the right not to be touched by dogs!"

Seeing the seriousness with which he spoke, I couldn't help thinking of something else, and asked, "The other day I saw you coming back from work and speaking to a boy aged three or four. Afterwards the child walked away feeling embarrassed. What on earth did you say to him?"

"He said, 'Hey, a foreigner, a foreigner,' as soon as he saw me. So I told him, 'You shouldn't say this in front of other people, it is impolite. Don't say that again in the future.' Actually, it's not the child's fault, no one ever told him before. That's all."

I admired his courage and his spirit of "loving to poke one's nose into others' business". Another time, on the way home in the evening, he saw a man robbing a woman's purse. He ran over and caught the robber on the run, took the purse and returned it to the woman.

"Were you scared then?" I asked.

"Of course, I was scared, but I didn't think too much. Actually, when you see something wrong happening, what need is there to be scared?"

"What's your deepest impression of China?"

"My deepest impression is the way people help others. When you need help, Beijing residents are the best. They are very warm-hearted. In a big city like this, we should try to help others. If you need directions, for example, Beijing people are the best. They are very patient, not like people in other cities, who are impatient because they're busy with something. But Beijing people also

have bad habits. When something bad happens, they always like to look on with folded arms, and seldom get involved or help to solve the problem."

"What are your plans for the future? What would you like to do the most?"

"Besides acting, the thing I'd like to do most is Sino-Indian cultural exchange." As soon as this topic is mentioned, Rizwan became immediately excited. "I'd like to increase the level of harmony and trust between the cultures of China and India. I'm not a politician, but I think culture is the leading force of society and politics. Culture comes first because there is no hatred in culture. It is an art, which everyone likes. Some Indian TV dramas are loved by Chinese audiences, while Chinese martial arts are very popular in India. There is no hatred in culture, and culture should come before politics."

During our talks I learned that the thing Rizwan is most proud of is being the first to introduce Indian TV dramas into China. All we had seen before were Indian movies like *Awara*, *Caravan* and so on. In 2004 *Koshish Ek Aasha* was broadcast on Beijing Television Station (BTV), the first Indian TV drama he introduced to China. Then followed it is another TV drama *Karishma* or *Miracle* recently shown on China Central Television (CCTV) Station introduced to China in 2006. Both TV dramas came to China with his help. He first looked for an appropriate company in China, then looked for the relevant companies in India, to discuss copyright issues, sign contracts and handle other things. He did all this for nothing. It was voluntary work and made no money for him. If the companies' business grew, they might give him an IOU or a commission. But, in Rizwan's words, "you can always make money."

At that moment, I heard a baby crying. "Oh, that's my son. He's almost one hundred days old," Rizwan said happily.

"Have you named him?"

"Yes, Mu Sa in Chinese, Musa in Arabic, and Moses in English. It's the name of a prophet."

"What would you like him to do in the future?"

"Whatever he likes. We will give him a very strict family education like I got, but we won't force him to do anything."

"What are you going to do in the future? Are you going to live in China for-ever?"

"As I said earlier, the thing I'd like to do most is cultural exchange. It doesn't matter where I live. I can't say that I have to do one thing or the other; our future is open. We've got a direction, but we won't have a fixed plan. This is the best choice. Everything is possible."

Looking at his bright eyes and smiling face, I'm praying silently in my heart that all his dreams will come true, that he will become a people's ambassa-dor of Sino-Indian cultural exchange by making full use of his advantages in the Chinese language.

Written and translated by Li Shujuan

Personal File

Name: Sabriye Tenberken

Nationality: German

Occupation: Teacher

Time in China: 10 years

Touching the Souls of Blind Tibetan Children

She is tender, perceptive, blessed with a sonorous voice that carries as far as she wills it to go. She can do perhaps most things a "normal" adult can, except drive a car. Her mind is crystal clear, and lights up the lives of the blind Tibetan children under her aegis. They flock around her, basking in her rays of warmth and affection. To them, she could be the reincarnation of a Bodhisattva; yet, she's but an ordinary mortal, a blind lady from Germany. She is Sabriye Tenberken.

*T*he Tibetan Training Center for the Blind in Lhasa has been in operation for about 10 years now.

Of Tibet's population of 2.6 million, 35,000 are visually impaired. This high percentage is attributable to both climate and hygiene: dust, strong winds, thick snow, ultraviolet radiation, soot and smoke from heating coal and yak dung, and vitamin A deficiency caused by poor nutrition. Inadequate social protection and the harsh physical environment conspire to set the blind back further. They have limited job opportunities, a lack of education and living skills, a gloomy outlook on life, in great part due to scant respect shown them by their communities.

Braille Without Borders, an international organization set up by Sabriye Tenberken, a visually challenged German lady, and Paul Kronenberg, a Dutch engineer, commits itself to the cause of training the blind. It seeks to empower them with knowledge and skills, so they can be absorbed into society as fully functional, respected citizens.

I interviewed Sabriye, Paul and their students at the Tibeten Training Center for the Blind at Jiangsu Road, Lhasa, on July 27, 2007.

Braille Without Borders is a story of love, aspiration and determination to overcome the odds. The school comprises 10 massage therapists, 114 students — 15 of whom have been transferred to ordinary schools — and a farm, used to train them in living skills.

Entering the World of Blind Children

"Strong hands, accurate with pressure points … your massage is so good that I've fallen asleep…."

Tashi is an old hand (pun intended) at receiving compliments such as these from his clients. Fortunate to have had teachers from countries as diverse as Switzerland, Vietnam and China, Tashi is skilled at a variety of massage: Thai, European, Chinese, as well as foot massage, weight loss treatment, and SPA treatment. The first medical massage center operated by the blind in Lhasa, the Medical Massage Clinic, Tibet, was founded in 2003. There are currently six massage therapists, four of them are now taking a more advanced training course in Beijing. The Clinic operates smoothly, with a monthly income of more than 5,000 *yuan*, and most of its clients are foreigners, perhaps because most of the therapists here speak English. During his massage sessions, Tashi feels no language barriers between his guests and him (although he did ask our correspondent to speak in English, as did some other interviewees).

Tenzin and Tashi were once classmates, and have now graduated to being colleagues. Tenzin was a yak herder before he joined the school for the blind.

One day in 1998, when he was out with his herd, he heard a conversation between Sabriye and his mother. Tenzin's mother was skeptical at first about the school, and also could not believe that the little dots (Braille) were alphabet characters.

"This foreign girl is a swindler," his mother said. "You would lose your strength if you went with her, eating and drinking well without doing any work."

However Sabriye did not give up. She told Tenzin's mother that she would pick him up seven days later, and asked her to make the decision after visiting the school.

Seven days later, Tenzin became the first student at the school for the blind. He started to learn massage therapy from the age of 14, and learned to support his family from that year on. On May 1, 2006, Tenzin introduced himself to his clients. "I am blind. I used to be quite self-conscious; however I became confident of myself once I learned English, because I am the only one in my hometown (Namu Township) who can speak English and has massaging skills."

At present, Tenzin is a massage therapist at the Medical Massage Clinic, and a teacher of Tibetan and physical exercises in the school. Tenzin's dream is to open a massage clinic of his own.

In Lhaze County, there resides a six-member family, once unique for nothing but the fact that four of them were visually impaired, and thus reviled and virtually ex-communicated by the rest of the village. Jampa, Derjee and Kyila, the three children, were born blind. In the year 2000, they enrolled in the school for the blind. They graduated three years later, and Jampa was the first to get a job, as an interpreter at the local Farmer's Hotel. She then moved to Lhasa, and is now an interpreter at an international medical organization.

Jampa is quite proud of the three of them, because they are the only ones who can speak English in the Lhaze County. Jampa plans to open a teahouse in the village to cater for foreigners; Kyila teaches English at the Tibetan Training Center for the Blind, and is in charge of translation and administrative matters there. She opened a Medical Massage Clinic in Lhasa with Dorjee in 2003. In 2005, she had the opportunity to learn English in the UK for one year, and her

language skills even surprised people there. Kyila now wishes to open a restaurant or coffee shop in Lhasa. She is also quite keen on business administration. Consequently Sabriye invited Matthew, the American economist, to teach business skills to the students interested in this vocation.

The three siblings, Jampa, Derjee and Kyila, once dependent on government support to survive, and the object of ridicule in their village, are now envied by everyone around. Their parents have reason to be proud of their children.

Derjee suffered more than children born blind or blinded at an early age. She was visually impaired at the age of 15, when her optic nerves suddenly began to shrink. She dropped out of school the same year, and struggled between death and renascence. At the age of 17, Derjee was enrolled in the school for the blind.

From the beginning she was an excellent student and did well in all the courses, thanks to her fundamentals. She is now a math teacher in the school. Moreover, from 2003 Derjee worked at the Medical Massage Clinic. Her double salary enables her to support her mother. In the beginning, when she lost her eyesight she worried that her mother would die before her, because she knew her brother and sister would not be able to support her. Now, she brings her mother from Shannan to Lhasa, and pays for her accommodation as well as living expenses.

Derjee has three wishes: to support her mother and cater to her needs and comfort until she passes away; to have a massage clinic in the west suburb of Lhasa, where the hotels are centralized; and to donate some of her income to orphanages and old people's homes. In 2004, Derjee was sent to Beijing to learn SPA treatment.

Before his enrollment in the school, Losung could only speak Tibetan. Eight months later, he had mastered Braille in Tibetan, English and Chinese, and also started to learn massage skills. Losung's dream: to open a bookstore in Braille, since there is no Braille bookstore in Lhasa at this moment.

Niyma Duwan studied English in Britain for one year. His excellent language skills convinced Sabriye that he was a born teacher.

Norbu and Chungla learned milking and cheese-making in Holland.

On August 8 this year, Jianqi went to Malaysia to learn about the production of educational school material in Braille, and then to Japan to study computers.

Sales of the disk, *Tell Me Why* far exceeded the school's expectations.

It was the opinion of several professionals that Suolang Wandui had a talent for the accordion. He was trained in the music department of Tibetan University, and now plays in a band. His ultimate objective is to be enrolled in the Central Conservatory of Music.

Norbu announced his ambition to his classmates at the age of 12. "I would like to be a driver." At the age of 19, he upgraded his ambition to "opening a taxi company in the future".

A boy of 17 said, seriously, "I would like to have a girlfriend."

Braille Without Borders: Traveling with Love

Sabriye contracted a degenerative retinal disease at the age of nine that rendered her almost completely blind by the time she was twelve. Yet, in the face of the misfortune, Sabriye's attitude is: "Normal people are led by their vision, however I am led by my senses; and perhaps sense is more attractive than vision."

With the help of Braille, Sabriye was able to study subjects such as English, computer science, history, and literature. She was accepted by the University of Bonn in 1992, and majored in Central Asian Culture; she also studied sociology, philosophy, Tibetology and Mongolian. In 1997, she traveled to Tibet on her own and rode through the countryside on horseback, wending her way into villages to observe how the Tibetan blind lived.

Sabriye was shocked and horrified by what she saw. Blindness here was treated as a curse, and the blind as lepers. This physical defect was rooted in superstition; the Tibetans believed that the law of karma was responsible for a person's blindness — that blindness was comeuppance, a punishment for one's

unfaithfulness to the Buddha or unlawful deeds in one's past life. In Lhasa, Sabriye met a blind beggar who had been abandoned by his parents when he were born; in Zigong, the locals hold to the belief that nine out of ten blind people are also deaf, and so the "normal" people seldom communicate with the blind, who are forbidden from leaving their homes. Sabriye once touched a blind child who had been confined to his bed for a long time, his decaying limbs and overall deathly condition move her to tears. She also met a blind child who suffered from grevious psychological wounds; as a result of being mistreated once too often, he had begun to regard everyone as the enemy, and threw stones and spit at anyone who ventured too near. A blind girl named Solang Bencuo, of the Mairi Village, Gongbujiada County, was stoned every time she went to fetch water. All she could do was cry all the way back home. She would plead with her parents to let her brother go out and fetch water instead of her.

The predicament of these Tibetan children drove Sabriye to strive to fight for their rights. She believed that training them in a special school would turn the tide of fortune their way, improve their living conditions, and strike at the heart of discrimination and prejudice rooted in people's minds.

Sabriye began to prepare for her Tibetan sojourn. She had devised a Tibetan Braille system, initially for her own use while studying Tibetology. She showed her script to a renowned Tibetan scholar, who pronounced it simple, understandable and easy to learn.

In May 1998, with funding from a German NGO, Sabriye started to implement her dream. She enrolled her first six students from the east of Tibet. They started from scratch. She taught the blind children how to use chopsticks, spoons, and canes, as well as toilets; she taught them how to distinguish directions, and to differentiate cars' directions; she corrected their bad habits such as throwing stones, spitting, their use of 'dirty' words, etc.

Describing her search for blind children, Sabriye uses one-one example to illustrate how people normally regarded the blind as good for nothing.... When she entered villages on horseback, the villagers could hardly believe that a blind person could ride a horse. Sabriye explained that the horse could lead her to

where she wanted to go. People laughed at her. Sabriye wrote in a letter to her mother: I would like to be transformed from a blind person who is able to do many things, to a headmistress who can teach blind children to be capable of doing many things.

Braille Without Borders was founded the same year with support from private funding companies and travelers from many places.

The "Three-Independence" Concept of the School for the Blind

The school enrolls students aged five to thirteen. Students are divided into four classes based on their age: Mouse, Rabbit, Snow Leopard and Tiger. Courses available include: Tibetan, Chinese, English, math, computer technology, music, and drawing (including kneading to strengthen the touching sense of fingers).

Sabriye's objectives for setting up this school are: to nurture an independent spirit in her blind students, and train them in special skills. These include practical skills such as fund-raising, PR, management, program designing. Adult students are trained in the following vocational skills: massage, music, animal husbandry (milk-, yogurt- and cheese-making), agriculture, horticulture, handicraft (weaving of carpets and sweaters, wood-carving, etc), clerical work (accounting, etc).

Mike, Sabriye's Canadian friend and member of an NGO, operates a school for the blind, as well as a farm, in Shigatse. The farm occupies 20 hectares of land, with a training center, a food processing factory and a printing factory for books in Braille.

"The operation of the farm acts as a tool to support the survival of the school," says Sabriye. The school in Shigatse mainly trains blind adults, and provides a survival test field for unemployed students, who use the farm as a rehearsal zone before getting jobs outside.

Sabriye motivates her newly-enrolled students every year with a three-pronged developmental program: Independent Spirit, Special Skills and DIY.

"Your parents will definitely die before you, and therefore you must depend on yourself to survive," she exhorts.

Zron, a Vietnamese doctor, now employed by the international NGO One Heart, is in agreement with the "Three-Independence" concept held by Sabriye. He understands that the school for the blind is not the Garden of Eden and the students must learn how to make a living for themselves. "Public welfare programs are just like the Bodhisattva, Guanyin, who taught people how to help themselves, and then she would disappear," he says. Zron teaches massage to the blind children.

When the Medical Massage Clinic was set up in 2003, Paul made it clear to Kyila, the person in charge of the clinic, that the initial investment was made by the school, and she had to repay it in the future. Paul thus put the onus on Kyila to depend on herself instead of relying on the school. When the time came for her to leave, however, her love for Sabriye and Paul, and her fear of the outside world led to her refusal to leave. She wanted to stay on as a volunteer worker but Sabriye turned down her request, and pushed both Kyila and Derjee into society. In 2005, the Clinic was transferred to Losung and then Tashi, and Paul gave them the same responsibility of repayment....

"Please throw away the crutch of the school as early as possible," Sabriye would tell the clinic, which is a partly independent affiliate of the school. Before the opening of the clinic, she asked Kyila, Tenzin and Tashi to contact the travel agency, design and distribute advertisements on the street and to hotels all by themselves, and thus promote the clinic. After the clinic was set up, she told them to deal with the relevant departments such as the electricity department, banks, the industry and commerce bureau, and tax bureau.

Whenever Derjee needed to come back to the school for some business, Ciluo would pick her up and drop her back. One day, Sabriye admonished Ciluo and told him that his help was not necessary. Since then, Derjee began to travel back and forth by herself.

The school for the blind is located on a busy street on Jiangsu Road, with

cars passing by quite frequently. Seizing the opportunity, Sabriye gave Losung an assignment, asking him to negotiate with the transportation police for a zebra crossing and traffic light near the school.

"I can't do that," the words escaped Losung's lips immediately. Sabriye countered by saying that if she could, then he definitely could as well. Losung gave in. Now studying massage therapy at a school for the blind in Beijing, Losung recalls that the captain was very nice…." I did not expect that everything would go so smoothly and successfully."

Cilo adds, "It seemed at the time that whatever Sabriye asked us to do exceeded our ability, but looking back, she was right, and she forced us to get away from inertia and cowardice as early as possible."

Discrimination towards these children was the primary obstacle to be overcome in order for them to survive. Although they had already been made aware that blindness was not divine punishment for their evil-doing in past lives or the result of demonic possession, but instead a product of genetic defects, illness and accidents, they realized that it was quite difficult to change local prejudices.

"My defective eyesight is inherited," Yuzhen once told villagers. During one summer vacation in his hometown, Tashi heard people pointing at him and calling him "Blindman". Tashi turned back and said, "I am not blind, my eyes are just invisible." Sometimes, he would challenge his antagonists with: "I can read in the dark, and I also know Chinese, English and computer skills. What about you?"

Their confidence stems, on one hand, from knowledge, and on the other hand from constant words of encouragement from Sabriye and Paul. "You are all Picasso," Paul would tell his drawing students.

As another form of encouragement, Sabriye invited Erik Weihenmayer, the first blind man to scale Mt. Everest, to lead six of the blind students in an attempt to climb one of the world's tallest and most challenging mountains, Lhakpa Ri, a peak on the northern side of Everest. Sabriye, Erik and six blind teenagers, as well as a team of guides and a film crew (for the documentary Blindsight), scaled the 7,045-meter peak successfully. One of the climbers, Dachung, said, "I had never thought of climbing before, but it really happened."

Knowledge begets confidence, confidence empowers one with the ability to fulfil one's dream, which in turn brings happiness. Sabriye has proved this time and again, with these children, as they chatter and laugh around her. "I believe they are quite happy," she says, with typical understatement. These blind children are familiar with her every movement and word. She often touches their shoulders and asks, "Are you happy?" and when she hears their laughter, she laughs in return, "Good, I am happy that you're happy."

The Tibetan Training Center for the Blind trained the first group of blind people in Tibet's history to read. In August 2001, the first school book and dictionary in Tibetan Braille was published; and on December 1, 2000, the Tibetan School for Special Training was established.

Sabriye published her first memoir, *My Path Leads to Tibet* in 2000, for which she received the Christopher Award four years later. On March 8, 2000, Sabriye was elected Woman of the Year by members of the International Lady's Club, Frankfurt, and presented the Charity Bambi Award by the German government the same year. In 2001, on behalf of the Queen of the Netherlands, H.E. Dr. Philip de Heer, ambassador of the Royal Netherlands Embassy to China, awarded Sabriye and Paul knight medals; in 2006, they both were awarded the "Friendship Medal" from the Chinese government.

The Color of Warmth Is Red

During the summer vacation this year, there were still a dozen students staying at the school. Kyila explained that none of them, except two orphans, wanted to go back home, because they all felt more comfortable in school. Kyila felt the same way.

These blind children were afraid of confronting their village people, with their prejudices and taunts. Kyila told it as it was, "We have already regarded the school as our home."

They also look up to 37-year-old Sabriye as their mother and 39-year-old

Paul as their father. Before every meal, they voluntarily express gratitude, straight from the heart, "Thanks to Mom and Dad for providing us with food." The children also call their nanny "Mom", and the chef "Dad". Tashi, who is quite relaxed in front of Paul and Sabriye, has a close kinship with them. Kyila says, "My life would have been destroyed if I had not met Sabriye." All the blind children expressed this simple idea during this interview: "Sabriye and Paul changed my destiny."

Kyila, who is now studying in Britain, was rather poetic in her feelings of gratitude towards Sabriye, "God closed my window, and Sabriye opened it for me again."

In 2003, when they earned their first salary, Kyila and Derjee invited their Mom and Dad (Sabriye and Paul) to have dinner at Xueyu Restaurant. The actual parents of these blind children regarded Sabriye and Paul as Buddhist idols.

The affection between the blind children and their headmistress is a cumulative one, accomplished over more than 3,000 days. In her drawing class, Sabriye taught students how to differentiate colors. She held their hands in the sun's rays and told them that warmth was red. She let them kneel to touch the earth, and said, "Soil is yellow." Water was colorless, while the sea was blue. Sabriye asked Niyma the colors of Lhasa and Shannan, and Niyma answered that Lhasa was yellow and Shannan blue. Sabriye admits it's a difficult task to teach blind children, and so she and the other teachers were extremely patient, and extremely careful.

In June this year, Ciqiong, a 17-year-old girl in Sa'gjia County, was diagnosed with brain cancer. A tearful Sabriye and Paul requested their friends abroad to look out for treatment possibilities, emphasizing that they would pay whatever it took to cure her.

Sabriye frequently exhorts the students, "Take the cane with you when you go out." She also warns adolescent students to stick with blind friends or risk being mistreated by sighted ones in future."

Paul likes to drive fast. Every time Sabriye is about to go out with Paul, the children beseech him to drive slowly. "How could we survive if you both were to have an accident?"

From 1998 to the present, 114 blind children have been trained in everything from Braille (Tibetan, Chinese and English) to proficiency in terms of reading, speaking and writing; 15 of them were enrolled in regular schools and all of them ranked first at some point in their English course; 10 students were trained in medical massage; and some of the others returned to their hometowns and began to employ their skills in agriculture or handicrafts. A survey made by Paul revealed that these blind children went from being a burden to the main sources of income for their families.

"Most importantly, Sabriye has turned these blind children from self-deprecatory to self-confident," says Ciluo. "Some training schools limit their freedom in consideration of their safety; however Sabriye taught them to try everything."

"What blindness ties up is vision, not mind." Sabriye inculcated her students year after year with this quotation from a blind Frenchman.

At present, the number of enrollment applications far exceeds the school's capacity. Moreover, insufficient funds and classrooms are bottlenecks to the further expansion of the school. Sabriye and Paul take time out each year to travel to other countries seeking donations, with the aid of Sabriye's presentations.

The school's logo depicts two hands, one facing up and one down, protecting an eye. Paul distributes the logo to visitors, saying "We hope your charity becomes the caring hand."

The Exotic Romance

The only tandem bicycle in Lhasa belongs to Paul and Sabriye. When they go out riding, they create quite a spectacle in Lhasa City, and people describe them as "riding wing to wing". Sabriye admits that she would have given up if not for Paul's support.

Paul holds degrees in mechanical engineering, computer science, commercial technology, and communication system science. His volunteer work includes working as a designer and construction coordinator for the Swiss Red

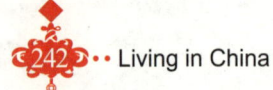
Cross to build up a catastrophe rescue center and a school for Tibetan medicine; constructing township primary schools in countries such as Zimbabwe, Botswana and Zambia; getting involved in designing projects for schools and residences in countries such as South Africa. In this school for the blind, Paul is in charge of training students in computers, bookkeeping and office work.

Paul emphasizes that his stay in Tibet is for the happiness in his heart. He says: "I am 'giving' rather than 'demanding', and what I demand is smiles from the others." Paul loves to see the children's happy faces, loves to feel their sincere gratitude. His happiest moment, he says, was when guests to the school saw the tremendous changes made. "When they first came to our school, they thought the children would not be able to do anything. Now, of course, it's a different story."

Paul and Sabriye first got to know each other at the Banak Shol Hotel in Lhasa, around August 1997. Paul's initial impressions of her were of a strong-willed, humorous girl. Sabriye told Paul that she planned to open a school for

the blind in Lhasa, and Paul replied that he would join her if she could manage the funding. Paul says: "We were just chatting and half joking at the time." Nine months later, on May 15, 1998, when Sabriye called Paul and informed him that she had already raised the funds and planned to go to Tibet, Paul predicted that the opportunity for a change was imminent. Five days after the call, Sabriye flew to Lhasa with Paul, who had resigned from his job.

It was only half a year after that they fell in love. One of Sabriye's requirements of her life companion was that he should be dark haired, and Paul, a natural blond, had to lie to Sabriye. The lie was discovered on his visit to Sabriye's home in Germany.

Paul told Sabriye's mother that the blind children in Tibet had given him the opportunity to meet and consort with Sabriye, and that he felt very lucky. Paul appreciates her for her courage and perseverance, and also for her "beautiful heart". As time goes by, Paul says, he is more and more attracted to these qualities and believes strongly that she will succeed.

Searching for the Source of Love

Sabriye's mother has visited Tibet several times. One day, Sabriye went on a picnic with the blind children and her mother, to the park. Upon reaching there, the children began to cover broken beer bottles with soil. When she saw this, Sabriye's mother pushed aside the soil with chopsticks and picked up the broken pieces one by one, then took off her hat and put the pieces in the hat.

Sabriye and Paul don't plan to have a baby just yet. Paul says it's because they "have regarded these blind children as our own". Sabriye says that since the founding of the school, the inner energy of the students has motivated her to seek more rights for them. According to Paul, Braille Without Borders has been a win-win program.

Sabriye has not taught for a year now, and is looking out for a successor. She has two choices: to leave Lhasa, or to extend her contract for five years. However, she has already seen to it that the school will be in good hands after

she leaves — in the hands of the graduates, the new teachers. Sabriye hopes for the school to exist forever, its existence proving that the world of the blind is not necessarily dark.

Sabriye and Paul plan to go to Kerala, in south India, to set up another Braille Without Borders there. Applications are now being accepted for the first batch in the summer of 2008. Students will be trained in computers, English, IT, management, fund-raising, public relations and engineering planning. Sabriye believes that only the blind can change people's prejudices towards them, through the exhibition of their talents.

By the end of the interview, I decided to use the title of a book by Helen Keller, *Three Days to See*, and asked Sabriye if she had any requests. She said, almost instantly, "I wish to see all of my pictures taken by Paul; I wish to see my lovely students; and I wish to see beautiful Lhasa."

(Thanks to Ren Linli for assistance during the interview.)

By Li Yanchun
Translated by Huang Junmei
Revised by K. Krishna

"Doctor Garbage"

He is a doctor, an expert in hydro-geology from Bavaria, Germany, but you can't help thinking he looks like a farmer. He is called "Doctor Garbage" because he is keen on collecting Chinese "junk". He is Hans Koller.

"Cola Man"

Hans, 56 years old, a doctor and an expert in hydro-geology from Bavaria, Germany, looks like a character from an old film with his goatee.

A few years ago, Hans, who has never liked to dress up formally, but on a business suit and came to Jinan City in Shandong Province to join an aid program, helping find water sources and dig for wells in drought-prone areas in the countryside. He was called "Doctor Garbage" by his colleagues. At first this struck us as very awkward, but later we learned that he was called this because he is keen on collecting Chinese "junk". He regards all this junk as treasure. We discovered upon entering his home that every corner was piled with junk. Although there was nothing costly in his home, the room was filled with containers, and looked like a storeroom.

It seems that Han's collection includes almost every type of junk. He has collected second-hand photo frames, wooden human images, used scrolls, waste copper coins, bamboo rods, zippers, iron locks, etc, and he even once had a human skeleton. Hans picked up a plastic statue of a seated Chairman Mao from a demolished building in a residential area. Hans regards this statue as a treasure; the statue was very dirty, and Hans told me later, quite proudly, that he had taken a bath with Chairman Mao.

I was quite proud of myself for giving Hans Koller the nickname "Cola

man". In my opinion, this name was perfectly suited to this cheerful man who rejected rank and fashion.

The German HNK Hydro-geology Co. is situated inside the Hydro-geology Center of Jinan City. Hans, who usually wears flip-flops and rides a bicycle, became a famous foreigner in that area. No matter where he went, there were always people who touched his shoulder and greeted him.

Hans' frugality doesn't seem very "German". At first, he was not fond of drinking and only drank a little, running only the first leg of the "beer marathon"; furthermore, he can't stay up too late at night; when his German colleagues were just starting their night life, he was already fast sleep.

"How strange! Right when things are getting exciting, this German has already fallen asleep." Many Chinese guests were quite puzzled by his behavior.

But no matter how loud the music is, or how noisy the party is, Hans' sweet dreams are never disturbed.

Hans usually gives others the impression that he is a farmer. With his red face and thin goatee, nothing about him is "upright" or "finely-cut", and he has no air of the expert. At first, when I heard people calling him Doctor Koller, I was always in a daze. However, my first impression disappeared so quickly: while enjoying tea, I chatted with Hans about Zen and Salvador Dali; he was so sensitive to musical instrument that he knew when a tone played on the violin decreased by half a beat or increased by half a beat. Sometimes he clapped big earphones on and wagged his head merrily, enjoying his job and the music of Mozart and Bach at the same time. Hans had a camera which looked like a machine-gun. The picture of a lotus he took with this camera would immediately remind people of the poem by Yu Guangzhong, "I'd like to stay, to accompany the lotus, to keep this small and boundless universe, and to keep this mystery." Hans, who hides himself under a peasant's coat, was actually brought up amid culture; however he is wise enough not to dress himself up as a civilized man, and simply displays his peasant characteristics under the sunshine.

Hans has such a passion for China that while he's here he feels he's at home.

While working in the countryside of Mengyin County, Hans fully tasted the attractiveness of Chinese food at his first dinner. He commandeered an entire chicken himself, with the result that he was still digesting the chicken at noon the next day (in fact, he was absent from the next two meals because of indigestion). Over the next few days, he kept going out into the sunshine during lunch time; it seemed he did not need food to replenish him with energy, and to recharge from the sunshine was enough for him. While he stretched his hands under the sunshine, we were just coming back from eating and drinking. Then, full of energy, he re-joined our group which was occupied with liquor; however, it was we, replenished with food, who had become lazy. We became quite accustomed to his "sun bathing" and now no one felt it was strange when Hans went absent during lunch time.

On our way to the open country, Hans always shrank into the back seat, where we kept the baggage, curling into the shape of a bag and sleeping the whole way while his Chinese colleagues sat normally in the regular seats. Hans told us that he had once ridden a jeep holding around 20 people when he was in India, of course some of the passengers sat on the top of the jeep. He seemed quite happy with his experience and gave no sense that he had endured hardship.

Hans resembles a person living in the 19th century: he ignores the existence of electronics, but is keen on mechanics and handiwork; his hands are scarred by labor, and the latest fashions are completely alien to him. He once appeared in an outdated image with a pocket watch, a worn straw hat, and a pair of square-toed shoes, quite out of touch with the reds and greens of modern civilization. The regard that people have for German experts is quite wasted on him. He was born to reject special treatment. His penchant for rejecting formal situations became so strong that he was incompatible with the typical German who emphasized forms. Hans made me feel as though he were just muddling along among his German colleagues, and I later understood that his "meticulousness chip" was typically German-made.

"Everything Is Under My Control"

Perhaps because he is fated to live a simple life, Hans got used to living in China soon after he arrived.

I always got the impression that Hans seemed to someone living on the margins. He was interested neither in chatting, nor smoking, drinking, shopping or partying. There were no sexual rumors about him. He paid no special attention to girls, and regarded all girls as either his younger or elder sisters. He had a "wife" who had no marriage contract with him. They had lived together for half a lifetime. His "wife" seemed to be a copy of Hans with her honest and sincere character.

A "fool" like Hans, out of touch with fashion and in search of "suffering" has no "word" among his German colleagues; on the other hand, he is a foreigner in the eyes of the Chinese around him, and is still unable to fit in with them.

Hans has many eccentric habits. He chooses to live in the office instead of a villa; he sleeps in a hammock instead of on a spring mattress; he sleeps on the balcony in the open every night and is woken up by the first sunshine; he never

eats at regular meal times, and spends two *jiao* for a pancake whenever he is hungry; he always goes to work in his flip-flops, and spends ten *yuan* for four shirts that he wears for the whole summer.

He once asked me to take him to a tailor to mend his pants. We found two tailors, but neither of them were interested in fixing his pants. The pants were just too worn-out and even a poor Chinese would throw them away immediately. But Hans was very reluctant to get rid of them. I, who have wasteful habits, was quite amazed by his frugal and conscientious attitude.

Other foreign experts in China usually drive around a Benz jeep allocated by their company with pride and exuberance, but Hans refuses to drive and gets around on his used bicycle every day. We could understand him, or figure out exactly what was wrong with him. But Hans' attitude was "If I reflect on myself and find myself to be right, then even if it be an army of one hundred thousand, I will go forward (from *Mencius*)", and he can't hide the satisfaction on his face.

Hans most loves to visit the open market at the foot of Hero Mountain. There is a bazaar there every Sunday, and almost all of Hans' items of daily necessity came from that market. You can find Hans there at seven o'clock every Sunday morning, and each time he comes to the market he roams around from booth to booth, occasionally staying to play with the dogs on sale. Moreover, Hans is quite good at bargaining when he sees something he likes. Hans has collected a pile of Chinese wooden images which are all quite vivid, simple and rudimentary. When his expert colleagues were attracted by these wooden images and planned to add something similar to their collections, they found that Hans had already bought all the images available in the market. Hans cleared off a corner of his table for the exhibition of these wooden images; he let the wooden images stand still, as though they were copies of the terra cotta warriors and horses. Everyone who visits has high praise for them.

One afternoon, we had all been at work for a long time, but Hans had not yet appeared. Our boss had asked about him several times, but we didn't say anything; nevertheless we were quite worried about his lateness. The sun was shining outside of the window; the distant mountains seemed quite clear and

close, so attractive that any one of them could have captured Hans' attention. Then there was the sound of flip-flops outside, and Hans appeared before us, sweating on his head. Our boss, so upset that his face seemed made of stone, snapped at Hans, "Why did you arrive so late for work?" Hans held back his smile, brought the boss to the window, pointed to the Qianfo Mountain and said, "Why should we work on such a beautiful day?" Our boss was nearly choked by his words.

It was obvious that our boss did not like Hans. He once stared at our group photo, pointed at Hans, gnashing his teeth, and said, "He is a bad boy, so how come he's always smiling?" For sure, Hans appeared as a smiling face in all the group photos, while our boss seldom smiled.

In China, Hans seemed to be a computer program that ran on auto. His most common phrase was, "Everything is under control", and it showed his confidence in everything. Hans and I sliced potatoes differently. I sliced them from top to bottom, while Hans sliced from bottom to top. He said jokingly that our different slicing methods showed the difference between the East and West:

the Easterners were not as confident as the Westerners. The Westerners were so confident that they were not afraid of hurting themselves — when slicing from bottom to top a person might accidently hurt himself, while an Easterners would only hurt the chopping board. I admired his smart and swift thought, and at the same time tried to think of a way to refute him, however I failed to think of anything.

Searching for Treasures in China

Hans' only hobby in China is collecting junk, and one of his interests is to search for treasure at building sites.

One time, a residential area in downtown city of Jinan was demolished and the buildings pulled down. It was raining heavily outside and it was muddy in the field. Hans went to the building sites to rescue the millstones and engraved stone bricks which would soon be destroyed. Although he was quite strong, it took a huge amount of effort to carry the millstones back. Even though the stones were too outdated to be used nowadays, their round and simple shapes looked like artwork.

After taking back one millstone, Hans was rewarded for his efforts: several of his German colleagues were so excited at the sight of the stone, that they also spent three days at the site and "salvaged" a dozen millstones and several dozen engraved stone bricks. Later these German experts decorated the courtyard with these stone works and made the courtyard a museum for engraved stone works. There are always people who like to have a seat in the courtyard and touch the stones.

Hans is in the habit of collecting waste paper and used envelopes for other purposes. He once called out loudly and seized from my hand a new envelope in which I was about to put a grilled chicken leg. Any items which were thrown away after only one use were always reused by Hans.

A German colleague once told me in a sarcastic voice that there were no more than three "Doctor Garbages" like Hans in Germany; but this remark made

me feel a little depressed. Hans always reminded me of Thoreau, an American who experienced happiness at Walden Lake and had no material needs. Human beings are throwing away more and more, and not only material commodities. Aren't we lucky to have people like Hans in our society?

When it was close to the day he would leave China, Hans separated himself from his German colleagues, leaving the newly-decorated apartment and sleeping in the office. His determination was quite simple: to refuse luxury and enjoy a simple life. His behavior was strongly challenged by his German colleagues; however, Hans still acted in his own way, and kept enjoying his sunshine and hammock. Just as the Chinese saying goes: people are easily satisfied when they have no demands, and they are strong when they have no desires. Hans was not troubled by his separation from his German colleagues.

Hans led the simple life of an ascetic, with a minimum of material demands. His household necessities seemed so shabby in others' eyes. Before he left China, due to his trust in me, he asked me to choose from the things in his home which he could not bring back to Germany. In order not to disappoint him, I chose one quilt which was not so worn-out. He later moved all his belongings into a vacant garage, but he was teased by the doorman. Perhaps all these belongings were thrown away as soon as Hans boarded the plane, and found their final place in the waste station. And now, "Doctor Garbage" has arrived at a suitable destination in others' eyes.

After Hans left, a series of montages continued to flash in front of my eyes: Hans, carrying his camera which looked like a machine-gun, tracking a peasant woman holding a piglet, the woman quite frightened by his behavior; in the peasant courtyard, Hans, holding a cup with a thick scum of tea leaves on the surface, chatting happily with the local peasants; Hans asking in detail about the number of cocks and hens while counting livestock; Hans stopping and smiling when he saw livestock alongside the roadside enjoying the sunshine; in the rain, everyone rushing home while Hans roams around and enjoys the rain…. Hans was born to connect with nature, although he knew nothing about singing of the moon and the wind, he is nature himself.

Hans bought a house after he went back to Germany. It was a down-to-earth single-story house and located in the open countryside. He also bought several milk cows and started to lead the life of a herder. He mailed several photos to me: his house was firm and simple; there was no garden, but there was a big tree full of "blond hair"; his milk cows appeared quite comfortable and satisfied, with smiles on their faces, the same smile that was on Hans' face. There were flowers on their necks; they were enjoying the kindness of their owner. Hans milked the cows and sold the milk, exchanging it for his bread.

He had found the most suitable role in his life. I felt quite happy for Hans; eventually, he was able to live his dream and did not need to skip work to enjoy the sunshine; although his dream life was scorned by the members of modern civilization, who slept on spring mattresses, and such closeness to nature was ignored by most other people, Hans was following just such a life in his patched and mended clothing. Although it was a little late, he has finally arrived and can spend his remaining life in this dream.

One Christmas, I drew a Christmas card to send to each of my German colleagues. I designed a residence for each of them on the cards: there were two stone lions in front of my boss' gate; Peter's home was located in a tall building in the city center; Wolfgang stayed in a temple; while Hans lived on a mountain, with two falcons keeping him company. Seen from far away, Hans owns nothing; seen from up close, there were trees everywhere. Hans overlooked the world of man from the mountain; while under the mountain, it was we who were rushing about with our hands full of things.

By Zhang Hong
Translated by Huang Junmei

Personal File

Name: Hussein Ismail

Nationality: Egyptian

Occupation: Senior Editor, Reporter

Time in China: 15 years

Seek Knowledge, Even in China

About 15 years ago, there was a particular trend among young Egyptians — to go abroad and seek out a personal path. One such youngster, unsure about where to go (most of his friends chose Europe or the US), suddenly recalled the prophet Mohamed's saying, "Seek knowledge, even in China." The young man's decision was made. His name is Hussein Ismail.

A New Movie Every Day

"Living in China is like watching a different movie every day," says Hussein, with a twinkle in his eye. "I never get tired of the changes taking place here."

He is the Arabic editor of *China Today* (China International Publishing Group), where he's worked for 15 years.

"One of my hobbies is just looking at Beijing: the streets, buildings, neon lights…. Everything in China is changing." What attracts Hussein most is the people. He says he likes to look at the eyes, ears, mouths of the Chinese. This might sound strange, until you realize that he just wants to know the differences in features between the Chinese and the Arabs, to find out why China has undergone such rapid economic development in the past 20 years.

"Many Chinese people have left a deep impression on me, from top leaders of the state to the common people I've met on the streets," he says. "I was impressed by Deng Xiaoping's theory, and the personalities of the former premier, Zhu Rongji, and the current premier, Wen Jiabao."

"China's reform and opening-up policy is driven by internal as well as external factors," he continues. "That is to say, the Chinese have a strong willingness to make changes." He points to the door and says, "For instance, it was as if people were locked up in this room. One day, the door opened and the people

inside rushed out, with their heady desires and aspirations." This is his metaphor for China.

"Where did this strong will come from?" This is what Hussein has been pondering for a long time. Recently he read the *Book of Changes*, a classic work of philosophy that was composed 3,000 years ago by a student of Taoism, and influenced philosophers such as Lao Zi (Lao Tzu) and Confucius. Hussein was pleasantly surprised to discover that there was such magnificent work done thousands of years ago in China. He also found that "the concept of poverty gives rise to a desire for change" and this was already deeply rooted in Chinese people's minds even then.

"Present-day China is a result of its long cultural history," he says, now satisfied that he's found the answer.

Muslim Commandment: Seek Knowledge, Even in China

Before he came to China, Hussein knew very little about the country. Now he is almost an expert. In fact he almost seems embarrassed to recall his first visit in 1992.

When Hussein graduated in 1987 from the Department of Political Science, Cairo University, he only knew about China from textbooks. He had read about China's foreign policy and its leaders, Mao Tse-tung and Zhou Enlai, for example; his grandfather had also told him of legends: Chinese women had long necks because they slept face-up on pillows; Chinese women had extraordinarily small feet because they put their feet in specially-made porcelain bottles to keep them from growing. Hussein learned later that cloth-binding was responsible for the size of their feet.

"At the time, I knew very little about China, and had no idea whether what I learned was true or wrong," he says.

Despite working at the Egyptian State Information Bureau after graduating, he had little knowledge of China.

So why did he come to China?

"Many Egyptian students were planning to go abroad after graduation. Most of my friends chose Western countries, and I was thinking of going to France. Very few people considered China, a country totally unfamiliar to them."

While he was deciding where to go, his grandfather said, "You should go to China! Mohamed said, 'Seek knowledge, even in China,' meaning that China is far away, but it is still a place where you could find knowledge."

"So, after thinking about it for a year, I finally decided to go to China. This was definitely a choice different from the others," says Hussein.

At 12 noon on September 30, 1992, Hussein arrived at Beijing Airport.

"Why do I still remember this day so accurately? Because it was the most important turning point in my life. I came to China!" Hussein says excitedly, his face shining.

China has been an integral aspect of his life from then on. One of his proudest moments came when he had the privilege of witnessing the gradual process

of China's opening up.

"I Was Taken Aback by Their Diligence"

As an editor and reporter, Hussein has visited many places in China. In 1998 when Ningxia Hui Autonomous Region celebrated its 40th anniversary, he was invited to attend the ceremony. He was thrilled.

"What attracted me to the place was its poverty, and the Hui Muslims," he says.

After arriving in Ningxia, he found that the communication facilities there were as good as those in Beijing. "You can communicate with any part of the world," he adds. "When I walked into the Telecommunication Center, I felt as if I was in a hotel. I was taken aback by the superb service of the staff there. The whole place was as if once hidden behind history.

"However, the poverty in the region was obvious."

How to reduce poverty became one of his preoccupations. Huaxi Village of Ningxia presented him with the best model of cooperation between the eastern and western regions in China, for a common distribution of wealth.

"Before visiting Huaxi Village in Ningxia, I had a chance to visit Huaxi Village in Jiangsu Province, the first village in China to achieve common wealth since the reform and opening-up," he says. "In fact, it's not right to call it a 'village', because its infrastructure, service, entertainment facilities and living standards are better than those in many cities. Huaxi Village in Ningxia was a model on East-West cooperation set up by the government to narrow the gap, to develop Huaxi Village in Ningxia with the help of Huaxi Village in Jiangsu. Han Guocai, the director of the village committee, thought it a good way to reduce poverty in Ningxia.

"I went to some farmers' homes, where I saw a dream situation. The village had encouraged people to develop a non-agricultural economy, so the villagers had started businesses with building materials, for instance, and were making a considerable income. Their living conditions had also improved." Hussein says

the head of the village also supported this kind of direct poverty-relief plan between the two villages, and this proved to be more effective than the poverty-relief plans laid out by the government. "The important thing is it eliminates poverty from people's minds," he says.

In Taqiao Village, in the suburbs of Yinchuan, capital of Ningxia, Hussein saw with his own eyes that this village, located within the most impoverished area in China, had become a model of common wealth. The furniture and electronic appliances in the villagers' homes were on par with those in posh hotels. Taqiao Village was a success, thanks to its emphasis on education, and assistance from the Islamic Development Bank.

"I was very impressed by the spirit of the people in Ningxia. Poor as they were, they were resilient, and confident," he says.

"This is why Ningxia touched me. Probably because there are Muslims here, I feel that I have melted into this piece of land," he declares.

While in Ningxia, he was awestruck to find as many as 6,000 minarets in 3,000 mosques, and saw that the two million Muslims there took true pride in their faith. Hussein learned from conversations with some elderly Muslims that China was now facing the same problem as many other countries: the loss of cultural and ethical values brought about by a rise in materialism.

After returning to Beijing, Hussein wrote two articles. One was *Achievements, Dreams and Problems — the 40th Anniversary of the Founding of Ningxia Hui Autonomous Region*, which told about the achievements Ningxia had made in the past 40 years, its hopes for the future and the problems it is faced with. The other article was *China's Muslim Headwear and Minaret*, about the lives and beliefs of Muslims in Ningxia.

Hussein says, "I found the answers to all my questions in Ningxia, including 'Where did their strong will come from?'"

After the articles were published, the heads of CIPG informed him that the articles had won the "Outstanding News" prize for the 40th anniversary of the founding of Ningxia.

"The regional government issued me a certificate," he says. "As if led by a dream, I visited Ningxia again in 2000."

In 1999, Hussein was awarded the "Friendship Medal" by the Chinese government to commemorate his work in China.

Self-Described Ambassador to China and Egypt

"What I am doing now is to promoting understanding and exchange between China and Egypt. I treasure every opportunity for communication between the two countries," says Hussein earnestly.

He once read a story in the Egyptian newspaper *Pyramid*, which said that in any given place in any Arab country, when a man and a woman met, there was always a third party at the scene. This third party was ... a Chinese commodity. Either the man or the woman would possess something made in China. Chinese goods have become a necessary part of an Arab's daily life.

Hussein was curious to know the truth behind some Arab media reports that China was dumping its goods in Arab countries, and that the Chinese working in these countries were threatening local employment.

To promote understanding and communication between China and Arab countries, Hussein and his colleagues quickly planned a series of titles around this topic. They wanted to express that all of mankind had common, beautiful dreams it pursued, and that the Chinese going to Arab countries or the Arabs coming to China all wanted to make their dreams come true.

Hussein made a special visit to Yiwu, a small commodities production base in southern China's Zhejiang Province. He interviewed the Arab businessmen there, and had heart-to-heart conversations with them. Back in Beijing, he and his colleagues wrote a series of stories, with the title: *The New Silk Road Where Dreams Come True*.

The articles first quoted the Arab media reports about large amounts of Chinese commodities flooding the market. Instead of criticizing these reports, the articles told of the experiences Arab businessmen had had in China, the help and care they had received from the Chinese government, and the win-win situation inherent in the economic exchange between the two regions. The articles also explained that small trade business was the foundation stone for big investment projects. The stories also frankly pointed out the problems and flaws existing in Chinese commodities. At the same time, it emphasized that economic exchange and trade between the two regions were promoting mutual and harmonious development.

When the article was published, the magazine received a large amount of feedback from the readers and attention from the Arab media.

The readers spoke highly of these stories, even calling from Yemen, Egypt, Syria and Iraq to express their love for China and concern for the Arabic people in China.

The New Silk Road Where Dreams Come True won the CIPG's "Oustanding Article" prize in 2006.

Hussein often describes himself as "the ambassador of Egypt to China and the ambassador of China to Egypt".

"When I write articles about China, I feel that I'm more than a Chinese; and when I write something about Egypt, I feel I'm more than an Egyptian," he states.

"I treasure every opportunity to establish communication between the two countries," he says.

Every time he hears of someone about to visit Egypt, or of Egyptian journalists visiting China, Hussein offers his assistance. He voluntarily provides information about China and Egypt, and makes suggestions regarding living and travel. Whenever he sees articles in the Egyptian media distorting or misunderstanding the facts about China, he immediately writes articles to reveal the truth.

Years of working and living in China have made him treasure the friendship between China and Egypt all the more. "The friendship between the two countries is true friendship," he says. "Friends in need are friends indeed."

Hussein believes that there is yet more space for the development of relations between China and Egypt.

"I think that there should be more cooperation between the two in

high-tech, industry, agriculture, training and joint projects in Africa," he says. "I wish to see more Chinese investments in Egypt, and more Egyptian investments in China. I want to see more 'Made-in-Egypt' commodities on the Chinese market, more Egyptian tourists coming to China, and more Chinese tourists going to Egypt."

The Life of an Egyptian in China

People are often curious about of the lives of Egyptians like Hussein Hussein in China.

"Language and cultural differences always produce jokes," he says.

He recalls how, during his first visit to China he was eager to use Chinese expressions as often as possible.

"One day, I visited a friend's home," he says. "After playing with his

daughter for a while, I asked her in Chinese, 'Ni Li Le Ma?' I intended to ask, 'Are you tired?' Hearing my words, the girl laughed. Her mother asked her why, and she repeated what I'd said to her mother, who told me that what I'd asked sounded like 'Have you divorced?' in Chinese."

Once, Hussein went to the Ministry of Culture on some business. At the gate, he was asked to register. He gave his ID to the guard, which had his name, occupation and home address on it. Then the guard helped him fill in the registration form. When he was about to fill in the blank next to "Sex", he asked Hussein: "Are you male or female?" (There was no this column on the ID) Hussein was not sure whether his clothes or hairstyle had confused the guard, so joked, "I'm female." The guard looked at him and smiled, "You are a man."

Hussein laughs and tells two more stories.

"One night, I was invited for dinner to a restaurant. Before dinner started, the waitress asked me what I would like to drink, and I answered in Arabic, 'Shuwoye', which means 'Wait a minute, please'. Two minutes later, the waitress served me with a glass of water. What I'd said sounded like 'Water' in Chinese.

"Another day I was out shopping. The seller thought that I was a tourist, and asked me to pay 300 *yuan* for something valued at only about 20 *yuan*. I pretended to accept the price. When he was sure that I would buy it, I said to him in Chinese, 'I will only pay 10 *yuan*.' We both laughed. He said to me, 'You are Chinese!' and I replied, 'You are a greedy merchant.'"

Many foreigners in China for the first time experience culture shock. Hussein, however, believes there's very little clash of cultures between China and Egypt, apart from a few differences. He sees both cultures as originating from the East, with the family as the basic unit and the age-old custom respecting the old and caring for the young.

"We can see similarities in the two cultures," he says. "In Egypt, during festivals, all the family members get together to enjoy food and share a togetherness, just as the Chinese do; the Egyptians sweep the tombs of the deceased to show respect for them, just as the Chinese do during the Qingming Festival.

"But their eating habits are different: the Chinese always eat at fixed times, but the Egyptians have lunch anytime from 2 to 5 in the afternoon. In addition, the ways they express their feelings are not the same. The Egyptians are comparatively more straight and open: when two friends meet, they hug and kiss each other, but the Chinese are rather conservative."

However, these superficial differences are not important. The important thing is that Hussein loves this country, and this love is apparent whenever he talks about China, or goes on holiday here. In July this year, he went to Beidaihe in North China's Hebei Province with his colleagues.

"The name 'Beidaihe' reminds me of many things, many faces, many places, plants, parks, flowers, beaches, shells, and conversations…. The last time I went to Beidaihe was in 2001, when I learned that Beijing had successfully bid to host the Olympic Games in 2008."

Hussein says that it took four hours to Beidaihe from Beijing by train in the 1990s, but today the distance is covered in an hour and a half. Beidaihe was also the favorite summer resort of Mao Tse-tung. Hussein once saw a picture of Mao swimming at Beidaihe, and when he swam there, he often imagined himself swimming in the same place Mao had been.

In Hussein's eyes, Beidaihe is no longer a pristine seashore city. It is now a gorgeous blend of China and its northern neighbor Russia.

"Almost all the shops, restaurants and hotels there bear Chinese characters and Russian letters," he says. "Chinese, Russian, Arabic and American songs can be heard from the speakers along the seashore. When I heard an Arabic tune from a BMW car I thought that the driver would be an Arab. But I finally found out he was an Azerbaijanian. He loved Arabic music."

Hussein sighs with emotion. "Beidaihe has become a mini United Nations, where people talk about politics, economy, culture, Iraq, George W. Bush, Gaza, Fatah and Israel as well as the global economic system, Islamism, Christianity and Judaism…."

"To me, Beidaihe is no longer just a place for holiday, but a world within which to broaden my views," he says thoughtfully. "It relieves me from daily life

full of people, shops, city noise and traffic jams."

Hussein is a person with independent views. This can be gauged from the fact that he has never given himself a Chinese name. He believes foreign names are not conducive for fostering communication.

He says, "Supposing I have a Chinese friend called Wang Hao, with the foreign name of Joseph. He works in a news agency in China, and I only know his foreign name. When I visit his office, nobody would know who I am looking for, if I mention the name Joseph. Likewise if I call his home number and say that I want to talk to Joseph, his family members wouldn't know whom to look for. Also, supposing I have a Chinese name called Zhang Zhou, it may be easy for my Chinese friends to remember. But when my Egyptian friends or my colleagues call me by my real name, few Chinese people will get it."

After more than ten years in China, Hussein has completely melted into the

Chinese lifestyle. His family is just like an ordinary Chinese family. In the day, the adults go to work and the children to school. In the evening, after dinner, the whole family sits and chats, and then goes to bed. On weekends, they go to a nearby supermarket to purchase enough food for the week. When friends come over, they go to the park and have dinner together.

"It is very important that my children know about Chinese culture," says Hussein. "My daughter and son are both studying in the Xiyi Primary School in Haidian District, in the third grade and first grade respectively."

Hussein encourages his children to learn about Chinese culture and art, for instance the Peking Opera, Chinese traditional dance and *kung fu*.

His children participate actively in the art shows organized by their school. In 2005, his daughter took part in the CCTV Peking Opera Contest for Pupils. Her wonderfully authentic performance won over the Chinese audience and she took the top prize. His son often demonstrates his *kung fu* in some Wushu contests, and often wows audiences with his style.

Hussein hopes his children grow up to become good, virtuous citizens, and of great use to society in the future.

When he's asked about his own plans for the future, he says, simply, "God knows."

"This has something to do with the Islam," he continues. "Only Allah arranges everything, so I don't think about the future."

By Zhang Hua
Translated by Xu Lin
Revised by K. Krishna

Personal File

Name: Maestro Roberto Vargas Lee

Chinese Name: Li Rongfu

Nationality: Cuban

Occupation: Coach, Businessman

Time in China: 1 years

A "Chinese" with a Strange Face

The first time he came to China, he had the feeling of coming home. He loves drinking oolong tea, practicing *Taiji*, and listening to the *guqin* (a seven-stringed plucked instrument). He looks like a foreigner, but has a Chinese heart. He is Roberto from Cuba.

A tall foreign-looking man is wearing a Chinese-style suit. He has a high-bridged nose and blue eyes but speaks fluent mandarin. I was stunned to see him and listen to him speak. His name is Maestro Roberto Vargas Lee, but he introduces himself as a Chinese from Cuba.

One eighth of his blood is Chinese. His Chinese name is Li Rongfu, which sounds like a shop boss's name. This name actually fits his identity — he is chief of the Cuba *Wushu* Association. You can see some of the toughness of the Caribbean and some of the elegance of Spain in him. At the conference, Li Rongfu is the only "Foreign-Chinese" among all 500 representatives. He writes notes in black ink and the notes are both in Chinese and Spanish. What a combination!

He drinks oolong tea, practices *Taiji*, listens to the *guqin* and believes in Lord Guan…. The 41-year-old Li Rongfu points at his own face and says with pride: "I may not look Chinese outside, but inside I am completely a Chinese person."

From Karate to Martial Arts

Li Rongfu grew up on the shore of the Caribbean Ocean, but it is in his genes to love traditional Chinese culture. His restaurant is named Tian Tan Restaurant after the Chinese-made essential balm brand, also Tian Tan (the Temple

of Heaven). The only two Chinese chefs in all of China Town work in his restaurant. Many important politicians have visited his restaurant, including Castro himself. Even Chinese leaders tasted their dishes when they visited Cuba. The Cuban law states that private restaurants can receive no more than 12 customers at a same time. Usually a private restaurant only has five small tables, and people will have to wait outside when there are too many customers. But his restaurant is far too famous. Because there are always important customers coming to eat, the government just lets it be.

Li Rongfu started to practice Karate when he was 12 years old. Once, the Chinese Ambassador saw his excellent Karate performance and after the performance an official went to meet him and ask him if he knew about *Wushu* (martial arts).

Li Rongfu shook his head.

"It is same as *kung fu*, *Wushu* and *kung fu* are the same thing."

Because of Bruce Lee's movies, Li Rongfu had known about *kung fu* since he was a small boy. In Cuba, the most mysterious *kung fu* was brought into Cuba

by Chinese people from Canton. He had heard of the Red Fist, and the Choy Lay Fut, but those martial arts were all really old, and the Cantonese weren't willing to teach people from other communities. The so-called Chinese martial arts were actually very rare in Cuba.

"*Wushu*…." Li Rongfu repeated this strange word again and again. Later, the Chinese Embassy helped him to get an exchange opportunity and sent him to study martial arts at the Beijing Sports University.

"It was miracle. The first time I came to China, I had the feeling of coming home," Li Rongfu remembered. He traveled to many places in China including the holy center of martial arts — Shaolin Temple. He thinks Henan Province is really beautiful, and its capital city Zhengzhou is pretty too. On the Lücheng Square in Zhengzhou, even the little children know about Castro and socialist Cuba, Li Rongfu thinks it is great.

When talking about China, Li Rongfu always feels like he's talking about his own hometown. Shaolin Temple is in the north, and Wudang Mountain is in

the south. He thinks it's a pity that he has never been to Wudang Mountain be-fore. When he heard that some foreigners are learning martial arts in the Taoism Mountain Wudang, Li Rongfu sees hopes and wants to join them immediately.

Karate and *Wushu* are two completely different martial arts. Once Li Rong-fu started practicing *Wushu*, he gradually lost interest in Karate. He says he likes *Wushu* more, because its purpose is not only to fight, it also contains some philo-sophical ideas.

There Is No Diploma for *Taiji*

"Did you realize that the posture and gaze of people who practice *Wushu* are different from normal people?" Li Rongfu reminds me, "People who practice *Wushu* sit more steadily and they are calmer."

Looking carefully at him, it is true that he looks healthy, sits steadily, and he behaves calmly.

At the Fourth Conference for Friendship of Overseas Chinese Association, this blue-eyed Chinese raised his hand several times and hoped to speak, but did not succeed because there were too many people in front of him. He was sitting in the last row. Although he raised his hand high, no one paid attention to him. But this did not affect his mood. He was patient. Once he got a chance, he would try his best to get it.

"I was not very patient before I began to practice *Taiji*. After I started, I felt that I was calmer, and my body was not stiff anymore." While he speaks, he as-sumes the starting position of *Taiji*.

In 1994, after 21 hours of flying, Li Rongfu came to Beijing and started his studies in the *Wushu* Department of Beijing Sports University. As soon as he stepped into the Chinese martial arts world, he was completely stunned by the performances of the excellent students in the school.

"It was just like in the movies," he said. At that time, he knew nothing about *Wushu*. He thought *Wushu* was great, and also felt discouraged. It was too difficult, how would he be able to learn it? His Chinese was not very good, so he

decided to choose *Taiji* to begin with, because it is relatively slow.

He is smart, and his master, Zhu Yuming, also helped him a lot. Ms. Zhu is a legend and once taught *Taiji* classes on TV. Li Rongfu had finally found his Chinese master, and felt very confident in learning and practicing.

It was hard to find the feeling of *Wushu* at beginning. He did not even sweat much. Language was one obstacle, and another was the stiffness of his body; he did not know how to relax. He said: "It is because you need to have a stiff body for Karate."

What could he do? To deal with the stiffness of his body, he could only work hard and practice a lot. Day after day, his sweat soaked his shirts, but he had made the decision to work hard and finally made a lot of progress.

"If a person's always nervous, then it will cause them bigger health problems in the future." Li Rongfu realized that practicing *Wushu* could help to reduce his spiritual tense. He used to have a short temper, but now he is calmer. His changes have given him extra confidence, and he thinks that now there is no problem that he cannot solve.

Three years later, he won second place in the University's contest.

Later, he gradually learned Long Fist, Knife, Spear and Southern Fist.

"I have never felt tired after practicing *Taiji*, on the contrary, I feel that I react quickly and I am more energetic. I am more sober and it is very good for my health. Now I have to practice *Taiji* every day, or I will feel really uncomfortable, as though I had skipped a meal."

The hard and soft of *Wushu*, the harmony of both inside and outside, have helped this foreign-looking Chinese to turn on his Chinese heart.

According to Li Rongfu, the reason why *Wushu* is good for the health is that when you are practicing, you can feel the changes in your body. In this way, your body tends to be healthier and you will also feel better.

Li Rongfu now practices *Wushu* every day. No matter how busy he is, he will at least practice the basic movements for at least seven minutes. When I ask him how far he has reached in the world of *Taiji*, he smiles and says modestly: "In *Taiji* you never get a diploma, there is always a long way to go." He says he will

never stop practicing martial arts and he will study them his whole life.

The United Nations of Martial Arts

Although Li Rongfu left Beijing, he did not give up *Wushu*. He brought the authentic oriental *kung fu* back to Cuba.

In 1995, after he went back to Cuba, Li Rongfu founded the Cuba *Wushu* Association. There were no martial arts school before that, and his school attracted a lot of attention.

He practices *Taiji*, *Taiji* Sword, and the *Taiji* Fan from 7 to 9 every morning. In the afternoon from 6 to 8, there are classes for children and youths. There are eight classes now in his school, and there are more than 100 people in each class. From Monday to Friday, he follows this schedule without any exception. On weekends, Li Rongfu likes to go fishing, diving, or dancing with his Chinese wife in Havana.

"It causes too much trouble!" laughs Li Rongfu when talking about his

identity in Havana. People always greet him on the street. He did a couple of TV programs about Chinese martial arts, and introduced Jackie Chan and Jet Lee. This made him a famous person in Havana.

His association has accepted more than 5,000 members since he founded it 12 years ago. The oldest member is about 80 years old, and the youngest is about 2 or 3 years old. Li's school is like a mini United Nations, besides local people, there are also people from Mexico, Italy, Spain, the Czech Republic and America. Talking about the tuition, Li told me that he is a communist party member and he follows the rules of communism — teaching for free.

In recent years, the *Wushu* association has often organized contests in Cuba and also some exchange activities between China and Cuba. The former Chief of the National Sports Bureau Yuan Weimin visited Cuba. Li Rongfu and his students performed for him. Mr. Yuan was very happy to see their performance, and gave the Cuba *Wushu* Association 100,000 *yuan* worth of equipment on behalf of China.

In 2005 Li Rongfu brought his team to Jiaozuo in Henan Province for the *Taijiquan* (Shadow Boxing) Annual Conference. There were more than 20 countries competing. Their team won the third place, and won four gold medals and six silver medals. Just after the ceremony, he called his wife and told her excitedly: "Dear, our team succeeded."

The average age of the members of his team is 20 years old. The young team members all love Chinese movies, for example *Crouching Tiger Hidden Dragon*. They love Chinese actors like Chow Yunfat, Bruce Lee, Jet Lee and Jackie Chan. Jet Lee is their favorite, because "he is the best at *kung fu*."

Li bought a five story building near the ocean in Havana. He has enough room to practice *kung fu* and it has always been the "major theme" of his home. He has also given his identity as a Chinese person to his 16-month-old daughter.

"She has learned how to stand like a martial artist." Li Rongfu opens his hands and poses like a martial artist. He plans to have his daughter start learning martial arts when she is two years old. He looks so happy as he talks about this.

By Zhang Hong
Translated by Ma Dongxiao

Personal File

Name: Dana Schuppert

Chinese Name: Female Zhuge Liang

Nationality: German

Occupation: Investor, Banker,
           Strategist

Time in China: 8 years

"Married" to China

She is a European lady, with the mixed blue blood of Germany and France. A chance trip to Beijing reminded her of her childhood life in China. So she decided to sell her car and the house where she had lived for many years with her parents, quit her job and cozy life, and come to China by herself, where she lives with her "two children" and "three boyfriends".

*T*his lady, with her unusual experiences, has been to several countries including Japan, India and Singapore; however, she finally settled down in China. As a romantic European with mixed French and German heritage, she tied herself to China and donated her love to it. Instead of being an occasional visitor to China, she chose China as her home.

She is Dr. Dana Schuppert, the Founder, President and CEO of Strategic European Investment Management Ltd. From interviews with her in magazines like *Business Weekly and Chinese Women*, we knew that she has an interesting Chinese name: Female Zhuge Liang. (Zhuge Liang was a wise man during the Three Kingdoms period in ancient China.)

We approached Dr. Dana full of respect. We will see what is happening in China through her beautiful and intelligent eyes….

Reading Chinese Philosophy at Six

One day afternoon in early 2007, by appointment, I entered an elegant office in the Beijing International Club. Amid its pleasant atmosphere, I interviewed Dr. Dana Schuppert on many topics, from her favorite places (Yunnan and Sichuan); to Lao Zi (Lao Tzu, circa 600-500 BC), Confucius and Sun Zi (Sun Tzu); from "reading thousands of books" to "traveling thousands of miles"; from

her love for Chinese classical poetry to her view of life. Her true love for China was evident in every word, as she recited the verses from Li Bai's poem: "From a pot of wine among the flowers I drank alone. There was no one with me — Till, raising my cup, I asked the bright moon to bring me my shadow and make us three."

As soon as I stepped into her office her assistant told me, "Dr. Dana Schuppert is a European lady, with the mixed blue blood of Germany and France. She has lived in China for many years. She is not only an investor, banker and strategist, but also a talented woman with the romance of the French, the precision of the German and the tolerance of the Chinese."

From our talk, I learned that she grew up in Europe. Her father was a famous medical scientist who was very familiar with the cultures of China and India. Her mother came from a noble French family, and was interested in Chinese art. When talking about her family background, Dana said proudly, "I am very lucky because I am probably the most perfect 'combination' in the world. I had great influence from my parents, and that has shaped my lifestyle since my childhood." In regard to her nationality, she answered, "I am a European with German nationality, and a background in both Germany and France. Europe was my most important background before I came to China."

Favorable living conditions provided Dana with free space for development, but she has "a Chinese heart". When she was six years old, she started to read Chinese philosophy in her father's study, became familiar with Chinese wisdom and art, and was deeply attracted by this mysterious nation. "I must go to this country one day," she said to her father, who was shocked by her idea. Many years later, she finally settled down in China, and made her childhood dream come true.

Dr. Dana Schuppert has a strong academic background with a master's degree from Paris University and two doctoral degrees in Human Science and Economics from University of Bonn. Established by the Prussian King William III in 1818, University of Bonn is one of the most famous universities in Germany, where Dana worked for five years as an associate professor. Thereafter, she

began to get involved in the investment banking industry, focusing on economic and political communications between Germany and France. She came to Asia in 1992 and has so far worked and lived in Asian countries like Japan, China, India and Singapore for 15 years.

In 1992, Dr. Dana Schuppert came from Japan to Beijing on a business trip. When she stepped out of the Beijing Capital International Airport, she suddenly felt a familiar smell brushing her face. Recalling that feeling, she said, "I don't know why, but I cannot describe it in words. It made me so comfortable, just like going back home!" It was this feeling which awakened her childhood memory of China and her strong attraction to Chinese philosophy, art, pottery and wisdom, and enabled her to make an important decision — China would be the country where she would live for the rest of her life!

One of the reasons why Dr. Dana Schuppert decided to settle down in China was her deep impression of Zhu Rongji. She saw Mr. Zhu, then the vice-premier of the State Council of China, for the first time at the annual conference of the World Economic Forum held in Davos, Switzerland in 1997. Mr. Zhu was invited to attend that conference and made a presentation on the theme of "China's Reform and Development" in fluent English. She recalled, "He was a government official who could make a speech in fluent English, without looking at his paper, before an audience of thousands, and still be full of wisdom and humor. He impressed me a lot." From then on, she was deeply attracted to China. She told Mr. Zhu, "Buddhism directs my lifestyle, so I will not get married. However, if one day you become the Chinese Premier, I will 'marry' China, because I have such strong feelings for her."

After that, she returned to Germany. Her parents had already passed away. Inspired by her true feelings and desires, she sold her car, the house where she had lived for many years with her parents, quit her job and cozy life, and came to China by herself. She expressed her feelings by saying, "I followed my own heart to China! I chose China as my home country so that I could do something for this country and its people."

When Zhu Rongji became the fifth premier of China in March, 1998, Dr.

Dana Schuppert listened to Premier Zhu's speech very carefully in the Great Hall of the People. She was moved by his words, which are still fresh in her memory: "No matter whether there is a land mine or a bottomless chasm in front of me, I will forge ahead bravely without any thought of turning back, and do my best to serve China and the Chinese people until my heart ceases to beat."

Two years later, in 2000, when Premier Zhu visited Germany, he met Dana who was then one of the strategic consultants for China-Germany political relations. In the meeting, she said to Premier Zhu, "You probably still remember me. Now I have 'married' China, and I have two children – Yunnan Province and Sichuan Province!" Premier Zhu was gratified by her words and smiled. The people around them also smiled approvingly. Because of this, some Chinese officials called her the "57th ethnic group" of China.

Dr. Dana Schuppert said that the mission of her business is to make effective use of available resources, and protect the environment and the precious culture of China. She also works to promote the sustainable development of the Chinese economy and society, and help companies in Europe, India and China seek cooperation partners and investment opportunities. She has done what she said she'd do.

She showed me an exhibition program of Yunnan Province, which she had planned and prepared for five years, as a window of Yunnan for Europeans and Indians to know more about the province. When asked about the reason of doing so, she answered, moving every Chinese: "Only because I love Yunnan so much!"

She personally invited Krishna Warrier, the former governor of Karnataka, also known as "the father of the Asian Silicon Valley", to China, where he paid successful visits to Beijing, Kunming, Chengdu and Shanghai.

She helped in the opening of the China-India High-level Cultural Exchange Conference, and founded the "21st Century China-India Cultural and Economic Exchange Center" in Lijiang, Yunnan Province.

......

She loves the cultures of China and India and hopes that the two neighboring

countries with similar cultural resources can cooperate well together. She would like to offer her help to further mutual understanding and cooperation between China and India. Based on her understanding of India and the life she had lived there, she gave herself an Indian name — Dana, which comes from the old Sanskrit language and means "happiness from giving" — a guideline for her life.

Dr. Dana Schuppert often says, "I am a European with a Chinese heart. I've married China and China is my home country. India is my brother and I have an Indian name." This is precisely why she spends her time and energy on promoting communication between China and India. One of the missions of her company Strategic European Investment Management Ltd. is to help companies from Europe, India and China seek cooperation partners and investment opportunities by integrating and balancing value differences between the East and West.

It is her personal ability and influence, especially her role as a strategic consultant in Yunnan and Sichuan provinces, that gave Dr. Dana Schuppert a Chinese nickname: the female Zhuge Liang.

Dana's "Three Boyfriends"

When speaking of traditional Chinese culture, Dana said in enthusiastic tones that the Chinese culture is the best in the world. It is its culture and its value that makes this country the most attractive nation.

Dr. Schuppert pointed out that Chinese philosophy is a practical philosophy. Unlike the abstract philosophies of Germany, people can recognize their own experiences in Chinese works like *The Classic of the Way and Virtue*, *The Analects of Confucius* and *The Art of War*. Chinese philosophy practically explains profound theories of life using simple sayings and proverbs, providing significant inspiration and valuable advice for our life and work. In fact, she read these works in German in her father's study when she was a young girl. She was deeply influenced by their profound ideas.

The Dao or *Way of Lao Zi*, though it speaks of infinity, tells people to follow current trends; Confucius (551-479 BC) tells people the importance of "moderation", "not going too far or staying too close". *The Art of War* has become a magic weapon for strategists. Because of these, Dana regards Lao Zi, Confucius and Sun Zi as her "three boyfriends". She said, "these three books are the best philosophic works, supplementing one another, and have become my life guidelines."

When asked about her expectation for life and the significance of life, Dr. Schuppert said, "traditional Chinese culture tells people that the best philosophy of life is to lead a life of health, knowledge and friendship." From this we see her own unique comprehension of life.

Dr. Schuppert thinks that traditional Chinese medicine (TCM) is a part of the traditional Chinese culture. She believes that herbs are the most natural medicine, and best suited to the circulatory function of the human body. She delivered a paper entitled "How Can the Traditional Chinese Medicine Industry Use European Capital" at the 20th Bozhou National TCM Trade Fair and the 1st Traditional Chinese Medicine Exposition held in China's Anhui Province in

August 2004, arousing much attention among the participates at the meeting.

During the interview, she recited verses from a poem written by Li Bai (701-762), a great poet of the Tang Dynasty (618-907), "From a pot of wine among the flowers I drank alone. There was no one with me — Till, raising my cup, I asked the bright moon to bring me my shadow and make us three." The verses express the exact feeling of the poet, she said. She also told me that this is one of her favorite poems of the Tang Dynasty.

In her view, Chinese people are so lucky to have such beautiful lines of poetry. Dana said that no other country in the world has an uninterrupted history of over 5,000 years, like China. A country with such a long and profound culture is sure to have a healthy and harmonious development in the future.

The Chinese culture has its own uniqueness and profundity. As a foreigner living in China, has Dr. Schuppert encountered any cultural conflicts? Are there any inconveniences in her life? "No, absolutely not," she replied. "I have completely adapted to the Chinese culture. It seems that it was fate that brought me to China."

Then we naturally came to the topic of the Starbucks coffee shop inside Beijing's Forbidden City, which had occasioned a debate on whether the Starbucks would do damage to the Forbidden City or whether it could be in harmony with the Forbidden City. Dana said resolutely in her clear but nonstandard Chinese: "No good, no good. The Starbucks doesn't fit with the Forbidden City. It should move out immediately. It damages Chinese culture."

Dr. Schuppert believes that "language is the key to culture and mutual understanding. Language and communication are most important to human life." She started to learn Chinese in 1992 when she first came to China. In her opinion, Chinese is a great language which is well linked with its history and culture. She likes the Chinese language very much.

Discussing her experience of learning Chinese, she said with a smile that she always tries to express herself in Chinese during her leisure time, no matter at the airport or the office. Although she can only use simple Chinese words and expressions, she has never doubted her ability to learn Chinese. She has a great gift for language learning, and can speak eight languages now.

When we talked about how to let foreigners better understand Chinese culture, she said, "Only those who have come to China and have experience in China can really understand Chinese culture. For those who don't have the chance to visit China, the media can play an important role in introducing the country."

According to her own experiences, Dr. Schuppert advised that the Chinese media should provide more information about China by means of newspapers, TV and radio stations, and audio-video products for foreign people who don't have the opportunity to come in person. It's different now, compared with the past. The Chinese media should have more exchanges of views with their foreign counterparts, and draw more inspiration from them.

She pointed out that the foundation of communication is respect — to respect each other's cultural backgrounds and manners of behavior. Without respect, all communication is impossible. Moreover, she suggested that, if possible, all publications for foreigners should be bilingual — in English and Chinese. This would be a way to improve China's image and to help more foreigners understand China.

Chinese Women Should Go to the Library More Often

Everyone has his/her own expectations for life. In Dana's eyes, the meaning of life is: Firstly, to know yourself; what advantages you have and what you want to get. Secondly, to pursue your spiritual goals instead of the satisfactions of material life only. Finally, to contribute as best you can to your family, your country, and others.

As she talked about her role in the economic, political and cultural exchanges between China and India, Dr. Schuppert smiled and said, China-India relations have always been one of her main tasks during her ten-year working experience in Asia.

In recent years, she was invited several times by top Chinese officials to visit Indian cities like Bangalore, Bombay and New Delhi, and also helped to

invite Krishna, the former governor of Karnataka, to pay a personal visit to China. As the "Father of the Asian Silicon Valley", Krishna outlined a development plan for Bangalore as early as 20 years ago, which led to it becoming the famous "Silicon Valley" of Southeast Asia.

On September 27, 2006, the "China-India Cultural Exchange & Discussion Conference" was held in Lijiang, Yunnan Province. Delegates from both sides made speeches suggesting possibilities for a joint project between Yunnan University and Bombay University to establish the China-India Cultural Exchange Institute. This is only one of the economic and cultural exchanges which have taken place between the two countries with Dana's help. She is eager to create opportunities and provide as much help as possible to advance the friendly cooperation between China and India, because the two countries have similar cultural origins and have successfully cooperated in the past.

Dana still clearly remembers the first time she traveled to Yunnan and Sichuan. She said, "They were located in the southwest of China. Unlike other cities which are more commercialized, the people here are pure and honest. I'm quite impressed by the diversity of cultures and ethnic groups, the abundant natural resources and the beautiful scenery here." Dana described Lijiang as "a place like heaven". She treats her beloved Yunnan and Sichuan provinces as her own "children" and tries to do her best for their future development.

What she has done has crossed national and regional boundaries, and beyond the normal feelings of human beings. All she has is love for China and India, especially for the western area of China.

She surprised me when she told me what she does in her spare time, "I don't have any spare time, and I even don't know what spare time is." She is fully occupied by her work every day, and never feels idle, with nothing to do. "Donating herself to work" is her entire life.

Of course, this does not mean that her life is boring. In fact, she combines her interests with her work and enjoys life while working. She has studied astrophysics, history, cosmology, nerve science, quantum physics and bioscience. She trained as a ballet dancer for 20 years, and loves to play piano and cello. She is also interested in interior design, and spent two years designing her office for a better working environment for her colleagues.

In the eyes of others, Dr. Schuppert leads an unusual life. She is full of love, but her love is not for particular people — no marriage and no children — but for different countries and provinces. She has enough money to enjoy life, but she donated the funds to the development of different regions, and their mutual exchange.

When asked whether other people understood her lifestyle, she said, "When I was an associate professor at the University of Bonn, I realized that everyone had his/her own lifestyle, and mine was different from others. I've never expected everyone understand me. I feel satisfied as long as I follow what is in my mind and what I value." "The wealth of knowledge, the enjoyment of perfection, the pursuit of wisdom and passion for study" are the mottos of her life.

Faced with such a successful business woman, I naturally wanted to know Dana's suggestions for Chinese women. Without hesitation she said, "Read, study and do research. Don't spend time on window shopping or make-up!" She advised Chinese women to have their own correct attitude of life, to respect themselves highly and keep true thoughts in their mind, to enjoy life and pursue knowledge, and make every minute significant and valuable. "Chinese women should increase their knowledge by going more often to the library, not going to parties."

Wu Yi, vice-premier of China, is the lady that Dana respects most, because the courage, frankness and resolution displayed by Wu Yi are necessary elements of success for everybody.

After the interview, Dr. Schuppert showed us around her delicately decorated office, and I was deeply moved by the strong sense of art in the office. The special design creates a harmonious atmosphere, decorated with cut flowers, bamboo, and beautiful pictures of Qinghai taken by herself. In addition, she told us that she was considering writing a book named *China, I Love You* based on what she had seen and experienced in China. She has stopped writing several times simply because of her busy work, but we believe this book, containing her

understanding and recognition of China, as well as her own dreams, will be published soon!

By Ma Xinjing
Translated by Xu Lin

Personal File

Name: David Deems

Chinese Name: Ding Dawei

Nationality: American

Occupation: Education Consultant

Time in China: 14 years

Spring Rain in Dongxiang

In 1994, a 6-foot 3-inch tall American came to China. In 2000, he plunged into Dongxiang, Gansu Province, at that time the province with the highest rates of illiteracy and the lowest levels of basic education in the nation, and he has now been living there for 7 years. Seven hundred *yuan* per month is his salary and all the money he has to support his family. Who is he? What kind of a person is he? In his own words, he is a person who "makes no money, pays no taxes, is a lousy consumer, rarely bathes or washes his clothes, but likes to pick his fingernails". He is David Deems, a young American man who volunteered to settle down in China.

The first time I met David Deems was at a conference sponsored by the US Ford Foundation. The conference organizers told me "that American guy, he's a rare bird. We offered to pay his flight here but he refused, and insisted on coming by train, hard seat, from Guangzhou all the way to Beijing. And he just went to the train station himself to buy a hard seat to go back to Gansu".

From what I learned, he's got a lot of hobbies and pursuits: sports, music, literature, education and "serving the people". He worked seven years teaching English at the Northwest University for Nationalities. He's been volunteering as an educational worker in Dongxiang Autonomous County, Gansu Province since 2000.

At that conference he passed around a little photo album, explaining ardently, "You all have no idea how cute our kids in Dongxiang are."

The next time I met David was in Lanzhou. As knowledgeable as any local, he led me across town on two buses to get to the south bus station, the starting point of our bus trip to Dongxiang. A driver standing in front of the station immediately came over to David and asked, "Going back?" After their brief discussion, David sent me off with the driver to buy a ticket. He wouldn't be getting on the bus in the station. Later I learned that Gansu bus regulations require foreigners to buy 40 *yuan* of insurance from inside the station. So David made arrangements with the driver to hold a seat, then got on after the bus was some ways out

of the station. He only had to pay the 10 *yuan* ticket price that way.

Lanzhou to Dongxiang is only 60 miles but it takes three hours. Having squeezed all six feet three inches of himself into the back row seats, his long legs somehow folded up, he showed me all the sights on the way. Like a true local host he explained how that road had been put in for the county's 50th anniversary, how this transmission tower was just installed, how far it is from this township to the county seat, etc, etc.

He always says, "Our Dongxiang."

"Treatment" Argument

When he applied at Northwest University for Nationalities in 1995 for his English teaching position, the school offered him a 1,200 *yuan* monthly salary. After checking out the school's situation, and discovering that his salary was higher than the Chinese teachers', David went to the school officials and asked for a 900 *yuan* salary. The school refused, insisting on 1,000 *yuan*. David thought a four digit number was too high, so after more "bargaining", all agreed

on 950 *yuan*.

And that wasn't David's first time demanding a lower salary.

In 1994, as an English teacher at the Zhuhai Enyi Private Primary School, David had a similar battle with the headmaster over a salary cut and a non-air conditioned room to ensure he received the same treatment as all the other teachers.

Just outside the Enyi School a local market was under construction. David pointed to the peasant workers there, saying how they were all cramped together, living in makeshift tents that were hot and stuffy inside with nowhere to bathe. He said if they could live like that, he was quite well off by comparison.

That headmaster still often talks about "that David, who likes to compare himself with peasant construction workers".

But now in Dongxiang his conditions are even worse, living without heating, a TV, a washing machine or even any plumbing. He claims, "The Dongxiang people live like this. Why in the world can't I?"

"Maybe it sounds weird but that's the way I see it." This was what David said after we arrived at his Dongxiang home. It's a 40 sq.ft. room with a desk, computer, three-person sofa, two filing cabinets and a board bed. By day this room is the office of the Bilingual Education Experimental Project in Dongxiang, funded by the Ford Foundation. It's David's home, sweet home at night.

I wondered how such a tall man could manage to sleep well on a standard length Chinese single bed. He says he's used to it: in 10 years' time in China he's never had a bed long enough. Our Chinese quilts are too short so he puts one on top of him and uses another to cover his feet. He jokes that this works for the best: he can't smell his stinky feet that way.

While discussing all this David is busy shredding some old newspapers and busting up some kindling with his feet for lighting the coal stove — quite necessary as evening was coming. Early March at 8,000 ft. above sea level was pretty cold.

With the fire well on its way we went out for dinner. As we entered a little local restaurant the boss and workers, quite familiar with the foreigner, all

greeted David in the Dongxiang language. One brought a plate of mutton and two bowls of noodles. Usually he'll just have a simple bowl of beef noodles and some bread, cheap at about 3 *yuan*. But to host me well he treated me to Dongxiang's famous boiled mutton.

The meal was 30 *yuan*. I stood to pay the bill, but he just sat and smiled smugly. "Go ahead and see if you can get them to take your money." The waiter took a careful look at David and took his money to pay the bill.

In our next few days together, under my pressure, David permitted us to take turns buying meals. Our meals, always something simple like noodles or dumplings, never exceeded 5 or 6 *yuan*, however.

In June 2002, at the end of his contract, David decided to leave Northwest University for Nationalities to devote himself to full time work in Dongxiang. The local education commission expressed a desire to hire him as an education consultant at 500 *yuan* a month. In Dongxiang even the local teachers can clear between 900 and 1,200 a month.

However, it took well over a year to get through the red tape necessary to hire this foreigner. In June, 2003, the Gansu Provincial Police, Foreign Affairs Office, Linxia Prefecture Police and many other administrative offices came together to Dongxiang to investigate David and his work. They reported, "He is asking for nothing in return, has overcome difficulty upon difficulty... his principles and behavior are truly impressive." Not until January, 2004, was he actually officially hired. Although he now has an officially recognized status, David has yet to enjoy receiving the 500 *yuan* monthly salary.

"No big rush. I can still keep living off my savings." He says he is neither a smoker nor a drinker, so food, phone calls and stamps for letters are his main expenses. Four or five hundred *yuan* a month covers all that just fine.

I joked with him, "Sounds like you are just totally without faults."

"Not a chance. I have lots of shortcomings," he quickly retorted. "I make no money. Pay no taxes. I'm a lousy consumer. I rarely bathe or wash my clothes. I pick my fingernails...."

David was born into an American middle class family in Cleveland, Ohio.

His father works in upper management for the largest tire manufacturer in the US. His mother had been a high school teacher but later was a full time mother to her four sons. Every summer they would take a family vacation to the Grand Canyon or Florida.

After high school, David chose to attend the College of William and Mary, America's second oldest university with over 300 years of history and an outstanding economics program.

As a college junior he went to study abroad at Peking University in Beijing in August 1989. Like all foreign students he also traveled quite a bit, getting a taste of all China has to offer. He became aware of his strong desire to become a teacher while getting his Master's in Ancient Literature from Asbury College in Kentucky. Upon graduation he went to teach in Japan for a year. In 1994 he returned to China to teach English at Zhuhai Enyi Private Primary School.

Hiring English teachers for the school one summer he discovered that four of his five selections had all come from Northwest China. If such quality people were leaving the northwest, who was there to take their place?

Thus David sent out his resume to several schools in the northwest. Having been offered jobs at Lanzhou University and Northwest Normal University, among other schools, David chose to work at Northwest University for Nationalities. His choice was purely logical: "These college students will graduate and return to their homes, the minority areas, to become teachers. Those are the places most in need."

This is the basic idea motivating many of David's later decisions: "Being a teacher you ought go to the places where you are most needed."

Conducting Classes Differently

At the Northwest University for Nationalities, David was not willing to live in the foreign experts building, instead choosing a small room in the students' dormitory. "I most certainly conduct my classes differently than other teachers."

Take his literature class for instance. In the first week he informed students

which authors and works they would cover. Then each student was required to choose an author, Dickens or Milton or whomever. From the second week until mid-term exams, every student got the chance to go before the class and teach, using whatever methodology he or she wished, effectively explaining what ought to be learned about his or her author. David sat among the students every week evaluating the results of the instruction and the choice of contents. The second half of the term was entirely dedicated to reading and discussing famous works. Which characters did you take a liking to? Were there any places you still didn't understand?

David converted one of his oral English classes into "Speech and Debate". Every week the students took a turn delivering English speeches or were given a topic to prepare in team debating.

In his mind, a teacher must possess his own thoughts and ideas. A teacher must clearly evaluate whether or not what is being taught has real value for the students. Foreign language is a kind of ability, a skill. Yet presently in China, foreign language education is mostly about passing compulsory examinations. Students lack the ability to speak, write or think in English.

At the Northwest University for Nationalities, David's classes gained notoriety for copious questions and discussion in class and mounds of homework. "I am aware of what the students face in their daily lives, like how much homework other teachers have given or whether the students are busy or free. If the school is having an activity some week, I will lighten the homework load accordingly." He found it hard to believe that some teachers of the writing class only required students to write five essays over the course of an entire school year. And those five included the two mid-term and two final examination essays!

A teacher has "homework" as well. That is to be aware of each student's ability, English level, and what he or she needs to work on. Students at Northwest University for Nationalities ranged from outstanding youths from Xi'an with fine English, to the countryside minority students who had never opened their mouths to speak a word of English before. When asking questions or encouraging students to speak, a good teacher has to be wise about what to ask

students, how difficult or easy to make things to meet that student's interest and ability. "That's quite a challenge," David admits.

Once, David was discussing students with one of the writing teachers.

"I've noticed that so-and-so expressed herself well in her writing but her grammar is pretty dreadful. What do you think?"

"Who's that? Which class?"

"You know, that class you are teaching."

"Oh, well, I'm not their homeroom teacher. Not sure who you mean."

The first class of each term David will devote time to clearly explaining how that class will go for the term. "They need to know what is expected of them. At the same time they ought to know what they can require of the teacher."

David told students that if he failed to examine their work adequately, simply adding a checkmark, for instance, or to correct the homework they hand in, that they need not do any homework the next time he asked for it. He said he couldn't require anything of students if he was not responsible for his part.

"You've checked every little detail of seven years of homework?" I asked a little incredulously.

"Yeah," he responded as if it were perfectly obvious.

"Oh, there was once…." One year David had three classes of "The Background of Western Culture" with 50 students in each class. If all three classes were given the same homework in the same week, he would inform one class that their homework would only be graded for content one week. Alternating classes, he could correct everything the next week. "But that was an exception. I wasn't really willing to have to do that."

He has one other valuable skill he often employs. "I never need to take attendance. One look and I can tell who's not there, because I know all my students. If anybody's missing I just ask his or her friends what's up, or if they are ill."

"Do that once or twice and all the students know they better not cut class."

"Education is purely an exchange among teacher and students." He believes that no matter what course is being taught — and especially at the primary

education level — having computers or multi-media instruction is not all that important. The people involved are the key.

"I saw a lot of stuff working in Guangdong Province. Maybe there's a kid whose parents have divorced and no one's checking up on his studies. If he doesn't study well the teacher just bawls him out for being lazy or something. But that kid doesn't need us telling him what two plus two is. He needs someone to care for his well being. He needs a good adult role model in his life to help him figure out life."

If exchange is so important, much respect for others must be shown. David has a great dislike for odd school activities that interrupt the students' studies. Classes are often canceled then, and he feels this is truly disrespectful to the students. David organized the "English Corner" for Northwest University for Nationalities to give students more opportunities to practice their English. But this English Corner has the special feature of having a weekly speaker. Every Sunday at three in the afternoon, David starts the corner by speaking for about 40 minutes on a topic, which leads to free discussion. To entice experts from other schools to attend his corner, David's policy was that any foreigner who stayed till after six would get a free dinner on him. You can guess for yourself how many free meals he had to give away in six and a half years. It amounted to

the greatest regular expense of David's life in Lanzhou.

Even with all this, David claims that he's not that good of an English teacher.

"I teach what I think is most necessary for them to learn. But even something like English Corner isn't really helping students pass the required national exams." His voice drops off upon saying this, his blue eyes looking down to his fingers, the nails of which show the scars and signs of the lack of vitamins in his Dongxiang diet.

Education Volunteer Work

One afternoon I rode a local bus with David from one of his schools back to the county seat. Once on the bus, the fellow taking the money said, "David, tell me, why did you leave Lanzhou to come here to Dongxiang?"

He replied teasingly, "Dongxiang's a swell place."

The young man couldn't comprehend this. "What are you talking about? Lanzhou's a lot better than here." David has faced such questions countless times.

In 2000 David began his "education volunteer work" in Dongxiang, coming to the county from Lanzhou for three days every week.

Gansu's Dongxiang Autonomous County is the only county in the nation especially for the Dongxiang nationality. It is also a nationally recognized impoverished county. According to the 1990 national census, the Dongxiang have the highest illiteracy rate of any group in China, a staggering 82.63%. The average person has only a second- or third-grade elementary education.

One of the main reasons David left the States to come to China as a teacher was that he felt it was a little redundant to teach in such a developed place. His choice to leave Lanzhou was based on the same logic.

"Lots of people are working in higher education now. The national government funds it. Northwest University for Nationalities now has seven foreign teachers. In comparison, basic education is quite neglected." He recalls an article

from the Economist which placed China second to last in the world for their emphasis on basic education. "The illiteracy rate tells all you need to know about the poor level of basic education in Dongxiang. If I'm supposed to think about staying in Lanzhou because the conditions there are better, I might as well just head back to the US. I'm not saying it's wrong to make places with decent education even better. First you just have to guarantee decent education for places that need it the most." He says it's just like cosmetic dentistry or some surgeries. They are not bad in and of themselves, but the basic provision of adequate health care for everyone ought to be the first priority.

Upon meeting David, I asked him, "So what is it exactly that you are going in Dongxiang?" With a queer little smile he replied in English with, "That's a good question," but didn't answer me.

Having followed him around Dongxiang for several days, I too am perplexed about how to explain all that he does.

One day we went to the post office to pick up mail and subscribe to a few magazines. Then we left to visit Machang Enyi School in Mianguchi Township and the six female teachers there.

Machang is about a 40-minute walk from the county seat. It was built in 2000 with investment from a Singaporean woman and the Zhuhai Enyi School. It presently has first through fourth grade and 240 students. David will purchase gifts for the teachers every year for International Women's Day. In the past it was quilt covers, bedsheets, or an alarm clock, but David couldn't come up with any good ideas this year. So he chose to get a few women's magazines sent to the school for them. He had planned to spend 100 *yuan*, and it came out to 109.

Another day was spent visiting Baoling Enyi School in Dongyuan Township. This school is quite far from the county seat, a half hour by local bus with a three mile walk on a mountain path. There was a dust storm that day as well. Upon arrival at the school David muttered, "Why isn't the national flag up?" Asking the headmaster, the reply came that it was taken down because of the dust storm, to prevent the flag being torn or blown away.

This school was originally built in 1956, but the buildings had fallen into

disrepair and were on the verge of collapse. One teacher would instruct the 20 students under the lone tree in the courtyard. In 2002, David collected 45,000 *yuan* from seven donors to rebuild the school. Now there are 110 students in five grade levels. Having just received a small donation in the mail the previous week, David brought the money to the school to give a small refund to the parents for their children's tuition. Tuition is 25 *yuan* a term, so the plan was to give back 5 *yuan* for each boy and 10 for each girl. On this visit David needed to get a list of the students who had received to mail to the donor along with a thank you letter.

On another day we went to Qiya School in Chuntai Township to discuss plans with the headmaster to get the children some school uniforms.

This is just a village schoolhouse located in the mountains about 30 minutes' walk from the county seat. They only have a first grade class there now, and the students have no Mandarin Chinese ability. The school is undertaking a small experiment with a new bilingual curriculum.

Once inside the school gate, David went first beside a classroom window to count the students present that day. He has a habit of doing this whenever he goes to these schools. I learned from the headmaster, who happens to be the only teacher at Qiya, that the school has 32 children. Last year there were 43 students but this number was inflated due to the countywide school enrollment drive.

The drive had temporarily brought in a few extra children last year, but this term those extras had all left the school.

David has to put up with a lot of such unpredictability. He's had to go to the local power company to complain about the 1.5 *yuan*/unit charge for the school's electricity (that's nearly three times the national legal standard price). He has spent time and energy to find a donor and handicapped school for a mute student in one of his schools. He made a visit to the county education commission to report on a trip David arranged and led, taking six Dongxiang teachers for a week of training at the Guangdong Enyi schools. He volunteers himself out to the Dongxiang Bilingual Education Experimental Project Office, doing much of their translation and paperwork for them.

Lots of people in Dongxiang know David as "the tall foreigner that always goes walking about". But as for what he actually does, few can say for sure.

"Even I am not so sure about everything I'm doing here." I sense tiredness and uncertainty in his voice as he says this. No one is requiring him to do anything, and neither does anyone instruct him as to what should be done.

"So do you think all this I'm doing has any real significance or value?" he asks me.

"I'm not here to be a so-called 'foreign expert' or to tell others what to do. I'm just a kind of laborer, willing to serve." He believes that the locals all know a lot better what their needs truly are. But he doesn't want to hear them just say, "We need money." Could they really want or need nothing besides more money?

Wherever David goes he always totes along a faded, worn-out document folder. He keeps all sorts of important papers inside: identification, a copy of his passport page, reports on money donations and school construction projects, documents from the education commission, the savings account passbook for the donations, his accounts ledger, school pictures, thank you letters, receipts to be mailed to donors to show where there money was used, etc, etc. He tells me in English, "This thing is my life here."

Don't Call Him "Lei Feng¹"or"Norman Bethune²"

Since David's story appeared in the media, he has became a famous person. He even appeared on the program "Tell It Like It Is" hosted by Cui Yongyuan. There has been a continual flow of letters and money donations sent to "Gansu, Dongxiang County, Ding Dawei" over the past few years. Donations have already exceeded the 100,000 *yuan* mark. Many people find it hard to believe David could still be in Dongxiang, so they mail letters from time to time just to see if he's still there.

"I probably get the most mail of anybody in Dongxiang." With such a high illiteracy rate, few locals write letters. The post office is busiest with money orders and delivers relatively few letters.

It becomes David's responsibility to determine how to best use these donations. "I don't want this money. Building schools, placing and paying teachers, ensuring all students can get an education, these are the government's responsibilities."

However, these donations come with his name on them. How can he refuse to be responsible for them?

Besides refunding tuition, buying needed equipment for the schools, and letting each student and teacher celebrate Teacher's Day or International Children's Day, David has also, for the last three winter holidays, taken teachers to Guangdong's Enyi Schools for training, exchange of ideas and even a chance to see the ocean.x

Ma Xiaohong is a teacher at Machang Enyi School. This Spring Festival she and five other Dongxiang teachers, led by David, together traveled two days and two nights on hard seat trains to Guangdong's Chaoyang Enyi School. Previous to this trip, Ma Xiaohong had never been to Lanzhou or been on a train. "Getting to see the ocean, my goodness, it was like forgetting all my troubles." As she spoke her great excitement about the trip was still clearly visible.

David was especially proud of the fact that, although he was taking six

people on a train journey during the Spring Festival, and had to change trains twice, he was still able to ensure each person a seat and only spent 143 *yuan* per person from Lanzhou to Guangzhou.

"How did you manage that?" I asked in disbelief.

He then took out a beat-up, dog-eared national train schedule book and explained how to buy "through tickets", how to pick trains that aren't expresses and have no air-conditioning (for a lower price), and then how to arrange with train conductors and station masters to board trains first and use his tall body to hold seats.

"The whole trip was a learning experience for these teachers," claimed David.

After returning to Dongxiang he collected all the tickets and receipts for the trip. These were used to verify how much money was used and for what purposes. They are sent along with explanatory thank-you letters mailed to the donors.

David writes such letters for all uses of money, not just for travel projects. The records are also kept in triplicate, one for himself, one for the schools and one for the education commission.

"No one requires you to do this. Why create so much trouble for yourself?" I asked while flipping through his ledger, which documented everything from construction fees totaling tens of thousands to telephone fees of a few *yuan*.

"How could I not do it? People donate their money to me. It's the least I can do to be responsible." This is said slightly louder than normal, he is seemingly a little angry with me.

Possibly because of his way of "being responsible", many donors continue to send money, with one individual having donated nine times already.

David's meticulousness and diligence can be seen in many other things he does.

At Qiya School he made sure to point out an old style amplifier to me. He claims to have found it at the Lanzhou second hand market. "It's a 1973 model, but it's just like new because it was never used; it was probably stored in some warehouse and forgotten. It's top quality and only 80 *yuan*." He has also bought

bookshelves from the used furniture market and bargained with an Internet bar to buy their old computer desks.

In 2002, an insurance firm in Shanghai donated six of their obsolete computers for Dongxiang through David. Truly a good thing for Dongxiang, right? Again, David couldn't refuse the responsibility.

In July, the six computers arrived in Lanzhou, and David headache began.

By the time the verification had arrived in Dongxiang, the goods had waited past the normal pick-up period. Just to retrieve them from the station, David had to pay an extra handling charge. But by that time the Dongxiang schools were already on summer holiday. It would be unwise to leave the computers in the schools unsupervised for the break. The two crates full of six computers thus occupied a place in the home of David's friends in Lanzhou for the summer.

He made use of each visit to Lanzhou to locate cheap computer desks from Internet bars. The Qiya School had been constructed only a short time earlier; the school was still without electricity. The other two schools' power supplies were far too unstable for computer use. With power outages common, each school would need a transformer or UPS. Power strips, electric cords, even dust cloths to protect the equipment from Dongxiang sand and dirt all had to be bought.

In October the insurance company called David to request a few photos of the students using the computers. David had to apologetically admit that the computers were not quite in use yet. The dissatisfied donors asked David if he couldn't possibly "find a little bit of time to attend to this matter".

A little later David was finally able to rent a truck and move the computers and desks into the places prepared for them: three at Machang, two in Baoling and one at Qiya.

The desks had to be disassembled for the trip so David put them together one at a time. The schools' teachers were all computer illiterate, not even knowing how to turn one on. David had to teach them one by one.

None of these schools has a telephone. Without a phone line, using the internet is out of the question. The computers are used for learning typing and using some educational software.

Yet there was still a problem: two of the computers had had their Windows system software erascd. What could be done with a '96 computer using DOS, without even a CD-Rom to install anything?

In the end David calculated that he had had to spend 2,500 *yuan* on the computers, not counting the value of all his time and effort.

Another time, 1,000 *yuan* had been given to David. He told the donating party that he planned to use the money to buy some plastic water piping to bring water to the Baoling School. The donor requested that, for accounting purposes, David send the official receipt of the purchase along with a certification, verified by the township and county governments!

"We're in the backwaters. Much of what goes on here is not done the way it is elsewhere." But the donor is always right, right? What can you do but just accept some hassles for the sake of the cause?

That day, on the way to Baoling, we passed by a small primary school called Yahujia. Seeing David from several hundred meters away, the children there began to holler, "Ding-Da-Wei!" The mountain road and the school are separated by a broad dry gully, so David hollered back that he'd stop by the school on his return trip. But the headmaster and several students still ran out from the school to cross the gully and exchange a few happy words with David.

The kids at the schools all like him, showing visible excitement whenever he is around. They enjoy having this giant grab them or hang some boy upside down by his legs. They like to crowd around and watch him spin a basketball on his finger.

And David is at his most relaxed and happy when messing around with these children.

The teachers also all like him. The female teachers often joke with him that it's no wonder he has yet to marry, since his feet stink so bad.

David is 37 this year (in 2004), according to the Dongxiang custom of calculating age, and says he was born in the year of the monkey. His mother, however, says that he is still just 35 because he hasn't had his birthday yet. He describes himself as "probably one of those people who doesn't often jump emotionally into things". At times he asks a few Chinese-style questions, like whether my residence permit is in Beijing or not, which are quite shocking to hear from a foreigner. He thinks it a natural thing.

"If you lived in some other country for ten years you'd be the same way."

He often sings or hums a tune while walking along. Once I heard him sing "Be Like Lei Feng", a song very popular during the Cultural Revolution (1966-1976), coming from his lips.

That tickled me. "You know that song?"

"I know a lot of songs." He claims, "If we go sing karaoke, I could keep singing Chinese songs all day without repeating myself." He knows the music of Tian Zhen and Sun Nan, as well as Sun Yanzi (Stefanie Sun) and even Zhou Jielun (Jay Zhou), who are all top pop singers in China. He used to listen to music often when living in Guangdong and Lanzhou. But Dongxiang is quite lacking in entertainment. He occasionally can snatch a newspaper like the *Lanzhou Evening Daily* from someone on the bus, and when he's done with it makes sure to pass it on to teachers at his schools. With his great love for basketball it's a pity he cannot see any NBA games in Dongxiang. But his father mails him sports magazines from home which he treasures.

David is considerate and caring. When walking together he makes sure to stand between you and the cars. He helps children and women with their bags on the bus. He'll talk with you about his family with truly deep feeling. At his English Corner, he never allows himself to repeat a speech topic, with the exception of Mother's Day, during which every year he relates stories of his mother, grandmother and his great-grandmother.

In public places he'll often run into those who find a foreigner an odd curiosity. When asked, "So what are you doing there? What kind of salary do you get?" he replies honestly, "Helping to build schools, but I'm not making any money."

The usual response is, "No money?! Okay, if you don't want to say then just forget it." Some in the county advise David to use his "celebrity" to do more promotion of his work, becoming better known and thus increasing donations.

"I don't want to do that." He said, "I just want to do what I am supposed to do. I don't intend to be labeled a Lei Feng or a Norman Bethune." He is not interested in being a role model and isn't out there to influence others.

The thing he desires most is a little more free time to improve his Dongxiang language ability. He also has a dream of taking a little trip to visit Qingdao and Mt. Tai with "Miss Right". He also is awaiting the day when the Dongxiang are no longer the most illiterate people in China.

"How much longer to you expect to stay here?"

"As long as they are still willing to employ me, I'll stay on," he replied with certainty.

David is a devoted Christian. But he also knows that in the world today the "religion" with the most influence is the so-called "American Dream" — striving to get a higher salary, better car, bigger house, more beautiful wife, etc.

But his earnest response to this is that everyone ought to ask themselves deep in their hearts if this is truly what they want and need. Will it bring them peace? Satisfaction? Fulfillment?

"Late late at night, when you can't get to sleep, your soul, your heart of hearts will try to talk to you. It will ask you what it is that you are living for. Don't just ignore this, or take a sleeping pill and try to drive it away." The deep calm in his blue eyes, as he sits on his little bed telling me this, makes me feel he is in possession of the entire world, the whole of life.

By Feng Yue in 2004
Translated by David Deems

Editor's Postscript

Realizing Chinese Dream

When compiling this book in 2007, I found this article written in 2004 by Feng Yue, a journalist at the *China Youth Daily*. Reading it, I was deeply moved by his spirit, and by his work in Dongxiang. Three years have passed since Feng Yue's interview. Is he still in Dongxiang? How is he getting on? I'm anxious to learn his recent situation.

How are your Dongxiang language studies coming on? Have you married your "Miss Right" from Dongxiang? My questions came flying out as soon as I met him.

"My Dongxiang language has improved a lot, but I haven't found a Dongxiang girl," David said, a little embarrassed. "They don't warm to me. There are mainly two reasons for that — one is because of who I am, the other is because of their ethnic group," David explained seriously. "I'm a poor guy with no money and no power, I'm only an employed worker. If I worked in the big city as a foreign expert with a high salary, high status, cars and a house, they might consider me. If you were a parent, you wouldn't marry your daughter to someone like me. Besides, you know, this is a minority region. Most of the people believe in Islam, while I'm a Christian. There is a difference of race and religion which of course makes it hard to resolve my personal matters."

"But I heard you got married," I asked.

"Yes, I got married in the summer of 2005. My wife is called Han Shidie. She's also an American. That is her Chinese name. Her English name is Stacy Deems.

Oh, I see. No wonder the words "Ding & Han" came at the end of his mobile phone message. "How did you meet? Was she willing to come here and be with you?" I continued to ask.

"We were introduced by a friend who studied Chinese as a foreign student at Qinghai Nationalitics Institute, and my wife worked there too at the time. Actually, she's had many experiences similar to mine. She came to China to study Chinese for a year for the first time in 1992. After returning home, she found that she loved China, and came here again in 1993 to teach English in Tianjin University. She went to Xinjiang and then went to teach in Qinghai Nationalities Institute in 2003. Later in 2005 we got married and she came here. You could say we are quite similar, with the same goals in life. "

David spoke in a plain and simple tone. But I know that for a foreigner to settle down here, in this remote region with its rough environment, is not easy. After marriage, he moved out from the office and rented a three-room apartment in the county seat. He no longer needs to light the coal stove, instead he uses an electric heater. He's got a kitchen, water and electricity, but it's not reliable. Sometimes the water and electricity are cut off. But for David, all is very satisfactory. He told me that in 2005 his salary was raised from 500 to 700 per month.

"700 *yuan*? Is it enough for rent and living?"

"Yes, more than enough," David said, smiling. "This house is only 100 *yuan* per month, and you don't know that in Dongxiang the average income of a household is only a little more than 1,100 *yuan* a year. We're much better off than they are. I don't teach in schools in the country now, but live in the county seat. The living conditions are very good, not like what you imagined."

I think he must feel very happy with his life now. His wife is his best assistant. She is now a full-time housewife and helps him to work for free every day. Before, he was responsible for communicating with school teachers, especially women teachers, and now they are taken care of by his wife. For example, in Machang School, there are 11 teachers, 10 of whom are women. "Because of religious reasons, men and women are separated, so I had a big problem before in communicating with them and taking them out to other schools for training. Now she is here, and I'm freed, and she is extremely good at dealing with them." Seeing David's delight shining in his face, I was deeply inspired. I felt very happy that he had found such a good companion, a true mate.

"What's your plan for the future? Will you stay here or…?

"I won't stay here for ever. Of course it depends on whether they will continue to employ me. However, in two or three years, 80 new schools funded by outside donors will be completed, and the goal of a school in every village will be realized. In addition, eight experimental schools practicing "Bilingual Teaching (Dongxiang and Mandarin)" now in Dongxiang will also be completed, and will be spread throughout the whole county by 2009. By that time, Dongxiang will no longer have the highest illiteracy-rate and the poorest level of basic education in the nation, and my work will be finished. I'll consider going to work in another backward place in China. I'll stay here for five or six years at most."

"What about your parents? They are getting older and older. Who will take care of them?"

"Yeah, they are about 70. Luckily my younger brother and eldest brother will take care of them."

Looking again at this American with his blue eyes and light hair in front of me, my heart is filled with respect and deeply touched.

His thoughts are younger than his age, and his heart is stronger than his body.

At the moment, a voice is ringing in my ears:

"A man's ability may be great or small, but if he has this spirit, he is already noble-minded and pure, a man of moral integrity and above vulgar interests, a man who is of value to the people." (From *Selected Works of Mao Tse-tung*)

Notes:

1. Lei Feng, (December 18, 1940 - August 15, 1962) was a soldier of the People's Liberation Army of the PRC. After his death he was characterized as a selfless and modest person who was devoted to Chairman Mao. In the posthumous "Learn from Comrade Lei Feng" (向雷锋同志学习) campaign, started by Mao in 1963, the youth of the country was indoctrinated to follow his example.

2. Norman Bethune, (1890-1939) born in Gravenhurst, Ontario, a distinguished Canadian surgeon and a member of the Canadian Communist Party. In the spring of 1938, in order to help the Chinese people in their War of Resistance

Against Japan, he came to China at the head of a medical team and arrived in Yan'an. Soon after he went to the Shanxi-Chahar-Hebei border area, where he formed the first mobile medical unit, which could be carried on two mules. Imbued with ardent internationalism and the great communist spirit, he served the army and the people of the Liberated Areas for nearly two years. He contracted blood poisoning while operating on wounded soldiers and died in Tangxian County, Hebei, on November 12, 1939. On the same day Mao Tse-tung wrote an article "In Memory of Norman Bethune" and called on every Communist and Chinese person to learn from him.

Written and Translated by Li Shujuan

Personal File

Name: Obinna

Chinese Name: Wangzi

Nationality: Nigerian

Occupation: Tailor

Time in China: 2 years

From an African "Prince" to a Beijing Tailor

He is Obinna, a young African man, good at needlework. While living in Beijing, running a dress store is his entertainment. But his skin color has brought him some trouble, that is, some customers would be scared away when they find out the seller is a black man. However, he still takes the aim of marrying a beautiful Chinese wife.

A few steps down the west of Dongsishitiao Bridge, a row of small stores stand on the street side, among which one deals in African clothes, not very eye-catching. The owner of the store hires an African assistant who is very good at tailoring work.

Do not underestimate this African fellow; his father was the chief of one African tribe in Nigeria and he was called Prince by the local people (the Chinese for "Prince" is "Wangzi"). Naturally "Wangzi" has become his Chinese name since he came to China. At present, Obinna is running this dress store with his Chinese partner. He said he enjoys the feeling of being unknown to the public as a superior African Prince.

Liking Using Hands Instead of Brains

Obinna's father has ten children: five boys and five girls. Being the fourth child of his family, Obinna does not have the responsibility of carrying on his father's cause. Thus he set out to make his own way in the world. Obinna majored in mechanical engineering and became an engineer earning good salary after graduation. However, he quickly realized that he did not like this job. He said, "I have been touching upon the art of tailoring since I was still a little pupil. I prefer this job, which can exert my handcraft to the engineering job, which would wreck my brains."

In 2005, Obinna came to Beijing for the sake of job. The next year he opened a dress store with his female Chinese partner. His partner is the owner of the store, and he is the assistant as well as the tailor. He is very proud of himself for their store is the only one specializing in African clothes in Beijing.

In this little store with limited space, all kinds of colorful African folk costumes are displayed, some of which are designed by Obinna himself. Instead of preparing design drafts, he always sets about tailoring directly; for he is afraid of that design drafts would confine his imagination. He enjoys trying new designs rather than repeating some fixed patterns.

Although pure hand-making limits the productivity of clothes, Obinna still insists on making clothes by hand because he believes the comfort and concern brought by hand making are impossible for machines to yield.

Selling Clothes by Dropping in Embassies

Although it is getting dark, the number of customers in this small store does

not seem to reduce. While chatting with the journalist, Obinna does not forget to attend to customers, but he does not promote his clothes on purpose.

"Some customers do not want to be bothered by persuasion; they like selecting their own favorable styles. I just need to wait for their questions. And there are some customers who just visit my store when passing, so it is futile to exert myself to sell. Yet I'm sure they will come to my store next time." Obinna has quite a lot to say about the art of business.

However, when he just came to Beijing two years ago, the situation was quite different. At that time, Obinna had to sell his clothes by dropping in embassies directly because he did not have his own store. He said even he himself could count how many embassies he had visited. After several months, he had earned a lot except for his Chinese proficiency.

For the time being, Obinna still uses the blend of English and Chinese to communicate with customers. As he has not taken any Chinese course, he learns

Chinese while working by treating customers as his teachers. Sometimes some people go to his store merely for the purpose of practicing their English with a foreigner. Although they will not buy anything, Obinna still welcomes them. He says, "Because most Chinese are too shy to speak English out, I would encourage them to do it. As a result, some of them have made friends with me, and some have become the buyers of my clothes." When being asked whether he would be an English teacher, shaking his head, he answers, "I've never thought about it, for teaching is really nerve-wrecking. I still enjoy being a tailor."

Doing Needlework Is an Entertainment

While making clothes, Obinna also has put a lot of thoughts into them. He has taken the need of Chinese customers into consideration and made some localized alternation to these African clothes. Picking up a silk dress, he says, "The design of this dress is African, but the fabric is native to China. Such kind of localized clothes sell rather well."

When there are few customers in the store, Obinna would do some needlework. It is really amazing and surprising to see that he could deftly make needlework with his big black hands. He says that doing needlework is basically female privilege in China, but in Africa both boys and girls need learn how to do needlework since primary school. He believes that he can do much better needlework than most girls.

In most cases, Obinna would bring the needlework back to his home in Beijing, so doing needlework becomes his major entertainment in the spare time. "The store closes at nine in the evening, so it would be very late when I finish my supper. I take doing needlework as a kind of entertainment, a kind of relaxation. Thus it is very natural that I would go to bed often at one in the morning." Obinna explains that he does not do needlework just for money; sometimes it would take him more than ten hours to make a handbag, yet he still can get fun from making it.

Being "Hurt" Because of My Black Face

At first Obinna was not good at bargaining, but when he came to China, he learned how to bargain, just as the saying goes "Do in Rome as the Romans do". Once a girl only got a discount of ten *yuan* with great effort. When they stroke the deal, she said, "You are really like the person from Wenzhou!" Obinna suddenly got the meaning of her words when someone explained that the people from Wenzhou are very shrewd in business and burst into laughter, "If you are not smart, you will lose your money when doing business. The older you are, the smarter you are. All the big mountains are piled up by small hills." At last Obinna's partner was sure that he was able to keep the store alone when he had been working there for one year.

If the customer gives a very low price, Obinna would say sincerely, "Look at the design and the quality, I guarantee that it will neither shrink nor fade." Sometimes he would invite the customer to watch the photos on the wall of him in folk clothes; sometimes he would put on the clothes designed by him. It is really fantastic when the black face matches the bright clothes.

However, Obinna's black face has also brought some trouble to his business. "Attracted by the clothes displayed in the shop window, a young lady came into my store and selected clothes directly. After picking out one, she raised her head to ask about the price. When she found out a black guy was coming toward her all of a sudden, she was scared to cry and run away." While talking about this experience, he burst into laughter, yet he says he still feels being hurt.

Some customers would just have a glimpse of the store at the door, and if they notice there is a black guy in it, they will drag their companions away. Obinna says these timid customers may never come back, but he has no way to change this situation. Sometimes he feels being hurt and even humiliated, "How could they ignore my clothes just because of my skin color?" Whereas he laughs again when considering this problem from another perspective, "For most of the time, my black face also confirms that my clothes are genuine: the customer

would believe that my clothes are really from Africa rather than some fake ones."

It might be due to his black face that more and more girls began to be fond of this store. Some regular customers will come here to seek after their favorite every month, even every week. Nowadays the tailor team, composed of Obinna and his four Chinese associates, has to be busy with cutting and sewing all day long in order to satisfy the needs of customers. And there are some customers who visit the store specially to order African folk costume, so Obinna decides to put forward the made-to-order service, which merely requires 30-50 *yuan* as the extra charge and promises the clothes will be ready in 2-8 days.

Doing Business with Clean Hands

Although his father was the chief of one tribe in charge of thousands of Nigerians and Obinna himself even owns a beautiful car, he does not want to either rely on the family success or lead a life without meaningful pursuit by marrying several wives. Since he came to Beijing, he has never tried to establish underhand connections with the embassy, for he looks down upon those who make fortunes by political nepotism. He says, "Some Africans have committed some

bad things in China and ruined the reputation of our country. I will try my best to restore our images with hard work."

"My hands are clean; those with sticky hands will be arrested by the police one day." Watching the thundershower outside the window, Obinna says, "Our Nigerians believe that the thunder is created by God and those with sticky hands would be struck to death by the thunder." According to Obinna, being a Christian, the first thing he did when he arrived in China was to go to church.

Marrying a Chinese Wife Is My Aim

Males should start career first and then get married in terms of the customs of African tribes. Obinna is also working hard to realize the two goals. He has found a Chinese girlfriend. When being asked about his girlfriend, Obinna seems to be a bit shy and simply wouldn't talk about this issue, because "it is too private".

As for the question whether he wants to marry a Chinese wife, Obinna answers, "Chinese people treat me as one member of their family, and I am obsessed with China." He takes great effort to explain the concept of "family": he has lived in the home of the female owner of the store for some time. The owner lives together with her brothers and parents, so Obinna feels as if he were living in his own home and so less homesick; besides, he is very busy with work, he has never returned to his own home yet since he came to China.

Although his father has already passed away, Obinna still bears his teaching in mind. For instance, "keep away from smoking and drinking", "make a lot of friends", "treat people with sincerity" and "do not go after money", etc. Obinna also learns from his father how to keep a low profile. He had never shown his high social status even in Nigeria. The only thing that could indicate his status was the tribe badge on his car.

Working Overtime for My Chinese Girl

Obinna's low profile let his Chinese friends feel he is very friendly, thus they invites him to have dinner quite often. But usually he would decline these invitations for he does not get off work until nine o'clock every night. Nevertheless, in the Spring Festival of 2006, he ate dumplings and watched fireworks with his Chinese friends. He says it is one of most unforgettable festivals he has spent.

In the past two years Obinna has visited many cities from the north to the south, like Tianjin, Shanghai, Guangzhou, etc. among which Beijing is still his favorite, for the public security is very good and he himself has never come across any scoundrel here. He says his life in Beijing is very comfortable and his career has taken root here. When his career is thriving, he will marry his beautiful Chinese bride.

According to Nigerian custom, the bridegroom does not need to spend any money on the issue of marrying wife: the bride would prepare the house and furniture; if the economic situation of the bridegroom is not very good, the bride will get everything ready for the wedding. But Obinna learns to follow the Chinese custom: in order to marry his Chinese girl, he is working hard to earn money. Presently Obinna will work until two o'clock in the morning at least twice a week. Perhaps because of this sweet dream, he has never felt tired. He says, "As long as I work hard, I will be able to afford the house and the car one day."

By Shan Jinliang
Translated by Chen Bing
Revised by P. K. Banerjea

Chasing the Sun

In the early 1980s, he was drawn towards China by some mysterious force. In the past 26 years here, he has been a student, a lawyer, a writer, and an investment consultant. Now he speaks fluent Mandarin and Cantonese, owns three courtyard houses, and devotes much of his time appealing to authorities for the protection of *hutongs*. Meet Laurence Brahm, an American rooted in the *hutongs* of Beijing, for whom Shangri-La is the ultimate spiritual realm.

$\mathscr{L}$aurence Brahm, an American with the Chinese name of Laurence, is a typical old Chinese hand. He is 6.1 feet tall, thin and graceful, with an expressive face under silken hair. He has spent more than half his 46 years in China; he has studied further, been a lawyer as well as an investment consultant for several international corporations. He has written over twenty books and made a documentary film.

His books are ideal guidebooks for Westerners wanting to enter the Chinese market. He has made great strides in both writing and business. The Nan Long Asia-Pacific Investment Co. Ltd., founded by him, may have achieved economic results, but it also emphasizes the sustainable development of culture. His speculations on philosophy and religion in the Qinghai-Tibet Plateau are widely read and talked about.

Upon meeting the interviewer, he asks at once, "What perspective will you take?" I laugh to myself: who the interviewer, who the interviewee?

Prelife Destiny

A conventional question put to an obviously unconventional person: "When did you begin to take an interest in China? Or, when did you begin to have a China complex?"

Without any hesitation, Laurence answered, "In my prelife."

An unexpected answer, to say the least. He smiles meaningfully, indicating that he's not joking. He tells us that he believes in Buddhist rebirth and he himself might have been a Chinese in his prelife. When asked what kind of person he would have been before, he says, unfathomably, "It's hard to tell."

Laurence Brahm was born in 1961, and spent his childhood in New York and Connecticut. His first contact with Chinese culture came from the Chinatowns in the two states. He completed his higher education at Duke University, North Carolina and learned Chinese for two years while pursuing his bachelor's degree in law. In 1981, he came to China for the first time, alone. For one thing, he was interested in Chinese culture; he was also more interested in Chinese reform.

It took him almost six hours from Beijing Capital International Airport to Nankai University of Tianjin, because the roads were really bad. The bus rumbled and jolted all the way to the university. This experience, however, did little to frustrate his ambitions, or sour his delight at finally having arrived in this country.

Laurence didn't know too much about China at the time, for "the American press gave people the impression that China was still in the Cultural Revolution and that the Red Guards were running around in the streets…."

When he set foot on this land, he found that China had already undergone a lot of changes in the post-Mao era. What impressed him most initially was a small free market he found in Tianjin.

"Some brave farmers brought their surplus products — for instance, peanuts and green soy beans — to the city and sold them on the sidewalks, and this set a precedent for free market," he says. "It was a microcosm of the Chinese economy, and from this you could foresee what road China's economy would take."

He took courses in Chinese at Nankai University with the aim of achieving complete fluency. Not one to stick to the straight and narrow, he didn't believe that reading aloud in class and practicing oral Chinese with overseas students like himself was the best way to learn Chinese. He would thus skip class and ride an old bike to visit small *hutongs*, where he would meet and chat with the people living there.

"I especially enjoy taking a stroll inside *hutongs*," he says. "The *hutongs* of Tianjin are quite different from those of Beijing. The buildings in the *hutongs* are typical northern style; yet sometimes when you step out of a *hutong*, you come to the front of a little square, which is typical Western style. It is really amazing."

However, the most interesting aspect was practicing oral Chinese with the locals. The people of Tianjin are warm-hearted and humorous, and often talk as glibly as talk-show hosts. This is confirmed by the fact that most crosstalk performers are from Tianjin. In the people of Tianjin, Laurence found a shortcut to improving his Chinese. Sometimes, to lure people into talking with him, he would perform small magic tricks.

"I liked communicating with the common people living in *hutongs*, for I could speak in Chinese and they understood me, which made me very happy," he says. "I often made mistakes, which amused them."

"This is communication, which is of vital importance," he continues. "Many big conflicts between China and America are caused by the lack of communication. Without communication, people would never get to know each other." It was thanks to his frequent communication with the locals that his Chinese made rapid improvement; he still had an American accent but was still completely understood by the Chinese.

Half a year later, he went to the Chinese University of Hong Kong to pursue a master's degree in law. In his spare time, he took on a part-time lawyer's job and continued to learn Mandarin; by now, he had also mastered Cantonese. He continued his study in the East-West Center of Hawaii for his doctor's degree in law.

During this period, he gave careful and serious thought to the China that was undergoing drastic transformation, the country whose legal system was gradually being improved. He traveled between Beijing, Hong Kong, and Hawaii by air. He wrote several papers of significance. In 1988, he published *Intellectual Property in China*, the first book in English to introduce the intellectual property situation in China; the book made quite a stir, and sold well.

Subsequently, he accumulated information while working as an investment counselor for international corporations, and wrote his second book, *NAGA China Pusiness Guide*. After that, he published *Banking and Finance in China*, *China Technology Transfer and Intellectual Property Guide*, *Foreign Exchange Controls in China, a Guide to Corporate Survival* and other books. These books were invaluable treasures for those who had attempted to enter the Chinese market but failed. His *Re-engineering China*, which spoke about the reform and change in Chinese state-owned enterprises, also aroused great interest among Western economists and investors.

A German ambassador once said that anyone who wanted to know about present-day China, especially those intending to invest in China, had to read the books written by Laurence Brahm.

At the time, Asian Development Bank was scouting for an eminently qualified person — someone who was familiar with the socialistic nations' financial system reform — to help Laos reform its economy. Laurence thus became president assistant of Laos Bank and formulated several new laws. He then became a consultant to Vietnam Center Bank as well. During this time, he often came to China to take tips from China Bank, and returned to Vietnam to popularize the stock-holding system. From then on, he traveled frequently between Beijing, Vientiane and Hanoi. This went on until 1991.

Since 1991 he has lived in Beijing, and the center of his work is now investment consultancy. In the mid–1990s, he carried out investment feasibility demonstrations for several foreign companies, including big international corporations.

"I was legal adviser when the Eastman Kodak Company set up its first and second joint ventures," he says. "I participated in the negotiations and drafted the contract for a joint venture.

"The biggest vitamin pharmaceutical company in the world also wanted to come into Chinese market. I persuaded them to move their investment center to Pudong in Shanghai. Finally, they moved their research center of the Asia-Pacific region from Hong Kong to Shanghai."

Big international corporations had begun to realize the value of his judgment, his business insight; they were now relying more and more on his acute understanding of Chinese culture and the Chinese economy.

The New Red Capitalism in the Courtyard House

In 1990, Laurence a Chinese friend who lived in a courtyard house, in Shijia Hutong, Dongcheng District. That day, he was told that the courtyard house next to his friend's was dormitory usually rented to foreign experts, and was available for rent at the time. The next day itself, he moved into the house. So began his sojourn in a traditional Chinese residence.

"It is said that the decision to arrest the Gang of Four was made here, in 1976," he says. "The series of important reforms that followed also started here. I am very interested in Chinese contemporary history, and so, naturally, I am interested in courtyard houses where important historical people have lived and important events taken place."

The legend of 1976 may be based on the fact that a top Chinese leader, who

decided to arrest the Gang of Four, was living in that house. Although the veracity of this event still needs to be investigated, it is indisputable that numerous historic events have taken place in various courtyard houses over the past hundreds of years.

Laurence was also told that many top Chinese leaders and celebrities were fond of living in these traditional houses. All of this added to his obsession with them.

"Afterwards I took an interest in the architecture of the courtyard house itself," he says. "Architecture is people's way of thinking in space. There must be some reason that courtyard houses take such a form."

In the process of discovering history, Laurence read books on ancient architecture, consulted experts, and visited a great deal of *hutongs*. As a result, he became something of an expert on courtyard houses himself, quite possibly able to put the younger natives of Beijing to shame in terms of knowledge.

"Courtyard houses embody Chinese culture quite well," he says. "When you enter a *hutong*, you can only see the outside grey wall. The grey wall is very serious, and you cannot know what is inside the wall. In contrast, if you walk outside a Western style house, you can see the garden and the house directly. You can easily tell whether the owner is rich or not from the size of the house."

The difference between endocentric Chinese culture and exocentric Western culture is clearly revealed in the architecture. "Walking in a Beijing *hutong*, people cannot see the inside of the wall, since all the walls look the same," he states. "Only the gate indicates the social status of the owner.

"During the Qing Dynasty (1644-1911), gates were ranked. The common people could not use the Broadview Gate; it was exclusively for mansions constructed for officials and royal families. However wealthy you were, you could not enter the gate. Ordinary intellectuals were allowed to use the Fortune Gate for their mansions."

Certainly, his thinking does not stop at the gate. "Having come through the gate, you have to turn a corner instead of going straight, for there is a screen wall in front of you; while, in the Western style building, a staircase behind the door leads to the owner's bedroom directly. In the Western style house, you can walk straight since there is no bend; while in the courtyard house, you can't: you may need to take several turns in order to go into the owner's bedroom."

He goes on to say that in a courtyard house, there is a dooryard, backyard, and sometimes multiple yards, and that this is quite similar to entering the Chinese market: you have to take turns instead of stepping into it directly.

His ability to think divergently is often quite amazing. Laurence's viewpoints are the reason he can write thesis upon thesis with such prolificity.

After moving out from Shijia Hutong, he bought three courtyard houses located in three *hutongs* in Dongcheng District, adjacent to each other. He invited the construction teams responsible for the repairing and maintaining of the Forbidden City and the Summer Palace, to recreate the original architecture of these dilapidated courtyard houses. By marrying the classic exterior with temperature control and the modern kitchen and toilet inside, he has realized his dream concept of blending the old and the new.

Laurence enjoys the elegance and grace of these houses, especially on dark, silent nights.

"In such silence, I feel much more relaxed," he says. "And I can think about things more clearly in such a state. I usually write something at night, instead of going to bed."

It was in the courtyard house that he wrote the influential book, *China As No. 1: The New Superpower Takes Centre Stage*, which predicted as early as in 1996 that China would grow into an economic powerhouse. In 1997, there was great international debate about whether Hong Kong would continue its capitalistic ways after rejoining the mainland. Consequently he wrote the book *Red Capital*, pointing out that the future of Hong Kong should depend on the red capital. The book created a great stir at the time.

Zhou Nan, the Director of Xinhua News Agency, Hong Kong Branch, even gave him a nickname: New Red Capital. Laurance accepted it willingly: not only did he pose as New Red Capital but named his hotel and restaurant Red Capital Residence.

The courtyard houses of Beijing proved conducive to much thought and creativity. His books, such as *Negotiation in China 36 Strategies*, *Sun Tzu's Art of Negotiating in China*, *Zhongnanhai*, *Zhu Rongji and the Transformation of Modern China*, are still quite popular.

In March 2001, he compiled *China's Century: The Awakening of the Next Economic Powerhouse*, which was prefaced by Premier Zhu Rongji and included the study of the development of the Chinese economy according to eight Chinese ministers, as well as several presidents and CEOs in the World Fortune 500.

"When this book was published, some Westerners criticized me; they said I was pro-China, pro-communism," he says. "But the ones who had lived in China for some time, or those who had been here frequently, agreed with me. Many foreigners who did business in China were willing to buy my books. Consequently I was interviewed by overseas media.

"Those who were practical and realistic believed that if someone wanted to know about China, he could not always trust *The Washington Post* which usually vilified China. The book was quite a success in Western countries."

"The fact has been proven that present-day China is the safest place for business investment and finance regulation," he adds. "Several events I predicted in the book have taken place."

Knowing that several of his friends admired his houses, he turned one into an inn and another into a restaurant. The third one is the headquarters of Nan Long Asia-Pacific Investment Co. Ltd., and his own residence. His company owns seven restaurants, three of which are in China: one in Beijing, another at the foot of the Great Wall, and the third in Bajiao Street, Lhasa.

His hotel and restaurant are filled with artifacts — some of which even came from Zhongnanhai. Old style telephones from the Mao Tse-tung era, ancient furniture, pictures, handicraft, are all displayed to great effect, creating a time warp of sorts.

A Hongqi (Red Flag) car is always parked outside the restaurant. Upon first glance, one would think it belonged to a central government leader from

the Mao era. Sitting at the table, drinking Red Capital wine, smoking Red Capital cigar, one feels as if one has entered a four-dimensional space where time has been condensed. The delicious food and wine, together with the ambience, creates a special flavor. Although Laurence has never advertised his restaurant, his restaurant enjoys a great fame; many foreigners and Chinese are attracted to it thanks to public praise. It is said that Red Capital is among the five most popular bars in Beijing.

The inn is also an exquisite yard, with carved beams and painted rafters. There is an artificial hill in the middle of the yard. Under the hill lies a hidden cavity, left from the time when Mao called upon people to dig deep holes and store their foodstuff. Laurence transformed it into an underground bar, which still retains its original coarse and unpolished style, and is reminiscent of the old film Tunnel Warfare. Spending a night at this inn, drinking, chatting with friends, watching projector films, would seem the perfect way to relax and unwind, even preferable to five-star luxury.

The yard gate is a standard Broadview Gate. Four extrusive pillars stand atop the gate tower, resembling the hair clasp worn by ancient people — and so the name, "gate clasp." Laurence says that he once saw gate clasps in Shijia

Hutong dating back to the Ming Dynasty (1368-1644). He was so taken by the clasps that he invited craftsmen to make copies. Although these copies were crudely made (since the workmanship required had been lost), Laurence managed to rescue the four wooden pillars in the nick of time when the courtyard was being demolished.

"If we hadn't rushed there that night, these gate clasps (now fixed on his own gate) would have been thrown away as rubbish," he says.

Having lived in China for more than 20 years, Laurence is familiar with its large-scale development projects, especially those in Beijing, famed as the "biggest construction site in the world". What distresses him, however, is the random demolition of buildings, in particular, the razing of courtyard houses and *hutongs*. If the price of development is the destruction of culture, he says, it's not worth it.

He reiterates this sentiment often. "A number of courtyard houses have been pulled down in Beijing, akin to cutting the wrists of culture. I don't understand what kind of Chinese culture these high buildings represent.

"As for constructing glass buildings with cement and steel, China will never surpass Los Angeles or Chicago. Even if you could, you still need to think about whether it is necessary. Why do you want to compete with others in terms of constructing high buildings? Why not bring your cultural advantage into play? Actually, if you can preserve the things which embody your culture, no foreign country can be compared to you. That is your own culture, and it is of crucial importance. You need to consider the next generation. They cannot know about Chinese culture without these culture carriers."

He continues in the same rueful vein, "The British magazine, *The Economist*, once published a paper about the pulling down of courtyard houses and *hutongs* in Beijing. It said that if the next generation wanted to know about the culture of Beijing, they would have to go to the museums and libraries in Taiwan, because the natives of Beijing would have already ruined their own culture."

"World famous cities like Paris and London go to great lengths to protect their own culture. The French and the Italians are proud of their ancient edifices. However, in Beijing, several old buildings are going to be pulled down! That's crazy!"

To protect courtyard houses, and publicly make his resentment felt, Laurence began to write articles, participate in televised debates, and visit the relevant government departments. His actions have been supported by many men of insight.

"Several foreigners come to China with the objective of savoring ancient Chinese culture," he says. "If they live in five-star hotels, there is no difference between staying here and living in Paris or New York: all five-star hotels are the same. They gain nothing from their trip to China.

"Isn't it a waste of our cultural resources? Beijing should try to preserve its courtyard houses to show its confidence in its own culture."

Laurence lives happily in his courtyard house, with his Chinese wife and two kids. The district they live in belongs to the 25 Historical Cultural Protective Districts, so they do not need to fear its demolition. His opinions, evidently, have had some impact. It is now fashionable for foreigners to live in courtyard houses, and possessing such a house has become a status symbol for the Chinese as well.

Media giant Rupert Murdoch and his wife Deng Wendi also reportedly intend to buy a courtyard house in Beijing. It is quite possible that Laurence will bump into the Murdochs one day while strolling down a *hutong*.

The Pursuer of Shangri-La

The Chinese call the age of 40 "the year without perplexity". But when Laurence hit 40, he was nothing if not perplexed.

"With its gradual economic reform and WTO status, China has become much internationalized," he says. "I personally haven't made any breakthrough in my career, except for earning some money via investment consultation. But I find that I have lost something in my spiritual world, compared with my material

possessions. I therefore want to spend my time pursuing spirituality."

Laurence believes that the Americanization and commercialization of China are caused by global economic integration. He calls such a phenomenon "oxidizing." "Oxidizing" expresses his qualms at a deep level, quite different from the poignancy indicated by "cutting wrists". As materialism mushrooms all over the world, every generation needs to think about how to keep the vigor and uniqueness of their own culture intact, and how to avoid being "oxidized".

The quest for the spiritual world set Laurence on his journey to Shangri-La.

In 1993, James Hilton published the novel *Lost Horizon*, in which he described a mysterious, beautiful earthly paradise called Shangri-La. For years, adventurers, poets, dreamers sought to discover whether this was a figment of his imagination or a real paradise.

Laurence was also curious about the truth behind this cultural myth. He traveled through several provinces and autonomous regions on the Qinghai-Tibet Plateau — Tibet, Qinghai Province, and Yunnan Province. He visited all kinds of people, artists, dancers, musicians, fashion designers, writers, pop singers, rock bands, environmental protectors, lamas engaged as assistants, the Living Buddha,

herdsmen and so on.

He recorded these people's understandings about Shangri-La; he also recorded what he had seen, heard, and pondered about on the journey. Subsequently, he published several books about Tibet in a series: *Searching for Shangri-La, New Age Sutra, Conversations with Sacred Mountains, Sage's Maxims, Shangbhala,* etc. He also filmed specials: *Searching for Shangri-La, Shangbhala,* etc. This is his progress as a spiritual being.

Jigme Gyaltsen, a lama in Qinghai Province, established a yak cheese factory with international aid, to help herdsmen become rich. Profits from the factory were used to run schools, so that the herdsmen's children had free education. Jigme unselfishly, altruistically sought benefits for the herdsmen, and this won Laurence's admiration.

Jigme told him, "By being kind-hearted, dedicated and good, you will find the real Shangri-La." Laurence was greatly moved by these words, and spurred on in his desire to discover the real Shangri-La.

He bought a *Shangbhala Lection* written by the 6th Bainqen Lama in Tibet. The location of Shangri-La, as described in this book, can be traced to the site of Guge Kingdom in Ali. However, what he saw was merely the ruins of this ancient city. Like the extinction of the Mayan civilization and the annihilation of ancient Pompeii, the glory of the Guge Kingdom vanished suddenly. For a while Laurence was lost.

A lama told him that only the 11th Bainqen Lama could tell him where Shangri-La was, because the 11th Bainqen Lama was the reincarnation of the 6th Bainqen Lama — the author of Shangbhala Lection.

Laurence had begun his tour from Zhashilunbu Temple in Tibet, through Qinghai and Yunnan, and now he returned to his starting point. This journey, for him, proved to be another trek across spiritual frontiers.

The young, sagacious Bainqen Lama answered all his questions about Shangri-La. According to him, the concept of Shangri-La could be dated back to India, where Buddha Shakyamuni was born. He said people saw Shangri-La as Xanadu, the earthly paradise; many famous Buddhist scholars, including the 1st,

6th, and 9th Bainqen Lamas, had talked and written about Shangri-La, describing it as a harmonious and happy place. It was hard to say whether one could arrive in Shangri-La, for it depended on people's determination and persistence. Only those who were sincere could find it, he said.

"Remember to do good even when encountering difficulties. This will bring peace to the world."

The Lama pointed out that many countries spent huge amounts of money acquiring weapons of mass destruction. These countries took it on themselves to ensure the safety of their own in this way, while wreaking havoc on the world. If these funds were used to help under-developed countries, to help the handicapped and students, or to purchase medical equipments, to promote medical research … then worldwide peace was possible.

The 11th Bainqen Lama hoped that the world would one day enjoy peace, and that all its people would love and respect one another, that different religions would tolerate each other and coexist peacefully.

On hearing the teachings of the 11th Bainqen Lama, Laurence suddenly felt refreshed. He realized that Shangri-La was hard to find geographically, but in the spiritual world of human beings, in philosophy, and in religion, it meant inner peace and wisdom and goodness.

Laurence is all praise for the profound wisdom and generosity of Tibetan Buddhism. He believes that the 11th Bainqen Lama will make great contributions to the world, as he has mastered the essence of Tibetan Buddhist culture, and is thus able to spread the morals and principles essential to a harmonious society in its pursuit of Shangri-La.

Laurence decided to devote more energy to the sustainable development of Tibetan culture on the Qinghai-Tibet Plateau.

"In Lhasa, I invested in building the Shangbala Hotel, originally a Tibetan-style building in the Bajiao Street," he says. "I also revived the traditional Tibetan lifestyle and culture in the course of restoring this ancient building.

"All the handicraft articles are made by the local Tibetan people, and these include curtains, carpets, pillows, Buddha beads, and so on. I ask the Tibetans

to put some fashion elements into these traditional handicrafts, so they look more modern. Some of the handicrafts are purchased by tourists, others are sold abroad. In this way, traditional culture can be promoted and at the same time, the Tibetans can make money."

He points at the artificial tiger-skin carpet under our feet and says, "Can you imagine that's woven with fleece? In the past, in order to make tiger-skin carpets, the English had to hunt tigers. Using fleece to make such carpets not only protects endangered animals but also carries forward the Tibetan tradition. The Tibetan people can make profits, as well as take pride in their culture. Isn't this the sustainable development of culture?"

He established the Shangbhala Foundation, affiliated to the Nan-Long Group, in Lhasa, and sent the Tibetan employees of his hotel to Beijing for training in business, Mandarin and English. They became the backbone of his company when they returned to Tibet.

Laurence also set up the Shangbhala School, providing free education to poor children. An old Chinese saying goes, "Teaching somebody to fish is better than giving him fish directly."

Laurence spends a third of the year in Beijing, and the remaining two-thirds

in Lhasa. He calls his Lhasa project "Himalaya Consensus".

"With this model, I hope that the Buddhist concepts of helping others, protecting humanity, and conserving natural resources can be applied to the economy, to solve the poverty problem and find a balance between material and spiritual civilization," he says.

In order to promote the concepts "harmonious society" and "sustainable development of culture", and introduce his Himalayan model, he made a newsreel *Stories in the Himalayas*. Recently, he has also written a book, *China After WTO* and is making a film, *The Man Who Is Chasing the Sun*. This could be said to be self-titled, since he has reached the roof of the world, the place nearest to the sun, in his pursuit of Shangri-La.

Laurence of the Himalayas

Sometimes Laurence travels to neighboring countries as consultant. In countries such as Pakistan, Nepal and Bengal, he has heard praises of his Chinese economic model. Governments and other groups seek valuable proposals from him, the old China hand; he himself is usually willing to provide strategic advice.

"Nowadays people like to talk about the Sino-US strategic partnership," he says. "But China should pay more attention to forming such partnerships with its neighboring South Asian countries. These countries are close to China geographically. In addition, they have the same economic development needs as China, and promote similar 'harmonious society' concepts.

"Cooperating with each together will also greatly promote the economy of this region. But when these countries learn from China, they also need to keep up with changing times. It doesn't matter whether it is socialism or capitalism; traditional models should be smashed and the experience should be emphasized."

Moreover, he believes, Hinduism, Islamism, and Chinese Buddhism can be combined together to form Asian values, because, he says, the concept of

"harmonious society" is embodied in the three religions. Culture should retain its diversity instead of staying fixed, and not be "oxidized" by the integration of global economy, he says.

"Most of the religions in the world — including Chinese Buddhism and Western Christianity — have originated from the Hinduism of the Himalayan foothills", he says, revealing his next amazing project. "I'm currently preparing to write a book, *The Dakini Code*, to explore the origins of religious schools, something which even *The Da Vinci Code* does not dare. It will be a subversive book."

His ability to come up with clever ideas and implement them successfully reminds one of the movie *Lawrence of Arabia*, in which the protagonist leads his people into battle. The Himalayan Laurence, however, by guiding the Tibetans towards peace and prosperity, seems a much more compelling figure.

Translated by Chen Bing and Gao Cuiming
Revised by K. Krishna

图书在版编目（CIP）数据

老外的中国情结＝ Living in China：英文／绿杨等著．
北京：新世界出版社，2008.1
（中外文化交流系列）
ISBN 978-7-80228-501-9

I. 老…　 II. 绿…　 III. 中国—概况—英文　 IV. K92

中国版本图书馆 CIP 数据核字（2007）第 170820 号

Living in China
老外的中国情结（英文版）

作　　者：绿杨 等
策　　划：李淑娟　张海鸥
责任编辑：李淑娟
责任校对：张民捷
封面设计：王天义
装帧设计：清鑫工作室
责任印制：李一鸣　黄厚清
出版发行：新世界出版社
社　　址：北京市西城区百万庄路 24 号（100037）
总编室电话：＋ 86 10 6899 5424　 68326679（传真）
发行部电话：＋ 86 10 6899 5968　 68998705（传真）
本社中文网址：hhtp://www.nwp.cn
本社英文网址：hhtp://www.newworld-press.com
本社电子信箱：nwpcn@public.bta.net.cn
版权部电子信箱：frank@nwp.com.cn
版权部电话：＋ 86 10 6899 6306
印刷：北京外文印刷厂
经销：新华书店
开本：787×1092　　 1/16
字数：170 千字　 印张：22
版次：2008 年 1 月第 1 版　 2008 年 1 月北京第 1 次印刷
书号：ISBN 978-7-80228-501-9
定价：78.00 元